QC
945
.J55
1993

Jiler, John.

Dark wind.

$21.95

DATE			

DARK

WIND

A True Account of

Hurricane Gloria's

Assault on Fire Island

JOHN JILER

St. Martin's Press

New York

DARK WIND

BOOK DESIGN BY JUDITH A. STAGNITTO

Library of Congress Cataloging-in-Publication Data

Jiler, John.
    Dark wind : a true account of Hurricane Gloria's assault on Fire
Island / John Jiler.
        p.   cm.
    ISBN 0-312-09311-X
    1. Hurricane Gloria, 1985.   2. Hurricanes—New York—Fire Island.
I. Title.
QC945.J55   1993
508.747'25—dc20   93-19223
                                                               CIP

First Edition: August 1993

10   9   8   7   6   5   4   3   2   1

For Daisy and Milton,
true islanders

C O N T E N T S

—

A C K N O W L E D G M E N T S

Dark Wind is the result of conversations with many generous people. Besides those whose stories are told in these pages, to whom I will always be grateful, there are many islanders whose stories are not told. The gift of their time has been no less valuable. My thanks to them: Mike Makos, the late Jimmy Viles, Virginia Lindsey, Mario Herrera, Chuck Doersam, Ted Drach, Frank Mc-Dermott, Walter Oakley, Chip Horton, Jerry Moore, Bill Roesch, Ted Minski, and John Hagerman.

    I have also benefited enormously from talking to islanders not specifically about Hurricane Gloria, but about Fire Island in general, about which their knowledge is deep and passionate—Isabel Adler, Jimmy Amster, Jill Warren, Bob and Geraldine Stretch, Artie Noren, Mabel Iverstrom, Lee Frey, and Walter Reich.

As a poor student of the natural sciences, I have been edu-
cated by great institutions and great people. Thanks firstly to the
Museum of Natural History and the Fire Island National Seashore,
Jim Ebert in particular, for making their resources so constantly
available. For my tutoring in the wonderful world of birds, I
thank Mary Laura Lamont and Laurie Farber; in that of deer,
Alan O'Connell; of meteorology, Stan Wasserman; of fish, Lou
Hess; . . . and of everything else, Rose Marie Becker, one of the
truly great naturalists of our time.

Thanks to the Ocean Beach Historical Society, Nancy Ro-
soff in particular.

For the title search, my thanks to Chris Tanner, Ray Leslee,
Lynn Fischer, John Miglietta, Mike Lawrence, Katrinka Moore,
and Jamie Moore Lawrence. And for work in the rock-and-roll
archives, Richard Gabbay.

This project has been greatly aided by the cartography of
Sue Ann Harkey, the calligraphy of Mary Lou Wittmer, the color-
ings of Roger Yogis, and the photography of Marty Heitner and
Layne Redmond—all friends and gifted artists.

My deep gratitude to those who read through this manu-
script and believed in it: Barbara Lowenstein, Sandi Gelles-Cole,
and particularly my valued friend Ben Camardi. Thanks to Dick
Ticktin, both for his enthusiastic read and sharp legal counsel and
to Fran Hovey, whose meticulous, thoughtful criticisms have been
a revelation.

Special thanks to the wonderful Danziger family: Matthew,
Peggy, and Bruce, who gave me shelter and dinner and companionship as I traipsed the beach during the dark autumn and winter
of '85.

Lastly I am indebted to Keith Kahla at St. Martin's Press,
my skillful editor Michael Denneny, and my wonderful agent Eric
Simonoff, who persevered until it happened.

And, of course, my continuing love and thanks to Elizabeth
Hovey, who has read through this a lot, and has endured its
shortcomings and my own on a daily basis.

Blow, winds, and crack your cheeks. Rage, blow.
You cataracts and hurricanoes, spout
Till you have drenched our steeples, drowned the cocks.
You sulph'rous and thought-executing fires,
Vaunt-couriers of oak-cleaving thunderbolts,
Singe my white head. And thou, all-shaking thunder,
Strike flat the thick rotundity o' th' world,
Crack Nature's moulds, all germains spill at once
That makes ingrateful man.

KING LEAR, III, ii

Gloria
        It's not Marie
Gloria
        It's not Cherie
Gloria . . . . . .
        Maybe she loves me,
        but who am I to know?

THE CADILLACS

PART I:
WHISPERS

O N E

Hot air rises. Cold air rushes in to replace it, and that rush is the wind. The wind is a gift from a God. It cools, it dries, it eases the mind, it fills a sail. It could power a city, if only we'd let it. It moves out the old, moves in the new. Without it, the world would be a stagnant hell. But the meteorologists, who spend their days looking above the clouds, who watch the great winds blow across the earth . . . they know that there is also such a thing as an ill wind. It fans a fire. It blows a ship onto a reef. It freezes a newborn lamb, wet and glistening, to death.

Hot air rises. Cold air rushes in to replace it. The hotter the hot air, the colder the cold air, the faster the rush, the bigger

—

the wind. The desert, with its scorched white days and frigid black nights, is a place of enormous wind. In Africa they have names for it. The Egyptian wind Khamsin raises walls of sand a hundred feet in the air and propels them along the Red Sea to Cairo, when the heat of April has begun to rise off the ancient streets. In its path Khamsin will rip apart the tents of the Bedouin and the Berber, and try to kill their plants, their animals, and their children.

In summer, the ill wind is called Sirocco. It blasts northward across the Sahara to the baking Libyan coast, skims the moisture off the top of the sea and then cloaks itself, hot and wet, over the southern cities of Europe. The people of Marseilles and Athens and all the towns of Sicily will feel, for months, as though they are locked in a windowless room with their own germs.

As autumn comes, and the sun moves back to the equator and beyond, lavishing its attention again on the grasslands and savannahs and lakes of Central Africa, the most dreaded enemy of all appears . . . the wind called Harmattan. Born on a cold starless night, Harmattan has no mercy.

On the Atlantic coast, the mountains and forests are green with the new drenching rains—the gift of a different wind, a benevolent one blowing in off the southern ocean. Harmattan will defy that wind. Gathering its force above the ancient capital of Timbuktu, Harmattan will scream down the forgotten trade routes, the same ones that camels once followed, bowed with ivory and ostrich feathers. Harmattan will wither the cacao fields of Mali, Harmattan will parch the mahogany forests of Senegal so badly the farmers will be sorry for every inch of rain they dared accept from the southern wind, and Harmattan will drape bustling Dakar with air so fetid it will beg for forgiveness. Then, as its final act, Harmattan will move out to sea where it will join forces with the darkest wind of all: Trade Wind, the same wind that took the Africans, in chains, away from their homeland.

Dana Wallace sits on the deck of his oceanfront home with a margarita in his hand. Unfortunately, he'll have to do without the salt. Doctor's orders. Wallace has lived life pretty fast and wide and now, at sixty-eight, after a heart bypass, he'll have to watch himself. Even the booze isn't a good idea.

But Dana Wallace drains his margarita anyhow, sucking the lime dry. He is a man of many triumphs in life, not the least of which is the seaside empire over which he now gazes. He did not come by those triumphs by backing off of things because they "weren't a good idea." People who do exercise that kind of caution are people who Wallace has never understood or trusted. They are the kind of people who enjoy paperwork, or who at least do paperwork when it's required of them. Dana Wallace starts his fires with paperwork. He thinks that young people who apply for a job and ask about the pension plan are sick, timid souls who miss the whole point of life.

Once on a train he met a man who was commuting to a job he had held for thirty years. Wallace was in a mischievous mood and he began computing, out loud, the number of hours in his life the man had spent on the train. The result was horrifying. The man was angry and embarrassed, so to make amends Wallace offered to buy him a drink once they got to Penn Station. Over the drink, the man not only forgave Wallace, but began to see his point. The man called in sick for the first time in thirty years, and they both went out to the racetrack. Wallace remembers it as one of his most joyous and positive days. He saved a soul.

Dana Wallace has had his joyous days, ripe and pulsing with the bounty of life, and he's had his miserable days, when the great risks didn't pay off, when the wide-open, big-hearted guy just got badly, painfully screwed.

Most of those times have had to do with women. He's had three wives and the most recent, a woman much younger than himself, left him because she had "some growing to do." Wallace tried to understand that notion, but now, six years later, still carrying the torch, he has bitterly concluded that "I have some growing to do" is a euphemism for "So long, sucker, don't forget the alimony." He's stuck on the point, but he's too smart to think that that makes him some kind of a noble romantic hero, some Bogart drinking under a ceiling fan. He knows that he's obsessed with someone who's long gone, and that he must get on with life. But he still loves her, he chases women who look like her, and he drinks far too much (he had been on the wagon for many years before she left him).

His old age is not shaping up the way it should, given his accomplishments, his money, and his zest for life. He is not as close to his only son as he might be. His friends are dying off. He has lost his enthusiasm for photography, once his vocation and his greatest passion (many of the great photos of World War II, the haunted faces on the beaches of Saipan and Salerno, are his). New developments in the human race, as he observes them from his deck, fill him with contempt and suspicion. The hippies were unkempt, disrespectful, soft, and girlish. The yuppies, soulless and immaculate, are worse.

What new trend will follow he cares not. For solace and companionship he turns to the animal world, to his faithful pair of black Labrador retrievers, and especially to his amazing stable of horses. Dana Wallace somehow coaxed an acre of grass out of this parched sandspit of an island, and to the envy and astonishment of other islanders, he has trained thoroughbreds here, to win allowance races at Belmont and to gallop through the surf at dawn with a hundred-and-eighty-pound man in the saddle. But even the horses are reminders of Maureen, the young third wife, who loved to ride them, who sat beside Dana in horse trailers as they'd roam state fairs across the South and take away the prize money and make love in motels beside the road.

Dana Wallace is a lonely man. But he won't go under. Rather than accept with grace the insults, infirmities, and sorrows of old age, he will face them squarely and say, "Fuck you."

* * *

The devil wind out of Africa, having spent its hot anger, has joined the gentle trade winds across the Atlantic. It is a complete change of character. Innocent, constant, almost playful, the trades push westward with no hint of their blast-furnace beginnings.

"Four days we sailed before the fresh trade breeze," wrote an inspired sailor. "The ocean was piled on end about us in white-crested ridges, flashing green on their sides, violet in the hollows. The sky was an unbroken sweep of crystalline ether, fading into neutral on the sea rim, while a glorious rush of pure keen air awoke weird music from every tight-strung shroud, and filled each cranny of the ship with life and freshness."

Frequently the lyrical journey belied the grim cargo, black flesh chained together in airless, malarial cells. When the trades failed, the nightmare was complete. The soon-to-be slaves were forced to take up oars and, with every aching stroke, row themselves farther from their homeland.

But even before the slave trade, other goods came to the New World in the holds of even smaller wooden sailing ships—gold, ebony, ostrich plumes, peppers, cloth, and chocolate crossed the African continent, and then the wide Atlantic. Earlier still, primitive men helped to spread the race by rigging crude papyrus sails to catch the wind, and hauling themselves and their families to the bulging coast of South America.

The trades have blown since man has lived on earth, and the principle behind them is the same principle that propels their hellish ancestor Harmattan across the desert. Hot air rises. Cooler air rushes in to replace it, and that rush is the wind. At the equator, the earth's greatest heat rises and flows north and south toward the poles. But by the time it has made even a third of that journey, by the time it has reached the latitude of, say, North Carolina, it has cooled to the point where it sinks. Then it rushes back to the equator to replace the hot air rising there. It's a complete cycle, and were there nothing more to it, the wind would blow due south to the equator.

But there *is* something more to it. The earth spins. There is a little "english" on the ball, as bowlers and pool sharks like to say. So the wind doesn't blow due south, but twists a bit with the spin of the earth and comes out of the east, and all the oceans of the earth are carved with broad twisting channels.

The same thing happens in the Southern Hemisphere, but in the opposite direction. There is an old wives' tale that if you poured water into a sink in Rio de Janeiro, its last eddies would be sucked down the drain in a clockwise motion, the opposite of what the water would do in your North American bathtub. If the sink and the tub were big enough, say hundreds of miles wide, the tale would be true. This is the Coriolis effect—the twist of the earth. It is what brings wind not from the north but from the east across the Atlantic, and blew the slaves and the plumes and the gold and the chocolate across the sea.

Dana Wallace finishes a second, smaller margarita, and pours the dregs down his kitchen sink, watching them disappear in a counterclockwise swirl. He is cutting short his ordinarily inviolable cocktail hour. He has work to do. It is September, time to clean up after the tourists.

Fire Island is a narrow ribbon of sand that runs from west to east almost at a right angle from the American coastline. An hour from New York, it is a favorite refuge from the summer oven of the city. By the thousands, New Yorkers young and old, fat and thin, famous and obscure pile on the tiny boats that ply the Great South Bay to the two dozen communities that punctuate the thirty miles of Fire Island. They trek across the narrow sandbar of an island and within minutes are on the wide white beach, basted with oils cheap and exotic as they roast to every hue of the human rainbow. Before them the Atlantic stretches endlessly. Were they to dive in and swim straight, they would not come ashore until Brazil. In the evening they retire to their bungalows and hotel rooms or remain by the sea—resting, contemplating, looking for cool breezes or hot sex.

As they do every summer, the islanders, the year-round residents, address themselves to the problem of where the tourists will eat and sleep and drink and defecate, of how their bicycles will be kept pumped up, of how the tiny shaded walkways will be kept free of their excesses.

All of this the islanders are happy to do . . . at a price. In Dana Wallace's case, the price has been handsome. Forty years ago, when he first got married, he began buying beachfront property. The four or five houses he now rents out to the tourists are enough to support him. For years, too, he took photos of the summer people on the dunes . . . family portraits. With his professional eye for composition and his native's feel for the terrain, the pictures rose far above the level of the family album. Dana Wallace taking pictures of your kids? It was like Picasso coming in and painting your living room. The public went for it in a big way, and many island end tables are still adorned with the dreamy, silver-lit portraits, "DW" scrawled in the corner. So Wallace has given to the summer people, as well as taken from them. He remains grateful to them not just for their dollars, but for the breath of the city they bring, the grain of culture, and the fast life without which his island world would be too bleak.

Still, he's glad to see them go. September on Fire Island is God's time. The streets and beaches are empty, and the ocean has heated to a tepid bath. The bluefish are beginning their great fall run to the South, and the striped bass won't be far behind. The sky is filling with birds, not just the gulls, terns, cormorants, and kingfishers that always dominate the seaward vista, but great caravans of migrant songbirds and plovers on their way from Canada to the sunny Central American forests and plateaus where they will winter; hawks and black-billed skimmers who live and nest on the island and now must cheat south a few more degrees of latitude to find winter food; and great squadrons of waterfowl, geese and ducks who have begun to abandon the tundra and frozen lakes of the North and will make Fire Island their winter home. All the low island bushes droop with fruit—the juicy purple beach plum, the inkberry, the bearberry, the cranberry, the rose hip, the bayberry. Even the stately holly tree sparkles with the bright red berries of early autumn.

It is a time of rest and of plenty. To be here in September, to bob in the warm ocean and watch the Indian summer sky, to squeeze a lemon over a broiled bluefish, to sweeten your bread with a spoonful of beach plum jam, to make love by an early harvest moon as snow geese path beneath it . . . this is what accrues to the islander when the tourists are gone.

Wallace rinses his cocktail glass and sets it to drain on his windowsill. The sky is fat with rain clouds, so he has decided on a fast trip to the village to get his mail. The weather makes a difference when you think about a trip out here, even the half-mile jaunt Dana contemplates into Ocean Beach, because there are no cars.

No cars.

Oh, the tradesmen, the construction men, the telephone and electrical linemen, have vans to transport themselves and their equipment along the thirty-mile length of beach. Most of the year-round residents have four-wheel drive vehicles so they can go shopping or keep from going stir-crazy, when the boats aren't running, by driving down the beach and over the only bridge that connects them to the mainland. But by and large there are *no cars*, and it is this fact that makes addicts of Fire Islanders, that brings them back year after year, that uncurls their nerves and dismantles, temporarily, their anxieties.

It is impossible to calculate, describe, or imagine the tranquility of life without the automobile. When a stranger first arrives here he knows something is different, but he can't say just what. He walks down the narrow, shaded walkways awhile, and then it hits him. The human being is king here. There's nothing to watch out for. Oh, an occasional bike might jostle you off the road, and a ten-year-old may careen recklessly down a slope on a red wooden wagon, but they will not intimidate you the way the steaming grill of a car will, even idling at a stoplight. There is nothing big and fast and metal to dominate the pace and sounds and smells of life. There is nothing louder than birdsong, or more pungent than the brine. There is nothing bigger and faster than you.

Wallace gets on his bike, an old Schwinn with no brakes, and heads for town. The well laid-out walkways offer a smorgasbord of architecture. Here is an old dormered Cape house, there a modern glass-and-steel box, beyond that an Adirondacks bungalow. In many of them there is activity, even though their owners have gone home or begun to limit their visits to weekends. Autumn is the time for reconstruction. Workers swarm over houses like bees. It is an ideal time to put on a roof, to slap some mortar on an old chimney, to build a new one. The people who own these houses, for the most part, are rich New Yorkers who want things done right, for their own comfort or for the rental value of the house. It is not unknown for a house to go for twenty-five thousand dollars just for the summer season. The roof can't leak for that kind of money. The construction workers are well paid because the traffic will bear it and because their wages must absorb, off the top, ferry fare to and from the mainland everyday. Everything costs more on an island.

As Wallace pedals past a new house under construction, a couple of workers on a roof wave to him, even though they don't really know him. Dana Wallace is a legend on Fire Island, particularly among these bandannaed young men who swing hammers for a living, and see themselves as marauders and soldiers of fortune. Many of them, of course, are not. In a couple of years they will settle into very predictable lives, if they haven't already. But there is something about swinging a hammer under that high sky, beside the pounding ocean, that makes you feel free. And it's well known among these young men that whatever Dana Wallace is or isn't, he *is* free. He does whatever he damn well pleases, no matter what kind of a price he's had to pay in loneliness, fluctuating fortunes, or friction with the law. On this last point, particularly, Dana Wallace is a model for the young marauder. There is authority all over the place on Fire Island—federal authority.

Many years ago the peace of the island was threatened by a force that seemed as unstoppable as any tidal wave that ever swept over it. A man wanted to build a road . . . for cars. He wanted to build a highway the length of the entire island, a thirty-mile expressway that would have shattered the peace into a memory, that would have sent the seabirds reeling back into the sea and turned the fragile chain of life into a chain of hot dog stands and gas stations. What made the threat so formidable was the personal power of the man who wanted to build it. His name was Robert Moses, and he had already been responsible for such prodigious urban constructions as the Triboro Bridge and the Holland Tunnel, both of which, in the public mind, had changed life for the better.

On the island, citizen's groups protested the rape of the fragile beach. Were they so selfish, countered Moses, that they couldn't share the place with everyone else? The citizens argued that the road would so bludgeon the environment that there would be nothing left to share. But Moses, a public relations genius who had scored points years earlier with the establishment of Camp Cheerful, a Fire Island retreat for retarded children, rode the selfishness issue hard; did a privileged few, he asked again and again, have a right to hoard paradise?

At last a compromise was reached. The citizens, who were not without political guile and muscle of their own, managed to get the entire island designated a "National Seashore." They were now protected from any incursions, including Moses's road. In return, the great man's ravenous ego was fed. The old state park at the west end was expanded and renamed Robert Moses State Park, and made accessible via a new bridge that spanned the Great South Bay. Its name? The Robert Moses Causeway.

Whether Moses was a vain Caesar or a visionary public servant is a debate that has yet to subside. But the islanders had been spared the assault of civilization. In its place, however, they had to endure a less tangible presence, one that to Dana Wallace was more irksome and threatening than all the automobiles Detroit ever turned out—the men and women in brown, the National Park Rangers.

Now that the federal government had declared Fire Island worthy of preserving, squadrons of well-trained and enthusiastic young people in uniform arrived to do just that. They began to oversee not just the slim parcels of land that were officially National Park wildlife sanctuaries, but the whole "ecosystem" (as they began to call it), including, and primarily, the fragile beach itself. No longer could islanders drive the beach with impunity. No longer could they, on a whim, pile into the pickup and head down to the west end to do a little surf casting. Oh, they could, of course, but it would have to be their only trip of the day. One to a customer. That was the new rule, and there were checkpoints and rangers to enforce it.

It was a dulling, a reining in of life, and it aroused feelings similar to the ones in old barnstorming biplane pilots who were suddenly told that they couldn't just land on their own oat field anymore, but must now land in a certain place, after flying only at certain altitudes, and this, and that, and the other thing. All the islanders bristled under the new authority, but most of them capitulated to it. Not Dana Wallace. In his opinion, the "ecological expertise" of these rangers was a bunch of crap they'd learned in their 4-H clubs back in Nebraska and it had nothing to do with Fire Island.

But among all the nit-picking and minutiae of the rangers, there was one idea, in particular, that Dana Wallace found more hateful and threatening than any other . . . an idea that he will fight with the last breath in his body.

It has to with the dunes, the twenty-foot-high ridges of sand that are the island's only protection against the ravages of the ocean. Erosion is real in this part of the world. Throughout Fire Island's history, the Atlantic has pounded its eastern tip, gouging away vast tonnage of sand, dragging it the length of the island, and finally depositing it on the west end. When Robert Moses first started snooping around Fire Island, he was startled to find the thin western finger a mile longer than it was on his map. It was almost as if the island were moving right in front of his eyes, and in the parlance of geologists, who speak of "migrating" barrier beaches, it was. The slim island seemed to be trying to fuse with the land it was protecting, the great whalelike Long Island.

But now the "migration" has stopped. The island's eastern and western tips have been stabilized by permanent channels, constantly re-dredged and re-fortified. The surf continues to

---

pound westward along the beach, scouring away sand, but with no place to put it back. So the thin island grows imperceptibly thinner. A tiny shaving, perhaps a foot a year. Hardly anything. Like in Las Vegas, the minuscule house percentage, which as every crapshooter knows will ultimately break you and send you home on a Greyhound bus.

How does the trembling homeowner cope as the ocean moves inexorably toward him? Erosion is a hot issue, as urgent as Indians in Dodge City or volcanic ash beside Mount Saint Helens, and everybody has a theory on what to do about it. The macho-agressive approach of the Army Corps of Engineers has been to build steel jetties to keep the sand from strafing its way down-island. The passive, ecological approach of the National Seashore has been to plant more beach grass and install more wooden-slatted snow fences, in order to hold the fragile dunes together.

As asinine as Wallace thinks the first approach is (the impotent steel jetties, before they get buried altogether, only succeed in briefly piling up the sand before it gets pushed on), he cannot countenance the second approach, the approach of the rangers in brown.

Oh, there is nothing wrong with planting beach grass (though Wallace has his own ideas about how to hold a dune together), but implicit in the rangers' approach is an idea he finds intolerable. In their heart of hearts, the rangers feel that erosion is a natural process, and should be allowed to play itself out. Man has built bulkheads and dredged channels to prevent the barrier beach from moving, and nature's payback for this arrogance will simply be to make the barrier beach disappear. As ye have sown, so shall ye reap.

But what about our property? the homeowners bellow. Nobody owns anything, the rangers respond. It's all on loan from Mother Earth.

And they have mustered political support for their point of view. Once the ocean has begun to destroy a house, the government is now empowered to tear down the rest of it. This is the new law, and it galls Dana Wallace to the core of his being. No one is going to tell him he can't live beside the sea, or in the goddamn sea if he chooses to.

Years ago when he was a young man, he drove four deep piles into the sand, great spruce logs floated down from Nova Scotia on the open sea, and built a house on top of them. It was a beachcomber's shack made out of driftwood and flotsam, and it was so close to the ocean that high tide soaked the floorboards. People told him he was crazy, that the ocean would take it away, and indeed the little place has been battered and gouged and flooded through the years.

But it's still there. In the evenings, sitting on the verandah of his two-story Cape house on the dunes, Wallace gazes on the shack and gets inspiration. Inside it he has made love by kerosene light to the rhythm of the surf, and inside it he has mourned the death of his first wife and the death of his last marriage. No brown-shirted Nebraskan with a piece of paper in his hand is going to tell him to tear it down. Wallace has made that clear, with axes and shotguns in his hands, to two generations of National Park Rangers.

You don't "allow" the beach to move, says Dana Wallace. You don't "go with the flow" and let the ocean swallow land and buildings you sweated and bled for. Dana Wallace keeps the ocean away with a fortress of dunes he has created and reinforced with the brush he has culled from a small pine forest he planted himself. It will stand until the end of time, and if by any chance it goes, he will go with it.

What he does in this life he will do within the sound of the big breakers.

T   W   O

As Dana Wallace pedals off into town, only
one construction worker does not wave to him. Bobby Ferguson
has no idols in the older generation, not even old marauders like
Wallace, to whom he is sometimes compared. Bobby's always had
problems with the adults in his life . . . any adults. Take the
faculty members of nearby Belmar High, his alma mater. Their
expectations were always too high. Basically, they wanted him to
do his homework and leave the cheerleaders alone. That was
simply an unrealistic demand on the slim, pubescent body of
Bobby Ferguson. Finally, when he got caught with Sarah the
student body president under the grandstands at midnight, naked
and mud-caked, the principal had had enough. He demanded an

—

apology, or an admission of guilt, or a long face, or *something*. Bobby just wouldn't offer it.

After three lengthy suspensions, Bobby gave up on the idea of high school and ventured out into the world. Nearby Fire Island, where misbehavior was rumored to be a way of life, seemed a natural place for him to light. He loved the days in the open air, swinging a hammer and working his lean body into the kind of object that would be in great demand during the long nights, when city girls forgot themselves and gave themselves over to pleasure.

But the best times of all, the purest times, were when the tourists had gone to bed, when all the pale desperate ones from the city were fast asleep and out of sight. Now, with the last bar closed, the last rock-and-roll chord played, the first pink streak of morning shooting out of the sky, Bobby Ferguson would take his surfboard down to the ocean. He would paddle out, swing around, and catch the big breakers that rolled out of the rising sun. Even if there were no waves, there he would sit, straddling his board, away from the bullshit. If Dana Wallace could live his life by the water, Bobby Ferguson would go him one better and live his life *in* the water.

He loved to be in the thin arms of a secretary from Queens whose name he didn't know, and he loved to be on a new roof with his shirt off smelling the fresh pine as he sank a nail into it, but nowhere did he love to be more than here, beyond the breakers.

For a while, Bobby had tried being a contractor, tried being the boss, but he lacked a crucial element. The rich city people had to be handled in a certain way. It wasn't just a matter of doing the job, which Bobby could do as well as anyone, but also of slinging the bullshit, of offering the glad hand, of making these people feel they were something other than chumps who didn't know what they wanted or how hard it was to do. At this last political skill Bobby Ferguson was no good at all. Even when he knew what his clients wanted to hear, he couldn't bring himself to say it.

Once, at the end of a long job, he was applying a finishing touch, a knob on a screen door, when his client tapped him on the shoulder and said she didn't like the color of the knob.

Another one could be gotten, Bobby said, but of course there would be an additional charge.

Why? the client wanted to know.

Because another knob would cost *him* another five dollars, said Bobby.

The client bristled. The Madison Avenue tradesmen with whom she did business in the city would have thrown in the knob, or any similar bric-a-brac, with a smile. But this was not Madison Avenue, and Bobby Ferguson was not some groveling courtier. The discussion escalated into an argument, and before the woman knew it, or could believe the young contractor's incendiary temper, the whole door had been ripped off at the hinges, and Bobby was stomping the hell out of it. Then he ran to the ocean, dove in, and swam out as far as he could, until his arms couldn't move anymore, out of sight of land, farther possibly than any human had ever been without a boat or a board. To this day he doesn't know how he got back. That was the end of Bobby's business, which thrives on this island only by word of mouth. So on this overcast September day, he swings a hammer for somebody else.

Dana Wallace turns the corner on his Schwinn, without returning the waves of the construction men. He doesn't approve of them. For all his individualism, for all the ornery streaks that run through him, Dana Wallace longs for the days when builders wore starched overalls and didn't let their beards grow. He is exercising the prerogative of an old man and wishing things were the way they once had been.

As the ageless village of Ocean Beach comes into view, with its green squares and brown clapboard shops, the feeling only grows. Fifty years ago, when Wallace was young and the American sky was beginning to fill with airplanes, there wasn't even electricity on this island. There were no telephones. There was only the soft ochre light from kerosene lamps, and the brown Western

Union tower run by Dotty Abrams, and everybody made do with it. While New York throbbed with the manic twenties and writhed with the depressed thirties, Fire Island baked in the sun, as innocent of civilization as it had been two hundred years before, when Secatogue Indians were the only copper-colored people on the beach.

The Secatogues were part of the Indian nation that roamed as far east as the wild cliffs of Montauk. But they found Fire Island uninhabitable, and used it only as a base of operations. From the bay side they would scour the sea bottom for quahogs, the hard clams with the purple spots that the Indian nation used for wampum. The Great South Bay was the Indian mint.

From the oceanside the Indians launched their canoes with a different purpose. Brandishing bone-tied harpoons, they went in search of the great whales that once teemed in these waters. They never missed. Even if a whale eluded the harpoon, he could always be harassed, cornered, forced into shallow water and bludgeoned to death.

But always, when the mission was done and the oil had been drained from the huge carcasses, the Secatogues would climb back into their canoes and cross the bay to the mainland, where their lodges stood serenely beside the flat water. To live on the thin outer island was unthinkable. Powerful spirits lived in the sea, spirits too wild to live comfortably beside. When circumstances forced them to spend the night on the island, they built great fires, both to keep away the dark spirits, and to communicate with their tribes on the mainland. Later the white man would use the same technique to warn oceangoing ships from running aground, and that is the most widely held theory of how Fire Island got its name.

The first white men on this island, however, were not that benevolent. They were pirates, the ruthless men who sailed beneath the Jolly Roger, and they gave concrete form to the evil the Indians had always felt coming off the wild ocean. Motionless, the Secatogues would squat behind the dunes and watch the pirates' excesses. From their black-sailed ships at anchor they

---

would land in launches full of squealing concubine women acquired at various ports of call . . . and rape them on the pink, sandy beach. They would haul great boxes of shimmering booty ashore, drag them across the sand, and bury them in a big hole.

Then, many months later, the Indians would see the black ship return and would be amazed to watch the pirates find the exact spot, unrecognizable now after a season of wind and sea, where they had buried their treasure. The pirates were using crude methods of triangulation, sighting treelines and small isthmuses on the mainland. The Indians thirsted for this knowledge, this magic. One day they would have it, at enormous cost to themselves.

After the Jolly Roger disappeared in tatters, civilized white men appeared on Fire Island. Their first overtures were cautious, as they drove their cattle across the bay at low tide to graze in the salt-rich seagrass that lined the north shore. But when the whaling industry boomed, Fire Island's days of innocence were over. The Northeast was suddenly whale-crazy. From the huge, sperm-oil powered lighthouse on Montauk Point, to the Manhattan shops that peddled whalebone souvenirs, the demand for product was insatiable.

Co-opting the Secatogue's technique, "refining" it to quadruple the catch, and finally using the Indian himself as cheap labor, the white man took over the island whaling industry. The Indians finally learned their triangulation technique, and with it learned to subordinate themselves to the will and the sorrows and the complexities and even the diseases of the white man. It was a story that repeated itself again and again in North America, but it seemed especially poignant on Fire Island for the speed with which it took place. It seemed as if one moment the proud Secatogue braves were moving swiftly through the breakers with their ivory harpoons, and the next that they slumped to work in the white man's factory, carrying their lunch pails, and turning out whalebone corsets by the thousands.

For a half-century, the once-pristine island belched black smoke and intolerable stench into the air. The great days of the

—

whaling industry were brief, but even after the North Atlantic had been whaled out, the refineries of Fire Island remained in production, crushing and distilling great numbers of the small silver Menhaden fish into potent farm fertilizer. Still, the place was considered uninhabitable by anyone with two nostrils.

Slowly, though, as the fish-oil workers began to settle there for their own convenience, reports began to filter back to the mainland of the crystal sea and the abundant game birds and the brimming berry bushes and the profound sense of peace once the factories had shut down for the day. Cautiously, the summer vacationer began to stick his big toe in the water. A couple of hotels sprang up to accommodate him. By the turn of the century, he was sitting stiffly on the beach in his modest bathing gear. It took a nationwide fad, however, to get him to dive in.

It was 1900 and the Chautauqua craze was sweeping the country. Originally intended as a sort of summer convention for Sunday-school teachers, the Chautauqua came to mean any sort of arrangement, or any sort of place, where people converged for self-improvement and entertainment, with an emphasis on the latter . . . especially near the capitol of frivolity and decadence, New York. So while a Chautauqua in Ohio may have taken on the character of a religious revival, or at the very least a reaffirmation of solemnity and faith, in New York it took on the character of a carnival midway.

On Fire Island, far-seeing promoters realized, it could also include the pleasure of the seaside. Fire Island became, for a brief, brilliant season or two, the greatest Chautauqua of all, a mélange of music, ventriloquism, ice cream, trained dogs, Japanese jugglers, magic, brightly lit boats anchored in the water, and saltwater taffy.

It burned itself out just as quickly as it began, and within a year the brightly colored tents were empty. But not before Fire Island had called itself to New York's attention as a place not only habitable, but exotic. Even as the flare of Chautauqua's brilliance dimmed in the years leading up to the First World War, little bungalows sprang up like wildflowers. In many of them, softly lit

by oil lamps, were the great faces of American culture, resting from the assault of the new twentieth century. Most of them were literary people, but as America entered the Jazz Age, so did the character of the American artist escaping to Fire Island.

Now, in the twenties, a soft summer night might find George Gershwin, in silk pajamas, ambling down a walkway smoking a Cuban cigar and working out a tune. At the head of the same street Fanny Brice, nude, might have been flinging herself into the waves for a midnight swim. Billy Rose may have been lying drunk in the dunes. An intense young Clifford Odets might have been stalking the marshes, frightening owls.

And young Dana Wallace, grappling with puberty, was wondering about the girl at the head of the street, in the little house called The Shells (for all the little bungalows had end-of-the-rainbow names, like Dunroamin' or My Blue Heaven). Every day young Dana would collect the laundry from her asthmatic mother, and there would be Peggy, lingering in the house just long enough to catch the visit of the freckled young laundryman. Dana remembers working up the nerve to ask her out, and digging clams all day to make a couple of bucks to take her to the movies. After the show they peeked into Sis Norris's bar, the China blue jukebox playing "Begin the Beguine," and watched raven-haired Sis pour amber-colored liquid for a pair of lovers. Wondering what it all might be like someday, Dana and Peggy snuggled together in silence.

Fifty years later, on a gray, late-September afternoon in 1985, Dana Wallace straddles his Schwinn and stares at the same building, now a singles discoteque boarded up for the winter. But before he can sink into his own particular mix of nostalgia and gloom, margarita-fueled, he is sharply interrupted. A small covey of black-billed skimmers squawk out of the boat basin—an uncharacteristically frantic episode for the sleek, even-tempered birds.

Now Wallace spots the reason. Far above the earth is a terrifying spectacle ... to a bird. Riding a hot-air current, her

huge striped wings barely moving, her hawk eyes strafing the shadows of the narrow island, a peregrine falcon soars eastward. Yesterday she left the Upper Hudson Bay, inside the Arctic Circle. Tomorrow she will skim the low cypresses on the Mississippi coast as she sets off across the Gulf of Mexico.

She is nature's fastest flying thing, and to other birds, the most dangerous. The falcon eats birds. Sometimes she will take a field mouse or a rabbit, but for the most part she'd prefer to dive at a bird with blurring speed and power, break its neck, sink her sharp talons into the bird's vitals, carry it off somewhere, pluck its feathers, tear it apart with her hooked beak, and eat it.

Although Dana Wallace is a lover of all birds, he doesn't hate or fear the falcon. He knows that she's only helping the race of birds by taking the slowest of them, and leaving the fastest to reproduce. And evolution aside, Wallace is simply in awe of the falcon's grace. During their mating dance, male and female soar in tandem at two hundred miles an hour, their power surpassed only by the delicacy with which they pass food back and forth from beak to beak. It would be like the pilot of one airplane lighting a cigarette for the pilot of another.

But the sky is full of graceful birds. What rivets Dana Wallace's attention to this one is the fact that she's almost gone. Like Wallace himself, she's the last of a breed. The feathered miracle of speed and power that Egyptians worshipped, that medieval kings held on gauntletted wrists, that once raced down country lanes and nested underneath the Brooklyn Bridge, this bird has just about had it. She's on top of what biologists call the food chain, meaning that she eats something that eats something else. The tragic result, in the case of the falcon, is an accumulation of the manmade poisons in the diets of its victims. The falcon is saturated with DDT past the point of being able to eliminate it. The poison weakens the calcium in a falcon's body, and the strength of its eggshells. Unhatched, chicks are crushed to death under the weight of their mother.

Instinctively the falcon avoids her executioner, man, by seeking out more and more remote spots. Now she nests within the

Arctic Circle, and winters on isolated South American plains. Still she cannot outdistance DDT, which the United States ships to South America by the containerload. So like Sarah Bernhardt on a farewell tour, she commands great attention these days in the theatre of nature.

Dana Wallace is no bleeding-heart liberal environmentalist. Show him a boatload of Greenpeace volunteers interfering with a nuclear test, and he will take great pleasure in pushing the button himself and blowing them to Venus. But the proud, fierce, remarkable bird that now flies over his head is a different matter. He will not move until her low *cjiek cjiek cjiek* fades from his hearing.

The eye of the huge hawk takes in the burly man's figure and moves on, racing east up the island. To her left the Great South Bay is as still as glass, punctuated by small fishing boats. To her right the Atlantic crests with whitecaps and gulls, which tempt her, but not much, since she feasted on an early-migrating duck in Rhode Island just this morning.

Now the falcon sees the houses end and a belt of green cover the narrow width of the island. The natives call this place the Sunken Forest. Were the bird to fly lower (as she would if her stomach were emptier), she would sense the ancient mysteries of this place, with its gnarled sassafras roots half-hidden in dark lagoons, its stately holly trees a hundred feet high, its pockets of marsh sludge teeming with life. But the bird will not linger here. The day is heating up, and the warm air currents coming off the land are making her flight effortless. She is on a roll. She watches the dark green band widen, then taper again, then disappear as another scattering of houses appear, the first she has seen since leaving the western settlement many miles before.

These structures are different. Architecturally, they are the same seaside bungalows. But they are laid out on winding wooden walkways that would give to human eyes the feeling of a toy town, or of some mythical kingdom of gingerbread cottages full of happy, singing peasants. Adding to this storybook feeling is the shock of color that comes off the place; many of the tiny

—

houses are brightly painted and festooned, and the gardens are redolent with late-blooming flowers.

The falcon dips, forsaking her free ride on the wind. Though she knows in her light airy bones that man and his poisons threaten her, she is attracted to this place. She lights on a large, eccentric building that dominates the tiny kingdom. It is the most fanciful place of all, full of high towers and turrets, something like the old European castles where the falcon's ancestors perched on royal wrists. So ornate is the building that the magnificent bird is barely noticed by the young men who scurry about its twisted walkways and moist, hidden grottos. The men mistake the falcon for part of the exotic design, just as the bird mistakes the men for the nude plaster Mercuries that stand about the garden.

They are statuesque, beautiful men. Naked themselves except for brightly colored shorts, they carry silver trays brimming with brioches, sweetbreads, preserves and marmalades, silver tea and coffeepots. Knocking on transomed, shuttered doors, the kind you see in old movies about the tropics, they are delivering breakfast to the guests of the Belvedere Hotel. Though many of the guests are up and about, lounging in the garden or already settled at the beach, some only begin to stir with the arrival of breakfast. They have been dancing all night, a common pursuit in the tiny township that surrounds the big hotel.

Like the servants, the guests of the hotel are predominantly men. Not all of them are beautiful, but they are well-groomed, like all the citizens of the town, and they look well for their age. They range in age from twenty to seventy. There are no children here. The townspeople do not reproduce. For their lovers they take other men.

This is Cherry Grove, a city of men. It is like no other city on earth. The falcon's-eye view of a mythical kingdom was apt. Everywhere are bursts of fantasy, color, and joy. Fence posts and walkways and birdbaths and chimneys are painted unlikely colors with care and delicacy. Around every bend in the roller-coaster wooden walkway is a creative surprise. A strange foreign tree leans across a path. A bright banner shades a tiny bungalow. A burst of music explodes out of the bushes. One house pretends to be a salamander, striped and iridescent, with a window for a mouth. Another bungalow, even smaller, is the Taj Mahal.

In the center of the town are two great restaurant-nightclubs that attract customers for miles around, even from across the bay. Here the creative fecundity comes to a hard focus. The food is imaginative and delicious. The china service is as tasteful as any empress ever laid out. And when those dishes are put aside and the dancing begins, the dance floor shudders with the sexual intensity of a thousand high school proms distilled into five hundred square feet. While disco music pounds like the heartbeat of hell, armies of men, nut-brown from the sun, pump, preen, stomp, churn, beg, and tease for each other's love.

And on Sunday, as the family men in Dana Wallace's end of the island file dully onto the boats in anticipation of the workweek ahead, these eastern men are only simmering. As Sunday afternoon (and the weekend) threaten to end, they will commence their greatest cultural rite, the Tea Dance. Demented from the intense sun, smashed on a couple of cocktails sloshing around an empty stomach, the men will rock the walls of the two nightclubs, The Monster and The Ice Palace, with their very souls.

Leading the frenzy is a diminuitive man in a loose silk chemise, which fills with the heated air like a sail. His name is Martin Quartararo, and he is the carburetor of this engine. Only his exhaustion will end the party, when hours from now he crawls to the door. To Monday morning, Martin and the men of Fire Island's Eastern Kingdom say, "Never!"

Out in the Atlantic, the gentle trade winds continue to blow as they always have and always will, moving white water west under blue skies. In the Southern Hemisphere their sister winds are their mirror image, twisting east with the spin of the earth. As a rule the winds meet at the equator, rise as hot air, and flow back toward their respective poles. The equator is known as a place of no wind at all, once called the Doldrums by frustrated sailing men who waited weeks at a time for a breeze to move their frigates.

In late September of 1985, however, there is an irregularity. The sun has spent the last three months giving the Northern Hemisphere its summer, and the hottest spot on earth is not the equator, but somewhere north of it. The southern trade wind has wandered across the equator looking for that hot spot, where she will lightly kiss her northern brother before they rise together and part company. But as she is lured across the equator, the southern wind is given a rude jolt. She will discover that things are done differently up here; just as milk swirls differently down the drain, wind twists differently.

The southern wind is jerked around to the west. Now, when she meets her northern brother, they will not deflect gently off each other and rise in Doldrum-like serenity. They will meet head on in a spinning, eddying dance. It is an intimate thing for brother and sister to do. Nevertheless, the meteorologists, the moralists of the sky, will not condemn it. It is a predictable occurrence up here in September, just as it is below the equator in March.

What will make the weathermen nervous, though, what will make them linger at their instruments through their coffee breaks, is the heat that cloaks the eastern Atlantic this particular September. Hot air rises. Cooler air rushes in to replace it, and that rush is the wind. The hotter the Atlantic where the two trade winds meet, the more likely their innocent sibling dance will turn into something wilder and more incestuous. The meteorologists have a name for this kind of atmospheric condition, where air is rushing around under a volatile sky, and it is a name that makes them uncomfortable to say and to hear. Low pressure. Everything is getting sucked up. There's nothing to push down, to keep a lid on things.

Oh, sometimes you need a little instability to shake things up when the air is oppressive, stifling, not moving—the kind of thing that anyone who has ever spent a summer in a coastal city knows very well. When it gets like that, you'd like nothing better than to have someone take the lid off the sky, suck it all out, and start over. The problem is that once the lid is off, and things start getting sucked up and out, it might get a little wilder and more chaotic than you'd like before someone finally wrestles the lid back on. Already, in this hot late September of 1985, the citizens of the Cape Verde Islands off the west coast of Africa have experienced this discomfort.

Preening on her timeless perch, the peregrine falcon has finally distinguished herself from the ornamentation of the Belvedere Hotel. Dozens of men have gathered in the courtyard, astonished by the bird's beauty.

But a half a century ago, her reception would have been very different. Not only was her classic profile more commonplace in the sky, but Cherry Grove itself was a sleepy middle-class community that didn't get excited about much of anything.

At that time, Fire Island's handful of homosexuals could be found in Ocean Beach, Dana Wallace's community in the western part of the island. When young Dana peeked inside Sis Norris's bar with young Peggy snuggled in the crook of his arm, he made no secret of his schoolboy yearnings; but Fanny Brice, cavorting in the midnight ocean, was obliged to hide the fact that she was a lesbian.

Ocean Beach was a place of great divisions and great tension. On the one hand were the homosexuals and the theatrical exotics, the Brices, the Gershwins, the Jimmy Durantes; on the other were working-class people—carpenters, sons of carpenters, all kinds of tradesmen that the Depression had driven to further and further extremes until here they were, trying to scratch a living out of the sand. The great in-between, the middle-class New Yorkers who would one day be the backbone of the population and act as a buffer between the two extremes, were nowhere to be found. The social rift was wide and tense.

An island population that winters together and then caters to a flamboyant summer clientele for a couple of months is often characterized by two things. The first is heavy drinking. The second is a complex kind of unity that is in turn made of two parts—an intense, often neurotic set of interrelationships, and a uniform hatred and mistrust of the summer people on whom they depend for their income. The natives of Fire Island's Western Kingdom in the thirties fit the profile well: a small, hard-drinking, church-going population of tradesmen and their families who lived only to serve the tourists. On first glance they would seem to have been cut from the same cloth as the sea-blistered Long Island fishermen who swept the bay floor for shellfish and hauled seine nets through the ocean—proud, independent, hard-working people who live out their lives in poverty and dignity.

But the fishermen only catch the fish; they don't have to smile and serve them up on a platter to city people. The grocers and carpenters and plumbers of Fire Island knew that their clientele would arrive in April and stay until September, parading down Main Street in exotic clothes and leading their purebred dogs on leashes.

Oh, Gershwin, a Brooklyn boy, and the well-camouflaged Miss Brice and the good-time Durante were acceptable and even popular. But famous theatre people were not the only exotics who poured off the boats from the mainland in the prewar years. There were people from the worlds of fashion and fabric design, people who had a product other than themselves . . . and did not have to be as circumspect about their public personality as the theatre people. In other words they could let it all hang out a little more, and they did; in the case of Antoine, too far.

Antoine was a man of many parts. He was one of Manhattan's best-known hairdressers. He invented Bains de Soleil, the leading suntan cream of the era. He entertained the Prince of Romania. He went to the beach every day with several servants and typed his autobiography under a huge umbrella. He led a life that was probably dazzling even to the Prince of Romania, and certainly to the natives of Fire Island. And to make matters worse, his house was right across the street from the Catholic church. Every Sunday the islanders would emerge from Mass to the spectacle of an Antoine excess, usually a lavish and decadent brunch that was just beginning to pick up steam.

—

But even that would have been all right if it weren't for the outdoor toilet. Though Antoine lived in the lap of luxury, with his grand piano and wall-to-wall carpeting (everyone else considered themselves lucky if they had enough kerosene to keep their cook stoves going), he did make one concession to "roughing it." He had an outdoor toilet. Not an ordinary one, but a roofless one—the better for the Oriental tree inside it to grow. And the door that protected the modesty of whoever was using the facility was minimal, kind of a swinging, saloon-type door that revealed the occupant from the knees down.

So the passerby would see Antoine's toilet (for the bold designer had insisted on placing it toward the front of the house in full public view), a silk kimono hanging on the swinging door, and beyond it the naked spindly legs of Antoine, the Prince of Romania, or some Manhattan creature of the night. It was too much. It pushed the natives' brittle pride beyond its breaking point, and gave them a focus for their frustrated vassalage and their long winter nights. What were their children supposed to think?

The faggots had to go. Oh, no one knew for sure that they were screwing each other on silk sheets in the royal inner bedchamber, but the natives felt they could make a pretty good guess about it.

First they set out to prove it, and once they did that, they would mete out some justice. An ad hoc committee of citizens was formed, what in the Old West would have been called a posse. They settled on a method still popular among authorities wishing to prove moral degeneracy of any kind, a method many feel is as immoral as the kind of behavior it seeks to expose. A decoy gets the victim to commit himself to the forbidden act and then arrests him for it. In this case the decoy chosen was the son of one of the posse members, an angelic teenager that the men thought would prove irresistible.

They were right. One night the teenager, a slow-witted boy with no real idea of what he was doing, was sent to Sis Norris's bar with an ascot around his neck. Sure enough, he found himself very shortly in conversation with a houseguest of Antoine's, a window dresser from Lord and Taylor's department store in Manhattan. As he had been instructed to do, the boy suggested they continue their discussion up by the ocean among the high dunes.

Once there, the moon and soft sea air worked their usual magic, and the smitten window dresser made a romantic suggestion. At this point the posse leapt up from behind a stand of beach grass and beat the hell out of him. The window dresser went to the hospital; the boy, in one of those strange twists of justice, found himself publicly ridiculed and was forced, with his family, to leave the island. Antoine's house was burned to the ground, and the gay population, a lost tribe led by a hairdresser, began to wander.

T H R E E

FIRE ISLAND, WEDNESDAY, SEPTEMBER 25, 1985, LATE AFTERNOON

Dana Wallace has not allowed bittersweet tequila memories to
deter him from his mission. He has picked up his mail from
Audrey the handsome, quiet postmistress and is pedaling back out
of Ocean Beach. Passing the shop just south of the old Goldie's
Bar, he feels a familiar tug at his innards. The bastards have turned
it into some kind of a trendy clothes store! Garish, cheap, of-the-
moment, the goods have about as much integrity as the owners, a
young couple Wallace has seen about town in matching parachute
jumpsuits. Let them jump out a plane for real into a swirl of
German anti-aircraft fire, he is thinking, and see how long the
smiles stay on their faces!

—

Of course, Wallace is not a stupid man and he sees quickly through his misanthropy to the real source of his anger. This used to be *his* photography shop! This windowful of crap is where he himself once displayed his wares: photographs, exquisite ones, luminous ones of the summer people perched on the dunes, the Atlantic behind them, the beach grass tickling their chins as they affected a distant gaze. Christ, he was talented. There wasn't a matron too fat or a child so vapid that Wallace couldn't ennoble in a photograph.

Plunged into gloom, he leaves the village. That his love affair with the camera should have left such a bitter legacy deeply disturbs him. He remembers his first camera better than his first lay. It was a Speed Graphic and he did in fact sleep with it . . . underneath the grandstands of the old Hialeah racetrack in Florida when he was twenty, newspapers stuffed in his clothes to keep warm. Then, in the misty dawn, he exercised racehorses to keep body and soul together until some kind of a photography break came, just like the waiter/actors do in New York.

And did it ever come! He remembers the very day. He was getting drunk with his mentor, an old photographer for the *Miami Herald*, when the phone call came from the City Desk: Rush out and get some shots of an eight-car accident on the old Tamiami Trail. The only trouble was the older man was too plastered to get out the front door, so who else but Dana Wallace fought his way through those police lines and got those pictures of death the public clamored for? There were people who thought he should have gotten a Pulitzer Prize for it!

There was really nothing he couldn't do with a camera. In fact, if the truth be known, it was really him and his pal Jimmy Jones who invented the first racetrack photo finish. All they did was rig a trip wire to Dana's old Speed Graphic and the first horse to cross the finish line took a picture of himself.

Hell, it revolutionized the sport! But then Dana went off to World War Two, and when he got back some conniving bastards had refined the technique, patented it, and were getting all the money and credit for it . . . while Dana Wallace was defending their pale asses overseas! That was justice for you.

—

Enough. Wallace knows how circular these bitter thoughts can be, and he resolves to entertain them no longer. He has no regrets about serving his country, and certainly doesn't think he squandered his talents in the South Pacific. Clutching his Speed Graphic in one hand and his weapon in the other, he took some of the great beach combat shots of the war. They were desperate pictures that defined the horror of the amphibious landing. The faces of those GI's pouring off the landing craft, frozen in the middle of terrified war cries, found their way to the pages of *Look* magazine . . . and became some of America's most indelible images of the Pacific Theatre of War.

No, Dana Wallace has no regrets. And even if he does, he will not admit them today. He is helped in this resolve by a magnificent sunset that has triumphed over the threatening rain clouds. If the sun can prevail, so can I, he thinks, pushing his rusty Schwinn up the walkway to his ocean home.

Dismounting, he scans his mail for something personal, a real letter, with his name and address written by a human hand with a fountain pen. No luck. Nothing but computer-feed-out bullshit. He'll have no trouble starting his fire tonight. But right now, with the astonishing dusk just at its peak, is no time to anticipate the darkness. In fact this is the high point of his day, more so even than cocktail hour. It's time for his evening gallop.

He makes his way down to the driftwood barn of his own design and construction, smiling inwardly. Of course, all the timid bastards told him at the beginning it was impossible. Horses on Fire Island? Thoroughbreds? How would you feed them? Where would they pasture? Where would they roam? Where would they train? Right there beside the big breakers was the answer. Wallace coaxed, sweated, and bled a layer of green grass from the sand, and got in a load of hay from the mainland for the winter. Pretty soon the naysayers were begging him to let their daughters have a ride.

And if Dana Wallace's prize colt could talk, he'd tell you that life is pretty good. Most of his competitors in the six-furlong sprint he will enter next week are at this moment packed into huge barns at Belmont Park that house forty or fifty other horses. Maelstrom, as Wallace has named him, ambles around his spacious corral by the sea. It is a leisurely life for a racehorse, but not a lazy one. He has a good chance to win next week. His legs and his heart are strong, the result of hours of pounding through the sand with a grown man on his back. When he enters the starting gate next week at Belmont, the bit cutting into his gums and the crowd buzzing in his ear, he will make Wallace proud of him, win or lose.

At the corral fence, Wallace lures Maelstrom over with a handful of grain and grabs the halter. He takes a moment to admire the classic profile. Financially, the racing game was futile, even disastrous, but simply existing next to these proud, fire-breathing creatures . . . that was reward enough for Dana Wallace. That and the trip upon which he was about to embark, *and*, of course, the pleasure of proving the timid bastards wrong.

He scans the beach, which is blessedly empty. On Friday the balmy weather will lure plenty of people out for an Indian Summer weekend. Then Dana Wallace will ride on the beach only at the risk of eliciting a complaint from someone. He is perfectly capable of handling those complaints, usually by ignoring them, but he vastly prefers the hassle-free kind of expedition this particular evening offers.

He tosses the saddle on the bay colt and swings himself up. Underneath him, Maelstrom bristles at the weight. The most he ever has to carry at Belmont is a hundred-and-ten-pound Latin wearing silks. And even then, he doesn't have to negotiate, ankle deep, the several miles of wet sand that now stretch in front of him. The colt would prefer a conventional racetrack.

Wallace gives him a kick in the ribs, and man and beast set out, Wallace's pair of black labrador retrievers plodding behind. Overhead, a dozen sea gulls hover, mildly irritating horse and rider by diving for the discarded rinds of an orange Wallace has begun to eat.

Many birds have a skittish, highly sensitized digestive system, but gulls, the good old boys of the sky, will take anything

—

at all. The twentieth century, with its sophisticated array of garbage, has been the sea gull's golden era. The bird haunts the Dumpsters and restaurant back alleys of Manhattan. He dives for a sandwich in the hands of a secretary on a sunny lunch hour.

And even here, in his unspoiled native habitat, he takes what's left. The loon may dive a fathom for a fish, the heron may trap one in shallow water and pierce it with its bill. The gull will wait until these efforts have been made, and feast on the discarded gristle and bone, swallowing a little sand along with it to grind the mess up for its long-suffering stomach. And when migration time comes (as it will any day now), the gull will go nowhere. As songbirds take off for the sunny South, the gull will wave goodbye and continue to scour the seaside for little bits of nothing . . . whatever the stingy winter coughs up.

And when spring comes, and the gulls go to their nesting island a mile or two inland, they will mate out in the open, in the midst of a vast colony. A gull doesn't need a private booth in a restaurant to make romance, and neither does Dana Wallace. In fact Wallace has consummated several love affairs among these dunes, as a pair of horses stood tethered to a shadbush and waited, mutely shocked by the thrashing about of their masters. Offer a woman a ride on a horse and you're halfway there, Wallace has always felt. As the last of the sun sinks beyond the dormered roofs of Point O' Woods, Wallace calls up a particularly saucy memory . . . a young woman, too young perhaps, in the wavy grass not far from this very spot. Meticulously, Wallace reconstructs in his mind the flawless body of the child-woman, and even remembers her smells.

The horn of a yellow van blares a few feet from his face, startling Wallace out of his erotic daydream. Maelstrom rears and nearly dumps his rider. Fighting to stay up, Wallace loudly curses the driver. But since the vehicle the man is driving is a school bus, and since Wallace wasn't looking where he was going, he stops himself just short of unloading all his bile on the driver. Bringing Maelstrom to hand, he discovers that the school bus is empty . . . except for the man behind the wheel.

—

The driver is James Lindsey, a man whose face Wallace knows well; they have both lived here longer than just about anybody. In fact, they are often compared to each other, but neither man relishes the comparison. There is always a bit of friction between them, and never much contact.

James Lindsey is a gull among gulls. He is a second-generation islander, the son of a carpenter and his wife who were forced by the Depression to the very edge of Long Island looking for work.

Then God stepped in, the way Bertha, Lindsey's mother, sees it. The call came for workers to build houses on a godforsaken little island that was acquiring some popularity as a summer resort. Pregnant with James, Bertha and her young husband got on a boat in the clear cold spring of 1930 and crossed the Great South Bay to Fire Island. While Bertha worked in the crew kitchen, her husband was framing some of the finest houses on Fire Island. Crawling over the naked rafters as the beach plums bloomed and the wild ocean roared and the air warmed, he fell in love with the place. When the job was over, the construction boss, a sour man named Bayliss, came by with their ferry tickets back to the mainland. The Lindseys declined them. They were staying here, they informed him.

But where would they live? Bayliss wanted to know.

In one of the houses they had framed, said the Lindseys.

But the houses were unfinished. There were no walls, no toilets, no lights. It was no place for a pregnant woman, said Bayliss.

It would suit them anyway, said the Lindseys.

But the houses belonged to someone else, said Bayliss. They had been commissioned by people from Manhattan.

When the owners arrived, the Lindseys assured him, they would find someplace else.

Bayliss shook his head and wandered away. These were headstrong people.

The Lindseys stayed, but they found that island life was not an automatic paradise. These gulls were facing into a tough wind.

The building jobs were slow to come; the Depression was still on. The day young James was born in early 1931, his father was out scouring the beach for light bulb filaments that could be sold for salvage. Not long afterward, Bertha herself was out on the frigid spring bay, mucking up the bottom with a pole, waking the startled flounders from their winter sleep . . . and hauling them back to her hungry family by the tubload.

Young James's first memory is of bread baking. Bertha baked six loaves at a time, and ordered her flour from the mainland in five-hundred-pound-barrels at a time, along with a tub of butter. As soon as the little boy could walk, he was dispatched to the Sunken Forest with a basket to fill with wild grapes, which would one day be the jam he spread on his mother's bread. These were country people. They kept pigs and cows, and coaxed corn and tomatoes and cucumbers from between the tough strands of beach grass up on the dunes, where they built the first house that was all theirs.

James often dreams about those days, now more than fifty years past, as he drives along the autumn beach behind the wheel of the school bus. This was the time of year when that corn would get ripe, and those brown corn silks would fly in the breeze like pennants on a yacht.

But on this day his reveries have been interrupted by an announcement on the car radio . . . an interruption that nearly caused the accident with Dana Wallace and his horse. The crackling voice on the radio called up another, jumbled image from Lindsey's childhood. It said that a low-pressure system had formed a "Tropical Disturbance" off the west coast of Africa, and that the meteorologists would keep an eye on it, lest it develop into a storm that might cause problems for the East Coast of the United States.

The report brought a smile to the face of the usually taciturn James Lindsey. He's been through more storms than he can count on this island, and most of them have been disappointing. By the time they get here they've usually nicked a dozen isthmuses on the way up the coast, and wind up doing nothing but dumping a few inches of pain-in-the-ass rain. The only one that lived up to its billing, for one thing because it didn't get any, was the hurricane that happened when he was a little boy, the hurricane of 1938. Lindsey is pitched back into memory as Dana Wallace and his horse, composure regained, amble up to him.

Young James remembers being sent for at school and racing home to find his mother scouring the horizon for him like a whaler's wife. He remembers the notch next to his street filling with water from bay to ocean, and families evacuating in rowboats. He remembers the top of Flynn's Bar down the road blowing off, and old man Flynn serving drinks to the weekend crowd anyway, as if the wild, wide-open sky above them wasn't drenching their smart linen clothes and rattling their mortal souls and diluting their whiskey. He remembers the streets filling with marauders, taking advantage of the tragedy and confusion by looting the smart summer houses.

But more than any other image of that dark Friday in 1938, there is an indelible one that shaped the rest of James Lindsey's life. It is the image of a man in uniform, a United States Coast Guard Officer, starting the engine of his power boat and taking off. The man had weakened and panicked and forgotten his vows and the traditions of his uniform, and was saving himself. As he gunned his engine, drowning out the voices of the people calling to him for help, his eyes met young James Lindsey's through the spray. James will never forget the terror and chaos in those eyes.

Ordinarily, Dana Wallace and James Lindsey might have aimed a few hot words at each other over the accident they just avoided. Both men have pretty short fuses. But since each feels himself to blame, they approach the other with neither blame nor apologies, but with the mute way of old islanders, which seems to say, "Well, here we are, we exist."

With horse and rider looming over the cab of the school bus, James Lindsey, not usually a gregarious man, is moved to share the radio reports and the story of the cowardly Coast Guardsman with Dana Wallace. It's a rare intimacy between the two men. There is an awkward pause. Then Wallace smiles widely and nods. Lindsey's tale has found a sympathetic audience. Both men hate the primping, officious Coast Guard, and in fact disrespect uniforms of any kind in the extreme. In this sense they fall into the category of Classic Conservatives. They believe utterly in the freedom of the individual. The chickens James Lindsey raises in his backyard are no different than the racehorse Dana Wallace sits atop. Both are symbols of freedom, as surely as they are in violation of laws, health codes, and fashionable neighbors.

But there are differences between the two men, profound enough to have kept them, these fifty-some-odd years, from becoming friends.

It involves the town of Point O' Woods, whose dormered roofs, purple now in the dusk, provide the backdrop for their conversation. Perched on the very edge of the Western Kingdom, Point O' Woods is the last outpost before the dense Sunken Forest. It also has a fence around it. Inside the fence are a collection of fine, weathered old Cape houses, a few of them built by the Lindseys themselves. Inside the houses are people almost exclusively of one ethnic profile: white Anglo-Saxon Protestants. These are the American aristocrats, families of old wealth and manners who assemble on their vast porches once the sun is past the yardarm (a moment open to individual interpretation) and toast each other with single-malt whiskey in Waterford stemware. To many they are harmless enough, with their blue blazers and their narrow, weakening gene pool. To others they are not.

It has to do with the fence.

On the other side of that fence, back in the volatile 1960s, there lived a couple of elderly Jewish concentration camp survivors. One night the old woman had a nightmare that she was back in Auschwitz. She sat bolt upright in bed, and there, out her window, was the jagged silhouette of the barbed-wire Point O' Woods fence.

She went berserk. Despite the efforts of her husband to calm her, she retreated into an emotional shell from which she was never to emerge. As she was taken off the island to a mainland hospital, news of the incident spread quickly through the Western

Kingdom, which then, as now, had more than its share of liberals and liberal journalists. The stage was set for the kind of inflamed theatrical event that enlivened that era. A group of protestors broke through the fence and spent the day marching up and down the forbidden streets of Point O' Woods just to show that they could if they wanted to.

Bemused, the WASPs watched the ragged exhibition from their dormered windows. Of course nothing changed, but the point, and the parameters of the argument about freedom had been drawn: Did *anyone* have a right, morally, ethically or legally, to be so *goddamn exclusive?*

To Dana Wallace, the answer is an emphatic no. In fact, he has taken pleasure in personally violating the privacy of Point O' Woods many times, most recently last week by jumping the dunes and galloping a big black mare through the prize begonia patch of some old aristocratic biddy.

As far as James Lindsey is concerned, the woman would have been within her rights to blow Wallace off the horse with a shotgun. Though he himself has no respect for the overbred ninnies he knows in Point O' Woods, Lindsey respects their right to private domain. In fact he thinks the place is a model of that principle. When a young WASP prince gets himself into trouble (as they often do, raising hell high on the drugs they've bought in Ocean Beach or over on the mainland) the matter is taken care of internally. Inside the fence. The law enforcement officials are not called in. The elders of the tribe deal with it, effectively and discreetly. That is very close to Lindsey's utopian vision of a world without uniforms. However, it is not a totally consistent view. There is a point at which the purity of James Lindsey's conservatism clouds over, and it has to do with the people who live beyond Point O' Woods and beyond Sunken Forest, in the Gay Eastern Kingdom of Fire Island.

Every so often Lindsey will be driving the school bus along the beach and perceive, in the distant dunes, the naked rear ends of two male lovers flailing away in the clear seaside air. Lindsey's instinct is to run them over.

—

To Wallace, famous for his sexual excesses, the right to screw, in the dunes or anywhere else, is an inalienable one. Though he is as full of macho bluster and contempt for gays as any of his Western Kingdom neighbors, he finds himself aligned with them, side by side, against the prudes of the world. That would include Lindsey.

"If you're so high on personal freedom," Wallace might say to him, "doesn't that include the freedom to screw in the dunes?"

"Not if my children have to watch it," the family man Lindsey would counter.

"They're free to turn their heads away," Dana Wallace would reply.

But on this particular afternoon the men are not having this kind of conversation. In fact rarely do they have any conversation, and Lindsey's story about the behavior of the Coast Guardsman in 1938 may be their lengthiest and most personal dialogue ever. Today they are in harmony. They remain on the darkening beach reacting to the radio feed about the "Tropical Disturbance" with equal contempt. The weathermen, buried by their charts, machines, satellites, and other bric-a-brac, are making something out of nothing, which is basically their job. Wallace and Lindsey gruffly acknowledge their mutual understanding of this fact, and part with manly grunts and chortles.

In fact, even the weathermen don't really expect the Tropical Disturbance to amount to anything. The trade winds off Africa frequently get caught up in low-pressure systems, especially in Septembers with this kind of heat. But the weathermen will publicize it anyway, because what they really don't want, what they must at all costs avoid, is a repeat performance of the most embarrassing episode in the history of their profession.

James Lindsey was spared the image of death in his child's storehouse of memories of the hurricane of '38, but the rest of the world was not. It was a world poised on the edge of the old and the new. The next year the New York World's Fair would reveal astonishing, unsettling visions of the world to come, but in 1938 waiters still wore black tail coats and royalty still ruled some of the countries of Europe. And it was the infancy of the science of meteorology. There were no satellite photographs of weather. People didn't know what was coming until it got there. The only warning came from ships unlucky enough to be caught in the middle of the ocean, and their only interest was in getting the hell out, not in counting the raindrops or gaging the wind.

In the fall of 1938 the coastal residents of the northeastern United States were cleaning up their summer cottages, only mildly diverted by the steady northeaster that had been pelting them with rain and warm wind for a couple of days. Within hours a thousand of them were dead, and the map of the coastline was changed forever. By the time the hurricane disappeared into the Canadian northwoods, still cutting a swath of uprooted pines a hundred miles wide, it had left a blanket of death over New England.

A wet, rotting blanket; death by drowning.

Oh, the wind took its toll, to be sure, slinging its lethal cargo everywhere at one hundred miles an hour; cutting throats with flying glass and leaving jugular veins to flow dry; ripping the roofs off houses and flinging them, like giant razor blades, to lop off ancient trees at the roots; impaling birds on weather vanes and nudging full school busses into ravines.

But the wind, when it deals death, is invisible and it is mercifully fast. Drowning is slow and it has a color.

The color is green. When a hurricane blows the top off the sky, not only does the air want to rush up and out, but so does everything else, even the water. The dreaded Low Pressure. Nothing stays down. The ocean swells and puckers, trying to climb out through the hole in the sky. The wind pushes the huge green swell forward until it swallows the land. When it's over, turtles and crabs are squirming on living room floors, and radios and Christmas tree ornaments are floating in the ocean. Mice chatter on floating screen doors as the turgid corpses of rats bob past them. And the pink lacy areoles of human lungs are suddenly engorged by what they were never meant to hold: water. Tongues are stiffened and blackened by a last, twisted gasp for a breath that will never come.

The green sea has invaded the land.

Images from '38:

A man pushes his brand-new Mercury to fifty miles an hour to try to outdistance the huge wave, but it catches him and neither he nor the car are ever seen again.

"I was sitting in my living room with my mother," wrote one survivor, "and we were both knitting. Suddenly the ocean burst into the hallway. I could hear the house breaking up around us. The water came into the living room and took my mother away. I never saw her again."

Sometimes summer cottagers, adept at water sports, could swim to safety, but their domestics could not.

"She was from the Bahamas," wrote a man of his maid, "but she'd never learned to swim. We were evacuating and she wanted to go back for her hat. I told her not to, but it was too late. The last I saw of her, as I reached for her, was her bright black face and the feather on the hat, all of it a swirl disappearing into the green water."

And then the occasional miracle.

"Our house was floating in the bay," a young Fire Island mother remembered, "and the water kept rising through it. I took my little boy into the attic and picked him up and held him to my chest and started singing to him. The water kept rising . . . to my ankles, my knees, and finally up to our necks. I kept singing. Then, at our chins the water stopped rising and started going back down again."

When the ocean finally receded from the land, like water being sucked down a drain, the world had been changed. Two-hundred-year-old trees, by now old friends recognizable in oil landscapes, were gone. Things of the Old World, things delicate and rickety and of another time, had been swept away. The threatening New World, with the Fascists prevailing in Spain and Hitler marching through Poland, was making good on its threats.

In the northeastern United States, the hurricane of 1938 had killed a thousand people. It had gouged pastoral valleys and crippled great cities. It had drowned five thousand cows, and it had torn up ten thousand miles of railroad tracks.

"I looked for my wife and daughter for days," said a man, "and I couldn't find them. I got back to the wreckage of our cottage and sat down on the front steps. I smelled death somewhere. They were keeping the bodies on the village green, where the band plays in the summer, so I'd gotten used to the smell.

I got up and looked under the steps and found the bodies of my family."

The following week was sunny and clear. "There's no better weather," said Ernest Hemingway, one of that era's most popular writers, "than hurricane season when you're not having a hurricane."

F   O   U   R

Nature's design is benevolent in ways that
take time to see. Hurricanes bring death and sorrow, but they
send fresh inlets roaring through into stagnant bays. The hurricane
of 1938 took more lives than the Chicago Fire, but like that sad
event, it created new opportunities.

In Chicago, a new city had to be built from the ground up
for a homeless population. Architects arrived from everywhere,
titillated by the blank canvas on which they could practice their
art and bankrolled by a million insurance settlements. The result
was an explosion of building that still dazzles the eye.

In 1938 in the eastern section of Fire Island, a small village
beside a grove of cherry trees was leveled by the storm. What
had been a pleasant middle-class community was suddenly a plain

—

of muck and splinters. Afterward, as the villagers picked through the rubble that had been their homes, a gaunt stranger in a white robe circulated among them. Several steps behind him, a group of intense young men followed.

It was Antoine the hairdresser and his persecuted, nomadic tribe of homosexuals. Wandering since their banishment from Ocean Beach, they had come to this fresh spot, scoured by the storm, to try to build new lives from the ground up. The villagers quaked. They were conservative people. The presence of the flamboyant tribe totally unnerved them.

But nature, as well as being demonic and benevolent, is also evenhanded. Over in the western section, far beyond the Sunken Forest, the village of Saltaire had also been devastated by the storm. Why not, reasoned the homeless middle-class people of Cherry Grove, rebuild in Saltaire? It was a solid family community that gave every appearance of remaining that way. So the population was reshuffled. The straights moved to Saltaire, and the gays settled into desolate Cherry Grove.

In the Galapagos, Darwin came upon finches who had been so long settled into various islands along the archipelago that, in the process of adaptation, they had become utterly unlike each other. In isolation the differences only grew. So now did Fire Islanders dig into their various niches along the barely traversable thirty-mile barrier beach. The WASPs had theirs, the Jews theirs, the middle-class Catholics theirs, and now, on barren land scoured even of its cherry trees, the gays, led by Antoine, their Moses, finally had theirs.

Soon gay celebrities flocked to the safe harbor. W. H. Auden came, the rumpled poet who ten years earlier had explored with Christopher Isherwood the decadence of Berlin. Now he was on Fire Island, on the threshold of an even greater, but sunnier decadence. Janet Flanner, the great lesbian journalist, arrived with her lover. It would be a city not just of men, but of all God's persecuted children. There were immigrants from the world of design, from the world of the theatre. What new fabric of a population was ever stitched together with such rich bolts of cloth! The peacock, so long frightened of fanning his magnificent tailfeathers, was opening them at last, and it was a dazzlement to the eye. At first the drag was discreet, and the fashion high. Young men could be seen wearing peach-colored silk pajamas and wide-brimmed straw hats, the latest things out of Paris. By the end of the forties, the fashion was to go even higher, and much, much lower. The point was that they could dress like the Queen of England, or a woman at a Hadassah luncheon, or a turnip. For the first time in their lives, they could do whatever they wanted.

Martin Quartararo is not a student of Cherry Grove's history, but he is certainly one of its great beneficiaries. As the small man flops down at his table on the gray flagstone patio of the Belvedere Hotel, with the peregrine falcon still perched on the turret overhead, he bellows for a cappuccino. He needs it desperately. The night, which has never really ended, was a rough, rough night. Through smudged, mascaraed eyes he notices the big, elegant bird and experiences his first calm for hours.

Whether stomping the dance floor of the Ice Palace, or recuperating from it on a patio, Martin is on the leading stylistic edge of the Eastern Kingdom. The term *gay* was made to describe him, whether you take it to mean the modern American homosexual or the way your grandmother did: gay . . . rapacious, devil-may-care, insouciant, will-o-the-wisp, merry, exuberant, and high-spirited.

Martin was born and raised in the French Quarter of New Orleans, a strange place for a boyhood, a place where, the wisdom goes, people go not only to put on a garish Mardi Gras mask but to take off the masks of their everyday lives.

It is hard in such a place to go undistracted about the daily business of boyhood, the shooting of marbles, the collecting of baseball cards, the skinning of knees. Most boys go through a period of harmlessly messing around with each other, sexually. Martin never grew out of it. By the time he was sixteen, he was dropping off his girlfriend, Grace, after a date, then wandering off into the French Quarter to seduce a businessman.

—

It was a tough place to be confused about your sexuality, because there were always people wanting to hurry you along one path or another for their own reasons. What made it tougher still for Martin was his homelife. His parents were not New Orleans bon vivants who could accept his deviations as youthful experiments or part of the civic live-and-let-live spirit of fun. They were Born Again Christians! They had a shop that sold religious curios *right in the middle of the French Quarter!*

Poor Martin. During Mardi Gras he would march past his parents' shop clutching his mask, praying they wouldn't recognize their only son prancing down St. Peter's Street in full lace drag. One year his mother came across his costume, a velvet evening gown, and covered a footstool with it! Aghast, horrified, and angry, Martin couldn't make a peep about it.

He had a job in the most familiar kind of tourist ripoff in the Quarter, the phony espresso joint. They run strong, regular coffee through an espresso machine with no insides. The tourists think it's the real thing and sip it out of tiny cups while someone takes a souvenir picture of them living it up. The cup of coffee and the snapshot cost five dollars each. It was a good place to meet people from other places, especially ones with money, and one night Martin met the man of his dreams. He was a traveling salesman with a nationally tested line of romantic bull. Martin swallowed it and fell in love with him. They had a torrid love affair, in the shadows of the Mississippi levee, on the shores of Lake Pontchartrain, in the little bistros of the Quarter. The only trouble was the interruptions. The salesman would be gone for weeks at a time on business trips.

Martin was starting to get a little strung out. Meanwhile, at the family home on St. Peter's Street, packed to the rafters with religious artifacts, the situation was becoming intolerable. And Grace, Martin's "high school sweetheart," the cover-up for his lascivious maraudings in the Quarter, had gotten married.

What a relief!

The problem was that his mother, anticipating his despair, was starting to fix him up with other girls! Martin groaned inwardly at the thought of it. And he languished morbidly during the long absences of the salesman. Well, his mother figured, he's still carrying a torch for Grace!

And she would plunge all the harder into the matchmaking.

Martin was going nuts. He needed some clarity and honesty in his life. At last, a phone call came from the salesman. He was back in town! As Martin rode the trolley to the old St. Charles Hotel, where the guy was staying, he was feeling clear about what he wanted for the first time in his life. He and the salesman would make a commitment to each other, and he would tell his parents. Open. Clean. Painful, but honest.

Martin sat on the edge of the hotel bed and began to speak in earnest, measured tones, even before the salesman could pour him a drink. By the time the boy was done, the man could barely contain his amusement.

Commitment? Honesty? What did Martin think the guy was doing on all those lonely nights in hotel rooms from New York to Tulsa? Curling up with a good book? Crocheting doilies for the home they would one day share? Get real! He was getting laid, as often and as happily as he could. The domestic dreams were for the suckers, just like the phony espresso. Martin was buying one, and dishing out the other. It was time he got smart.

The boy ran from the hotel room in tears. He ran the full length of gracious, wooded old St. Charles Avenue until he was back in the garish Quarter, his own demented hometown. He spotted the familiar filthy marquee of Dixie's, with its punched-out bulbs. It was a depressing place run by an old lesbian band-leader from the thirties, and a perfect reflection of his mood. He was just about to go in and indulge himself in some ugly sex or some pretty cocktails, when an old gray Dodge pulled up beside him. He recognized the driver as a furtive lay from his teenage days. The man said he'd seen Martin running down the street crying and wondered what was wrong. Could he be of help, somehow? Martin remembered him now, a sympathetic older man named Bill who always had a big crush on him. They drove awhile,

—

and Martin poured out his true confessions. The man nodded and comforted. Finally Martin said, "Will you take me home please?"

"That's what I'm doing," said Bill, peering at the street signs on the tiny Old World corners of the Quarter.

"I mean your home," said Martin.

Bill burned rubber making his U-turn. Back in his sprawling place on the Esplanade, he bathed Martin in an antique tub with legs, talcumed him, fed him, and tucked him in. An hour earlier Martin had been in Love's hammerlock; obsessed, insecure, demanding through tears. In no time at all he had executed a complete reversal. Now he was on top, and any desperate behavior would come from the other guy. There was no doubt which way he liked it better.

As Martin sips his cappuccino at the Belvedere and remembers Bill with a sad smile, Dana Wallace is washing down Maelstrom after the ocean gallop, and James Lindsey is turning off the ignition key of his school bus. And far away, an event is happening that renders obsolete the announcement on Lindsey's radio. Within the past couple of hours, the Tropical Disturbance off the coast of Africa has deteriorated past the point where it can comfortably be called a "disturbance."

When we last observed them, the southern trade winds had been lured across the equator by the heat of the northern summer, and the twist of the earth had sucked them into a kind of eddying waltz with their northern brother.

Now, the innocent dance of brother and sister has begun to lose its innocence. It has begun to resemble nothing so much as the frantic whirling gambols into which the celibate Shakers poured all their dammed-up sexual energies. Now, it has an element of the dark and demonic about it. What has brought it to this level, which the meteorologists must bring themselves to call not a Tropical Disturbance but an outright Tropical Storm, is the vast Atlantic itself.

Hot air rises. Cooler air rushes in to replace it. But when

---

that rising air is not only hot but wet, its molecules, contracting in the thin upper air, dump a load of rain. That is the process of condensation. It creates heat, which only sucks the air in more intensely. Now it doesn't rise so much as it flies upward. More air rushes in to fill the vacuum, more rain falls, and the storm becomes its own self-contained little slice of hell. It creates its own heat, and its own vortex of twisting air. Now it exists independent of the trade winds and the African heat that spawned it, and is liable to do anything it wants, either in terms of direction or intensity. It may take a few wild convoluted spins around itself and die, or it may head west toward the Americas, and accelerate to a higher level . . . perhaps, conceivably, even the highest level.

Of course, it probably will not. Devoutly, the weathermen pray that it will not. But there is simply no way to predict what will happen next. For all their space-age techniques, the scientists have now been reduced to observers. The thing will do whatever it likes, then let us know about it.

Oblivious to any weather except the weather of the moment, Martin Quartararo finishes his cappuccino and prepares to take reluctant leave of the Belvedere. Alas, Martin is not a registered guest and may not return to a transomed room and imagine himself to be Jean Harlow in the film *Red Dust*, waiting for the return of Clark Gable. Instead, Martin must leave the Belvedere and face reality, though there are those who would call the lush toy town of Cherry Grove anything but that.

One such naysayer would be Ivan Bekoff, who passes by at this moment on his way to the hardware store. Ivan does not live in Cherry Grove and rarely visits it, but today he is in vital need of a plumbing part, and here he is. Spotting him, Martin sees a way to extend his idle on the Belvedere patio, and invites him for a cappuccino. Ivan agrees, reluctantly. The decadent Belvedere is not a place where he feels comfortable, but rather than snub an old (and now rarely encountered) acquaintance, Ivan will sit and sip. Martin calls Ivan's attention to the falcon, and the two men spend the first ten minutes in silence, observing the bird along with the small crowd shuffling on the flagstone.

That suits Ivan fine. Small talk is not his specialty. In fact the spectacle of him at the table with Martin, who is pixieish, petite, and still heavily made up from the night before, is a stunning study in contrasts. Ivan, gaunt, ragged, and bearded, is as uncomfortable as Daniel Boone in a parlor. In fact Ivan *is* a bit of an explorer and a pioneer, especially with respect to the gay eastern settlement of Fire Island.

Ivan is older than Martin, and can remember a time when homosexuals paid a far higher price for being different than they do now. He looks back on his young manhood not as an endless bacchanal among the wild and beautiful, but as a lonely and bitter trial. The words applied to him were not *gay*, but *faggot, sissy, queer, fairy*, and other things reserved also for rapists, lepers, deserters, niggers, dogs without owners, or the recently defeated Japs and Krauts. When men like Ivan Bekoff passed, women hid their children's eyes and strong men became uneasy, or violent. Homosexuals seemed to bring out some senseless, bottomless rage in people.

And with the arrogance of twentieth-century medicine came the approach of homosexuality as disease. "It's a great pity that Oscar Wilde isn't alive today," lamented an ambitious psychiatrist prominent in Ivan's youth. "We would have radiated his overactive thymus, atrophied the gland, and suppressed its overactivity."

Psychiatry felt that homosexuality was something to be corrected, and its methods were brutal. As recently as 1960, when Ivan made his first trip to Fire Island, gay patients were being lobotomized or given electric-shock treatments to alleviate their symptoms. But even worse than the treatments were its implications, that homosexuals had a disease. And even worse than the implications was the degree to which the victims themselves believed it. Already disastrously low on self-esteem, with their dirty little secret to hide, the thousands of sensitive young men from Tampa to Tacoma hung their heads even lower; they were not only immoral, they were also mentally ill. Morbid self-doubt and self-loathing became the gay's enemies from within, and they were more formidable than all the other forces arrayed against him.

The extent to which Ivan has triumphed over these thoughts are a measure of his personal happiness, but they do little to enliven his current encounter with Martin Quartararo. As the shadows lengthen over the Belvedere, the possibilities for conversation between the two men grow as cold as the cappuccino. It seems to be a friendship that has, over the years, exhausted itself. At a certain point they chose widely divergent paths in life, and that was that. Ivan tries to excuse himself as gracefully as possible.

"Will I see you tonight at the Ice Palace? The band is supposed to be fabulous," says Martin.

"I doubt it," comes the answer.

"What about the Sonja Henie film festival this weekend?"

"Maybe," says Ivan, squirming to be gone.

"Well then, how about . . ." But Ivan has lurched off to the east. As he disappears, Martin's smile creases into a frown. The older Ivan gets, the less fun he is.

Ivan vanishes into a stand of shadbush and heads home. He does not live in Cherry Grove, but well beyond it. To get there, he must pass through a famous area of scrub brush. Botanically, it is a standard swale area, not nearly as interesting as the lush Sunken Forest that separates Cherry Grove from the straight towns of the west, where Dana Wallace and James Lindsey live.

In the swale, short for "sweltering lens," the undulating dunes concentrate the sun's heat. Only the heartiest things survive here, things like the tough gray dusty miller plant, the false heather, the low, gnarling bearberry. Not only must they eke their nutrients out of the sand and withstand the intense heat, but they must somehow resist the burning saltspray that whips in off the water— nature's harsh way of pruning.

Eventually, as generations of the crude plants die and decompose, they will enrich the ground to the point where things of greater sophistication can grow—the beach plum (bright purple

—

now in its ripeness), the elegant bayberry, the shiny, dangerous poison ivy. In the same way, the sacrifices of early homosexuals paved the way for men like Ivan, and he in turn has made life easier for Martin Quartararo.

But the swale is more than a metaphor for gay history; it is also the place where much of it was played out. This strip of low brush has been the sexual bazaar. It is hard to imagine a more decadent, lurid, sensual chapter in the history of men on earth than the one that has transpired here. A layer of semen lies over the sand. Men went in here to get laid, relaid, or parlayed. At any hour of the day or night, someone was waiting behind a scrub pine to do just what one wanted to have done. Denied hearth and family, condemned from the pulpit, gay men flooded in here to see how good they could feel, and how many times. Some wags called the swale the Judy Garland Memorial Park; but others, the ones who didn't like romantic veils pulled over things, gave it the name that would stick: the Meatrack.

Now, on a September afternoon, Ivan Bekoff moves through the Meatrack on his way home. A couple of men are arrayed on the dunes like Italian countesses, offering lascivious invitations. Ivan keeps his head down, trying not to meet their eyes. The place makes him extremely uncomfortable these days. If he knew another way home, he would take it. As his eyes dart about the brush for other, less-traveled paths, he remembers the first time he walked through here, when the Meatrack was little more than a wilderness.

Ivan doesn't remember much about how he first got to Fire Island on that day back in 1960: a phone call from a buddy on his way back from boot camp, a moonlight drive, then the morning sun hitting his face in an old black Plymouth with two big Italian guys sprawled on the hood. He rubbed his eyes and looked around. A wide sable beach, a China blue sea, a thousand beautiful men! He climbed the dunes and had a cup of coffee at the yacht club. Watching the waves roll in, he had to pinch himself. Coffee at the yacht club! Blond, green-eyed waiters?! Was this the same skinny kid who'd hidden his dark sexual yearnings in the back of a synagogue?

Ivan was in the Promised Land. But the wildness of Cherry Grove, the floating cocktail parties, and the hothouse sex were not strictly speaking his cup of tea. He had been raised in a traditional Jewish household, with an emphasis on craftsmanship, learning, and dignity. Never could he totally shake these values. Yes, he had the hormones of a young man and could not resist the sensual maraudings of the Martin Quartararos of the world. But he was by nature a different sort of man, and he resolved finally to make his home not in Cherry Grove, but farther to the east, where a wall of forest beckoned him.

He foraged past what is now the Meatrack but what was then just a tangled knot in nature. He cleared a little piece of land for himself in a stand of low shads, just south of the bay. He loved the wild terrain, the twisted woods, the bashful deer, the throaty birds. He relished the idea of building a house with his own hands. He was surrounded by a vast welter of gnarled sassafras and shadroot, a bog, a jungle . . . still full, two decades later, of the debris of the hurricane of 1938. A handful of other hardy campers and squatters dug in among the swamp maples and the toads and the red fox, and formed a pioneer community. They picked wild grapes, and for their only comforts they culled the storm's flotsam. One couple, good friends of Ivan's, lived in a grove of trees with only a storm-tossed toilet and piano (had they been Gershwin's?). All of them made their fires against the night, like the proud Secatogues.

But eyes were watching their campfires. Mainland realtors were beginning to comprehend the potential of Fire Island, even the wilderness areas. A man named Smadbeck finally acquired the impenetrable three-mile tract east of Cherry Grove, and began parceling it into long bay-to-ocean strips, and then into lots. Paradise lost, packaged, and sold. Ivan and several other gay squatters promptly offered to buy the property on which they squatted, but Smadbeck refused. He was looking to sell to the vast, land-hungry straight population, and he had no desire to compromise his asking price by having to explain about the pioneer homosexuals. The lesson of the Western Kingdom had been learned; once gays got in they were as tough to get out as the catbrier that bit into your legs as you tried to clear your land.

At the newly dredged Pines harbor, a sign was erected. "This is a family community," it began. "We believe certain things."

These were code phrases. They meant "Faggots, keep out."

The great Battle of the Pines was about to begin.

Cherry Grove was bursting at the seams. The fast life was not for everyone. Not all gays enjoyed dressing as women and roaming the tiny walkways with cocktails, looking for someone to love. Many of them, like Ivan, were serene, serious human beings who had come to the island searching for just that, serenity. To the west was the Sunken Forest, now inviolable National Park land. So like Ivan they covetously eyed the new community to the east, where purple martins and mourning doves weaved through the silence of the twisting shadbush and swamp maples.

"All we want to do," they told Smadbeck and his cadre of developers, "is live in peace in the woods." Smadbeck, who assumed all gays were silly, immoral, and effeminate, didn't believe them. The gays pressed their argument; if heterosexuals shared common ground simply because of their heterosexuality, would Knute Rockne and Mahatma Gandi therefore be close friends?

Smadbeck wouldn't listen, and wouldn't budge from his position. Ivan and the other squatters were expelled, and straight settlers from the mainland began buying the land hand over fist. The gays countered by buying lots secretly through straight representatives. When the ruse was discovered, all hell broke loose. The Battle of the Pines escalated. The leaders of the burgeoning straight community threatened to have the gays arrested. The crime? Sodomy, still illegal in the State of New York. The gays retaliated by exposing the straights' marital infidelities, learned of through the instant grapevine of the mainland hairdressing salons. The battle raged bitterly.

When after years of warfare a nervous settlement was finally reached, full of resentment and instantly regretted by the straights,

—

it had been engineered by the Great Compromiser: hard cash. The simple truth was that four gay men, some or all of them pulling in big money from the design world, or the entertainment world, or the insurance world, or *any* world (that was another reason they were resented, for their success) could live together and pay far more for a house than an ordinary straight family of four.

And so the moral position of the straight settlers softened. Many of them were made offers they couldn't refuse, and they sold out. Now the immigration of gays across the Meatrack was rapid. By the mid-1960s they were a presence, though the straights still sought to keep them an invisible one. At close quarters, the tension heightened. Ivan and his friends were warned to behave themselves on the beach. They were told not to wear tight pants to the supermarket. They bristled but obeyed. Soon, though, as the straights began to taste that Manhattan cash, they sold out more and more rapidly. The gays became a vocal minority, and finally a majority. The Battle of the Pines had been won, and the whole five-mile stretch, from the edge of the Sunken Forest through the eccentric hamlet of Cherry Grove, through the wilderness Meatrack and now the sprawling Fire Island Pines, was a Gay Nation.

It was a development that coincided with an event on the mainland that gay Americans consider the single most dramatic moment in their history. On a summer night in 1969, a group of men lounged in a gay bar called the Stonewall on New York's Christopher Street. Without warning, they were subjected to a brutal humiliation to which they had become sadly accustomed: a police raid.

The difference was that this time, rather than meekly bowing their heads and saying, "Go ahead, we deserve it," they fought back. The police, who had looked forward to another routine shakedown, were suddenly confronted by people upon whom a new idea was dawning, that no matter what anyone thought of the way they led their lives, they had the legal right to lead them.

When Antoine first led them into the rubble of Cherry

Grove, the gays at last proclaimed, "This is what I am." Now they added ". . . and I have these civil rights." No longer did they have to pay outrageous rents to occupy the same housing as straight people, or huddle on a tiny island for the privilege of "being themselves," or endure whimsical clubbings by the police. It was the last step in the long, torturous evolution of the gay American. And it was the hardest step, because it meant erasing the last self-doubt, the one that whispered, even through success and beauty and wealth and fame, "There's something wrong with me."

Now, finally and emphatically, the voice of Ivan Bekoff, along with thousands of others, said, "No, there isn't." They blinked in the sunlight and realized, barely believing it, that they no longer had anything to hide. It was the inestimable thrill of human dignity restored, or for the first time conferred.

It was as if an opera star had all her life been muffled. Now, when she sang at last, what an aria would sound! It would be a song of freedom, and a bittersweet requiem for all the casualties that had gone before, for the sensitive souls from California to Canarsie whose spirits had withered and died under the assault of bigotry. But most of all it would be a call to celebration. It was time for the greatest party ever thrown, and what better place for it, shouted the celebrants, than the new Gay Nation . . . the Eastern Kingdom of Fire Island?

—

To throw the greatest party ever thrown is a tall order. The competition doesn't come from Louis XVI, or Hollywood, or anyplace farther away than staid old New England, the ancestral home of the WASPs who live in Point O' Woods ... people whose dour reputations, it turns out, are undeserved.

Newport, Rhode Island, is kind of a sad place these days. Without the America's Cup, it is notable only for the great mansions that line the sweeping coastal nook north of the city. Through their marble halls pass small groups of chattering tourists by day and solitary security guards by night. But these are the halls that held the most opulent parties ever thrown. The houses were built by steel and coal magnates to contain and amuse their wives—many of them intelligent, frustrated creatures who de-

—

cided that if parties were to be their only creative outlet, then so be it.

"There are only four hundred people," said grand, old Mamie Fisk, the greatest hostess of all, "who are truly at home in a ballroom." Before she was through, she would take the four hundred to the extremes of the elegant and the grotesque.

One evening her guests arrived to find the grounds of the Fisk estate transformed into a wonderland. A huge miniature train system had been built, overnight, to carry around footmen with cocktails and tea services. Out in the bay, for no other reason than to amuse the guests, a dozen ghost-white sailing ships sat at anchor. At various locations on the huge lawn, the entire casts of New York operas and musicales, their regular performances canceled, sang their hearts out for the strolling guests. It was all extraordinary and it left the four hundred wondering what her next party would be like.

It would be very different. Mamie Fisk had a dark side. When it got the better of her, she expressed it through her only creative outlet, her parties.

The famous Dogs' Dinner took place on her enormous sloping lawn on a perfect turn-of-the-century afternoon. The four hundred socialites, answering an invitation to an alfresco dinner, were led to a huge, round, delightfully festooned table built especially for the occasion. A short distance away, inexplicably, was a smaller table of the same shape, its contents hidden by a silk coverlet. The guests began nibbling on a magnificent pâté as a string quartet serenaded them.

Then, on a signal from Mamie, a footman ripped the cover off the small table to reveal a mountain of dogfood. Simultaneously, four hundred mutts—rounded up earlier off the slum streets of the harbor—were released.

Through the afternoon, the dogs savagely devoured their meal as the aristocrats picked disconcertedly at theirs.

It was an extraordinary era in party giving, but a sardonic one tinged by the boredom and desperation and loneliness of its hostesses.

—

The great Fire Island Pines parties were another matter. They may have had their share of desperation sexually, but no one was bored, and no one was lonely for long. There was money and taste and opulence, as in Newport, but in Fire Island Pines the party machine ran on spiritual fuel. These events were festivals of generosity, of freedom, of light over darkness; they were celebrations of the Promised Land, and their most perfect symbol was a man named Ferron Bell. He was the Mamie Fisk of Fire Island.

If Dana Wallace, with his last-of-a-breed macho bluster, can be called the high priest of the Western Kingdom, then Ferron Bell, creative, gentle, and eccentric, is the high priest of the East. Whenever a young man arrives in the Eastern Kingdom, he hears instantly of Bell, and if the newcomer is terribly lucky, he may be granted a private audience with him. These days it might be at the beach, or in the dusk shade of the willows by the bay, but ten years ago it would have been at night, at one of the amazing parties. It isn't so much that Ferron Bell personally gave the great parties of Fire Island Pines, or even that he went to them all, but that like the New Year's Baby, in diaper and top hat, he was their perfect incarnation.

Born in California during World War Two, Ferron was the son of the gardener at the Wrigley mansion in Pasadena, an opulent old place that is now the headquarters for the Tournament of Roses Parade. Redolent with hyacinth and bouganvillea, it was a private park for the growing Ferron. He trailed his father about, playing with the expensive toys the Wrigley children had grown tired of. But when he grew too old to play, Pasadena made him restless. When he turned eighteen, he joined the navy.

It didn't agree with him. He was searching for something not only absent in the military code, but antithetical to it. Discharge papers in hand, he set off through the California hills, looking for he knew not what. As darkness fell on the first day of his journey, he found himself outside a religious hermitage. He knocked on the thick wooden door and a Brother of the Order of St. Basil opened it. He asked him for shelter, and it was granted. Months passed before he left.

—

Behind the cloistered walls and among the soft singing voices of the old Russian monks, he felt truly at home for the first time. He performed his tasks in the laundry room in silence, and lived the spare life of a young novice. He devoured the readings of Thomas Merton, who from a dark monk's cell in Kentucky cast a spell of simplicity, flame-light, and devotion for an entire generation. Ferron Bell fell deeply under that spell.

But it wasn't until a visit from some old women down the road that the young man's transformation was complete. The Sisters of St. Basil had all the faith and mystery of their brothers, and more. Their faces were a million years old. Their eyes were as deep as the sea. Their fingers were the color and shape of the vines that climbed the Abbey walls. And the fingers had a skill that Ferron Bell begged to be taught.

The skill was painting icons.

When their first church was built in Russia by Czar Alexander in 1838, the Sisters had already been painting for hundreds of years. When the Bolsheviks drove them into Siberia to make them pay for their allegiance to the Czar, they passed the endless winter by painting. When they escaped through Manchuria, losing half their number to the mountains and the murderous cold, they distracted themselves by painting. When they crossed the Bering Strait to Alaska, they were still, by the midnight sun, painting. When they moved down the coast and discovered the mild valley of Sitka, where they could make food grow out of the ground, which for the first time in their collective memory was not frozen, they celebrated by painting. And when God finally set them in the sunny hills of California, they moved their worktables and their icons outside, and painted. The impressionable young pilgrim Ferron Bell seized on it. He'd found his life's work. He was an artist.

Meanwhile, outside the thick walls of the monastery, back in the real world, the sixties were exploding. The eyes of the nation were on nearby San Francisco, where the well-educated white youth of America, in lustrous clothes, were letting their hair grow long, pumping their brains with chemical colors, and blasting open their skulls with rock-and-roll chords that resonated a week later. Black men were being photographed in wicker chairs with machine guns in their laps. And in the shadow of all this, emboldened by it, certain bars on Castro Street were beginning to openly advertise themselves as homosexual.

The real world was exerting a pull that the artist in him couldn't resist, so Ferron Bell said a sad good-bye to the Order of St. Basil and went to San Francisco. He got a job as a dancer in a Bavarian bar, wearing cowbells and alpine shorts. Soon he was getting stares from men, and following them up, and confirming what he had always thought about himself. It was his first great explosion of sexuality, the first flush of "This is what I am" and the choice of ten thousand California men.

But there was a furtiveness about Castro Street, a leering and a self-loathing that disturbed him. The joyous affirmation of the Stonewall incident was still years away. Ferron, the young artist fresh from a cloister, had more in common with the wildly idealistic hippies, exploding in music and color. But most of *them*, Ferron knew, would become very conventional adults once their anger and confusion had spent itself. Looking for an answer, a synthesis, the pilgrim set out again, in the only direction the continent stretched before him . . . east. This time his mecca was a village on a tiny spit of land that curved like a giant question mark off the coast of Massachusetts.

Ferron didn't know much about Provincetown, only that it was by the sea and that gay people enjoyed a certain amount of freedom there. As he traveled the last few miles, the land tapering, the silver sea on either side, he felt as if he'd finally gotten where he was meant to be. Gay people were everywhere, and they seemed to have none of the darkness or the guilt of their California brothers. Nor was the cruising as tense or pressured.

There was a natural feeling about it, as there was about everything in this simple seaside village. The streets wound up and down hills past lovely little clapboard houses, some of them three hundred years old. There was permanence here and there were values. It was a revelation to the California boy with a heritage of fast food and tract housing.

And above all, there was painting. Provincetown was an artist's colony. Sex and art no longer had to be mutually exclusive, the one frivolous and furtive, the other profound and serious. He was meeting gay men he could respect. He was home at last, he thought. But he was to discover that there was another side to the New England mentality besides the one that lovingly tended the village green and generously tolerated homosexuality. These people were descended from Puritans.

Shortly after he arrived, Ferron got another of his unusual jobs, as the town crier of Provincetown. Attractive and outgoing, he was a natural for the position, largely a ceremonial one, that involved calling out the time of day, announcing the special events, lighting the gaslamps, and whatever else the town fathers wanted him to do. The problem was the uniform; Ferron found it a little baggy. Could the colonial breeches be tapered? he wondered. A bit more flattering? The town fathers bristled. The venerable position of town crier would not be a perch from which a homosexual would do his advertising.

To a great extent the fathers had made their peace with the gays, mostly because the town economy depended on them; but certain things were sacred. The breeches would not be altered. The issue was not crucial to Ferron, who would have left the pants alone or quit the job, either one, to avoid a fatal rupture with the straight community. But this was the sixties and any issue, no matter how small, was resonant and symbolic of the loss of freedom anywhere and of oppression and tyranny everywhere. The desire of Ferron Bell to mold a costume around his genitals was no different, some felt, than James Meredith trying to enter the University of Mississippi . . . or, to go back to the origins of the costume itself, than Nathan Hale, in the shadow of the gallows, spitting in the face of the British.

Local agitators seized on the issue and a media event was organized. Ferron would make a month-long solitary march to

Boston, a distance of a hundred miles . . . in costume. In every hamlet through which he passed, there would be cameras and microphones and fife and drum corps. It would become a national issue.

But Ferron wanted no part of it. He was not a political creature. He had a mission, he was now certain, and it was not confrontational but spiritual. In the middle of the hubbub, he slipped quietly out of town.

As the Sisters of St. Basil continued their nomadic journey down the West Coast a hundred years earlier, so did Ferron Bell continue his down the East Coast, certain that the true nature of his mission was about to reveal itself. This time his destination was a place he had always felt pointed toward, as if he and the place were operating in the same magnetic field. The place scared him, but that made him all the surer he was meant to go there.

New York City. Huge, raw, and unforgiving. The art there was not in tasteful boutiques but in giant, gaping holes in the concrete, in empty truck garages, old lofts, and warehouses where a thousand refrigerators had once been stored or a thousand seamstresses had bent over their work. In one gallery, a forest of birch trees grew! In another, an artist had been chained to the wall for six months! These were the paintings! In yet another a huge ceramic bowl the size of a village green was displayed. Where was there an oven big enough to bake it? The city would not answer these questions. It demanded that you simply be astonished. It was telling you there were no answers, at least not the ones you'd been settling for. It was grabbing you by the lapels and shaking the complacency out of you. It wanted your nerve endings standing at attention.

And the gay scene was on fire. It was boiling up toward the explosion of Stonewall, and one could dig in anywhere one wanted to. One could wear leather and get into the rough trade down by the river. One could take an older lover and go shopping at Bloomingdale's. One could do both. One could do anything in between.

Ferron Bell did neither. Through the winter, he slept in the park. He was in a sacred city, he felt, and all around him were temples of art. It was as if in the nineteenth century a Sister of St. Basil had been magically plucked out of the frozen Russian countryside and set down at the Hermitage museum in St. Petersburg. She would absorb the genius around her with tears of gratitude and humility. She would shun the bright lights and the tempting sweets of the bakeries and eat crusts of bread and save her pennies so as to be readmitted again and again to the museum, arriving when it opened, leaving when it closed. That is the life that Ferron Bell lived in New York.

He made only a few cautious contacts in the city's mysterious social world, but when summer came and the city became a concrete prison, he followed them out to Fire Island.

The young man made a brilliant debut. A buzz went through the cotillion world of the Newport 400 when a girl came out with the right social credentials, and talent and looks to boot, and the genes hadn't crossed to make an idiot out of her. Such the stir was created by Ferron Bell on Fire Island. He was beautiful, he was gifted, and of almost greater importance, he was untouched. There was an innocence about him as simple and elegant as the wild swans that traversed the Pines harbor, and every man wanted him, from the hoariest, wiliest old queen, to the hottest young stud. He found himself with enormous power, enough power to bring his spirituality to bear on the great party-going era of the Eastern Kingdom, and shape the Gay Nation in his own image. It was a confluence of the man and the moment—Lincoln and the Civil War, Napoleon and post-revolutionary France, Ferron Bell and Fire Island Pines.

The soul of the place was up for grabs. The Battle of the Pines had been won, the straight realtors had been defeated, and as the decade of the seventies began, Fire Island Pines was establishing a character of its own . . . far different than its neighboring Cherry Grove, where little bungalows winked at each other across fading, roller-coaster walkways.

Ivan Bekoff's tiny, hand-hewn shack had quickly become

an anomaly, dwarfed by the wealth and size of the remarkable structures that sprang up around it. Many of them were invisible, blocked from the walkway and from each other by thick woods of sassafras and chokeberry, their very existence indicated only by freestanding gateways.

The houses, where they allowed themselves to be seen, were the sleekest kind the school of beach architecture offered. The Pines made Malibu look like a Country Seat in Iowa. Many of them were not so much houses as ideas, or feelings, or mood swings of an architect. One house was a slash, the next a sigh. The next was a question mark. This was not the same wood, floated down from Nova Scotia in the nineteenth century, that James Lindsey's father used to build the houses of the Western Kingdom. All the exotic wood in the Pines seemed to have come from the Philippines, packed in Styrofoam, yesterday. Though no house was farther than fifty yards from the bay or the ocean (here or anywhere else on the snakelike island), many of them had swimming pools.

You rang a lighted doorbell on an ingenious wrought-iron-and-sassafras-root-threaded gate and it swung open to reveal a wooden pathway disappearing into a shroud of catbrier and shad tree. You thought you were in an Uncle Remus fairy tale, or in the middle of nowhere, and suddenly there was the house, a two-million-dollar Bergdorf's hatbox, made out of redwood and guarded by a thousand-pound black jade lynx.

The occupant was a man of means and power. His name might be found on a shampoo bottle, or a dress label, or a musical score. Perhaps he had moved here from Cherry Grove when he could afford to, in the same way that Ivan's parents, having immigrated to Brooklyn, finally moved out to Scarsdale. Or perhaps he was a millionaire who was willing to come out of the closet for the first time, as long as he could do it in such opulence.

In no time at all, Fire Island Pines had become one of the richest communities on earth.

—

* * *

But the place was without a soul. The Battle of the Pines was over, and so was the first flush of triumph and purpose. The place was an opulent wilderness. Without Ferron Bell the great party-giving era might have been remarkable for nothing but its vulgarity and excess: beautiful people wolfing down incredible food in magnificent surroundings.

Not that the party goers weren't creative people; many of them made their living by being just that. But Ferron Bell took it a layer deeper. Mamie Fisk and Thomas Merton rolled into one, he filled the moment with style and innocence simultaneously. He took the creativity and hammered it into a hot golden arrow that everyone could grab on to as it raced across the evening summer sky.

There were storybook parties, where everyone stepped out of a child's dream. Five men came in a bush as Sherwood Forest. Ten men came as Bo Peep and nine of her sheep. A man rose out of the Great South Bay, fluorescent green, as King Neptune. Carried by a dozen nubian slaves, Cleopatra arrived lolling in a milk bath. At midnight, a Broadway dancer rode in nude on a silver surfboard. The costumes were exquisite, many of them put together by men who designed for a living. That would be half the fun of it; gathering during the day, chattering on somebody's sun deck smashed on the drug of the week, listening to show tunes, sewing your costume for that night.

There was the Heavenly Bodies' party, where everyone was the moon or the sun or a Greek or Roman god in a constellation, in a costume of solid silver with hair and beards electrified by a hundred tiny lights.

At one party five hundred doves were released at midnight.

At another, phony diamonds were hung like teardrops from every tree, illuminated by a purple beacon that washed up and down the length of the party from out in the bay, so that it looked like magic dust was being sprinkled from above.

At another party, quite unannounced, a dozen naked

Norsemen seized a makeshift stage and acted out the plot of a whole Wagnerian opera to the throbbing of a disco hit, then the soft cooing of a Barbara Cook song about lost love.

At the Red Party, everything was red—from the invitations, to the caviar, to your fingernail polish, to your costume (if you had one) or your body (if you didn't), to the wine, to the lobster and the cherries jubilee, to the huge banners that flew in the trees above the party, to the canvas tent where the slides were being projected, to the raft out in the bay where one could swim (guided by red buoys) to make romance, to the color of the paper that joints were rolled in, to the wrappings of the chocolate mints to be picked off the trees, to the color of lips themselves. Red, red, red, red.

The air was soft and warm, the sea was lit up and rolling in, you were beautiful and strange and so was he, and the world was red.

FIRE ISLAND, SEPTEMBER 26, 1985; MORNING

Fire Island Pines is empty. The harbor is placid. Nothing ripples the water but the resident pair of white swans, their gray gaggle of young behind them. Up by the ocean the peculiar million-dollar redwood improvisation that is Calvin Klein's house bakes dully in the late sun. Down the next walkway, the disco loudspeakers on the deck of the Botel are cemetery-still. The weekend will see some action, but right now all is clear. It is a situation that might encourage trespassers or looters, but there isn't much problem with crime here anymore. Many of the places are patroled electronically, some with guard dogs.

If we could see it with the peregrine falcon's eye, as she finally soars off the island now toward the south, we might mistake the Pines for any wealthy, wooded American suburb. Grosse Pointe, Michigan, for example.

Grrrrrreeeahhhh coos a voice. *Kah kah kah Greeeeeeeeee.* With the departure of the falcon, an all-clear sounds from the throat of a warbler, and the songbirds come out of hiding.

The great Party Era of the Pines is long gone, a piece of history. The birds are the ones now whose song stylings lift spirits and ease old wounds, who dazzle with their wild spring costumes. When the ice leaves the bay and the beach plum bushes explode into white blossoms, the birds return from their tropical winters and blow everyone's mind with taxi yellow, indigo, scarlet, and sapphire.

As the days lengthened over the teeming rain forests and flat coastal plains of Central and South America, nature pushed bright plumages through their breasts, the better for them to win mates when they arrived north at their breeding grounds.

When they get here, they have only to puff out their chests, or spread their gaudy tails to get a mate for a lifetime, or just a fast feathery fling. But that is enough to saddle them with father-hood for the coming season. Bird spring is so hot with sex, the ovaries so wet, spongy, and coiled like springs, like fat globules on the end of a Q-Tip, that once is enough.

If puffing out your chest doesn't get it, then maybe you show off by swooping through some aerial stunt that begins high in the air, then cascades and tumbles in a big wide swirl that winds up in a maddened blur, expect for the demisecond when you hover beside your intended, and show her your underside (which soon can be hers).

And if you don't go for that macho hard sell, if you want to go Park Avenue, there's always a little dance you can do, a little mincing step she can join you in, right to the bedroom door.

But *display*, the word that bird people use to describe these pickup techniques, is only the smallest part of the story of the wild springtime sex carnival. There is an old Hollywood movie where Fred Astaire and Bing Crosby are both after the same girl.

Crosby croons, "I'll capture her heart . . . singing . . ."

Astaire replies, "Not when I go into my dance," and beats out a hot wild tattoo with his feet.

Crosby gets the girl. Bird song is the most beautiful sound on earth. It may be the high trill of a Spanish soprano or the low moan of a big fat Delta blues singer. It may mean "Please be mine" or it may mean "I saw that worm first, you bastard!"

"Canada," the meadowlark seems to sing at dawn. "Pure sweet Canada Canada Canada . . ."

Now a curtain of birds parts to reveal the creature who is sounding the all-clear. Greeeeeeeeee comes the call again. "Kah kah greeeee!" A deep sound for a songbird. What's this? The sound is coming not from the throat of a bird . . . but of a man! Now we make out his figure, as the birds define it by perching on his knees and shoulders. Portlier than the sleek pilgrim who took the secrets of the Sisters of St. Basil from the hills of California, Ferron Bell sits on a dune by the ocean. All around him, hovering, squatting, taking bits of food from his palm, are his old friends from the West, the songbirds. They filled his childhood days on the big lawns of the Wrigley estate and now they trust him to sit among them.

He in turn trusts them . . . far more, these days, than he trusts men. The great party era of the Pines has indeed ended—and in such a way that has thrown Ferron Bell into a reclusive middle age. Rarely does he socialize anymore, and new intimacies are unheard of.

Perhaps maturity would have dimmed this man's beacon anyway. But far more likely it has to do with the swift, brutal end of the golden party era of Fire Island Pines. For Ferron Bell, it was like a kick in the stomach . . . or a dark wind through the soul.

At Woodstock it seemed as if the hippies, and all of mankind, had achieved some kind of harmony and perfection. A month later the Rolling Stones gave a concert at Altamont, in California, that ended in ugliness, rioting, and death. Chroniclers of that era trace its decline to that moment.

For Fire Island Pines, the Altamont was called "Beach." It was to be the great Pines party of the late seventies, an extravaganza of classic, sprawling proportions. A quarter mile of Atlantic oceanfront was roped off. Along it, illuminated by torchlight, would be live music, flame eaters, palm readers, greased acrobats, telescopes, masseurs, and an incredible array of exotic food and drink. Beach would be a summation of all the Pines grandeur that preceded it, and even an echo of the nineteenth-century Chautauqua.

The problem was the gate crashers. For a while now, straight teenagers from the mainland had been an annoyance. They were showing up at the Sunday Tea Dances to ogle the weirdos, get high and party. At first they were just a self-conscious minority. But as their numbers grew, so did their boldness and truculence, and their girlfriends were even nastier. It had gotten so bad that the Tea Dances had become dominated by them and had lost all meaning for the original participants. The gays were now holding "high teas" elsewhere; quiet cocktail parties behind curtains of shad trees.

The night of Beach, it seemed like every drunken, lurching teenager on earth was there, smashed on beer and cheap whiskey. They marauded along the narrow walkways, throwing rocks at houses and insults at gay couples. The gays shouted back and the scene escalated quickly and badly. Many of them were beaten up, as they had been back in the Western Kingdom in the thirties. What was to have been a benign summer saturnalia turned into a crowd leaving a prizefight at Madison Square Garden.

At the end of *The Glass Menagerie*, by Tennessee Williams, himself a frequent visitor to Fire Island, a man accidentally breaks a glass unicorn, the most precious belonging of a sensitive young woman. For her and the author the act can never truly be atoned for and life is forever afterward shaded by menace and sadness.

Such a night was Beach for the Eastern Kingdom. The parties continued, but invitations were now checked at the door by beefy security guards. Once inside, the party goer noticed a difference in tone. People came in costume, as Rita Hayworth or Joan Crawford, but no one came as Bo Peep anymore.

—

* * *

Ferron Bell does not go to parties these days. He has a monk's penchant for solitude, and he has the song of the birds. These things have guided him into middle age. Long after the disco speakers have been wrapped in plastic against the frost of winter, Ferron Bell will walk these pathways, sketching snowbanks, painting the wild December ocean. In that bleakness, he finds sensuality—in the air that stings the lungs, in the low-riding sun that blinds the eye.

Now, in 1985, in the conventionally sensual time of Indian summer, he finds pain. Now he must say good-bye to the birds. Their berries and their worms are gone and they are going south for more. Every bit of strength will be needed for the journey, so the sex hothouse is closed up, the gonads are shrunken and dried. The golden throats have fallen silent, and the coats have faded to dull browns and grays. This is the party that Ferron now hates to see end.

Oh, a few will stick out the winter on this thin island, hammering bark with their forged steel bills 'til every last insect has been dislodged or frozen to death. The sparrow and the chickadee and the nuthatch and of course the gulls will be around. But Ferron's favorite bird, of all the thousands that fly the earth, is leaving . . . any day now, he feels in his bones. That is what has brought him here, to this lonely dune on the edge of town . . . to say good-bye to the American redstart.

The redstart is a strange, lonely bird. Look for it in the highest branches of the deadest trees, in the thickest forests beside the wildest oceans. In Europe they call them birds of decay, because they trill their sad song from the crumbling walls of old abbeys. Maybe that is the connection to Bell, the former monastic. For its friends, the redstart chooses not its mindlessly chirping cousins in the warbler family, but the haunted, nightflying whippoorwill, its companion in the dark woods. Disturb the whippoorwill in its moist bog and it will chill you on a summer day with a look from its yellow eyes. Disturb the nest of a redstart, so much as lay a finger on a chick, and its mother will let it starve to death.

74

Put one in a cage, and it will starve itself. Death before bondage. The proudest bird in the sky.

"*Arabia,*" the redstarts seem to wail. "*Inky Inky Arabia, Arabia.*"

Why Ferron Bell has fallen in love with them, it is hard to say. He can rarely manage to find them. He knows only this; that in the early spring they will be making love in the dead branches of the Sunken Forest, their black hoods, tangerine bellies and salmon-tipped wings bobbing and fluttering. But now, in the shortening days of autumn, they are here on the dunes in the mornings, staring south, aloof and melancholy, contemplating their journey.

Today he sits among them.

This will be their mute farewell. Watching the ocean, neither they nor he move.

Suddenly, the birds scatter. The juniper bushes part, and through them rushes Ferron's friend Harry, a squat, exuberant man with generous green eyes, another veteran of the great days of the Pines. His round face is full of urgency. He has been looking for his friend

"Ferron," he says, breathless, "a hurricane is coming."

S   I   X

The dance of brother and sister trade winds, once an innocent waltz, has become a dance of madness, of moist, hot sex, a dance of death.

Hot air rises. Cooler air rushes in to replace it, and that rush is the wind. And wet, hot air, its molecules contracting in the thin upper atmosphere, dumps a load of rain, an act which in itself creates heat, which only sucks in the air more intensely. But on this particular September in the mid-Atlantic, the brutal, hellish heat has transformed the act of condensation. The air doesn't rise; it soars upward, ripping the top off the sky. More air rushes in to fill the vacuum, to plug the hole with a wild urgency. More rain cascades on the steaming ocean. The storm has become a monstrous engine that revs itself to a higher whine with each combustion. More heat, more madly spinning air, spinning more madly. For a thousand miles around, the sky is a swirl, chasing itself in furiously diminishing circles to a single point where there is no sky, and steam explodes into the black universe. And that point is moving inexorably across the water.

This is a hurricane. It is quite simply the strongest force in nature. The energy it generates in a day, if somehow harnessed (what a thought!), would supply the power needs for the United States for six months. And in keeping with its extraordinary power, it will make up its own mind about what to do—and a dark, irrational mind it is, striking out blindly, viciously, madly, randomly at the world. The meteorologists would prefer, here in the late twentieth century, not to attribute human evil to a storm. It is a force of weather measurable by their instruments. But even the most conservative weatherman, at times like this, must concede the possibility of a resolutely ill wind.

For a while, they can predict, Gloria (as they have named it) will travel due west, chastened and kept on course by the permanent stability of the area known as the Bermuda High, which a hurricane will avoid (they like to say) the way a whore avoids a church. After that, nobody knows. Will it veer left and terrorize fat golden Florida and the sultry towns along the Gulf of Mexico, or will it careen along a sliding arc to New England? Or will it curve back on itself and spend its fury on the open sea? None of the complex machines can say. It can go wherever it wants and do whatever it wants, so long as the ocean provides the liquor for its dark joyride. Nothing can stop it but dry land, which it hasn't seen since its native Africa.

There was a belief among early-American slaves that hurricanes were sent from Africa as a retribution, that the big winds were seeking the plantation owners and would not rest until the antebellum mansions, built on the backs of black men, were reduced to rubble . . . mausoleums for their swinish occupants. Even to the most sophisticated weatherman, that now seems as good

—

an explanation as any. Because until the storm finds land again, blessed, parched dry land, it will go and go and go. There must be human sacrifices before the thing will quit.

FIRE ISLAND; THURSDAY, SEPTEMBER 26, 1985; NOON

Dana Wallace is flushed and titillated as he lets himself in the door of his house, which he never locks. Mucking out the barn, he has heard the announcement on a transistor radio. A hurricane! Hell breaking loose! Bravo!

Nor can he think of a more perfect name for a death-dealing storm than Gloria. The intimate connection between sex and death has never eluded him for a second. He always found the Weather Service's practice of naming all storms after women amusing, and was unhappy when feminists forced them to change their policy.

Already the ocean seems to be roiling up, and Wallace feels his blood surge. The ocean is his religion. It alone retains its undiluted power in the modern world and it alone (along with the snow geese) can be counted on for its comings and goings. It has been his enemy and his lover both, and he has always felt, as a kid on the beach, as a hotshot in the navy, and now as an old man, that someday it would come to take him away. Not that it had more guts, just that it had more time. It's the same lesson he learned the hard way at Hialeah about playing horses. The house, with its huge bankroll, can withstand a longer losing streak than the little guy, so the little guy goes and the house stays.

Once, many years ago, he lost a house to the sea.

Back from World War Two on Fire Island, Wallace was down on his luck, a navy photographer without a job. He was reduced to wintering in his father's summerhouse, a bitter pill to swallow. Not only did he hate to take a handout from the old man, but the place was huge, damp, unheatable, and full of ghosts. It was the house he was born in. Having to shiver through the winter there with his wife and new baby, he felt like an abject failure. He felt like he was going backward.

In the spring, taking long walks on the beach to thaw out and think things over, he finally came up with a plan. He'd gotten back from the war expecting to cash in on his racetrack photo-finish idea, but he'd gotten screwed out of that. Nursing his bitterness, he'd spent the winter shooting portraits of his newborn baby, Dana Junior. The pictures turned out brilliantly. Now, on one particularly bright walk, the whole thing came together in his head. Beyond the dunes he spotted a perfect little cottage, with a half-moon carved on the door, sitting behind a FOR SALE sign. At last he had his postwar angle! He would photograph the children of the summer people on the dunes, capture the little darlings (and their parents' money) with the same strong composi-tions and seaside natural lighting he'd used on the haunted faces of the war!

But he needed money to finance the deal; he needed the perfect little cottage with the half-moon door, for his family and for his darkroom, and he needed the land around it.

As innocent of officialdom then as now, Wallace hitchhiked to Manhattan and strode into the Reconstruction Finance Corpo-ration to present his case. The receptionist suppressed a smile. The RFC, created by Herbert Hoover to bolster a depression economy, floated loans to banks, railroads, and insurance compa-nies ... not strung-out G.I.'s with get-rich schemes. Wallace's voice began to rise in anger, as it always does when he is frustrated by rules and well-dressed people behind desks. But as a security guard prepared to throw him out, Dana Wallace caught a break. A high official of the RFC, sauntering by, overheard the whole thing. The official was an older man who felt enormous gratitude to returning servicemen, and considerable cynicism about the mammoth, frequently corrupt businesses the RFC was bailing out. With the official championing him, the dazed Wallace, smelling of salt air and oysters, was ushered fluidly through the corridors of power. An hour later he was standing on the street with the first loan ever granted by the Reconstruction Finance Corporation to an individual.

He fired off a telegram, which Dotty Abrams copied down in the brown-shingled Western Union office in Ocean Beach and brought up to Peggy. It said "Open the door, Richard." It was a lyric of a popular song of the day, but what it meant in this context was "That little cottage on the dunes is ours."

Wallace hitchhiked back across the Fifty-ninth Street Bridge and out to Long Island. It was long after dark, so he had to pay a fisherman to ferry him across the bay to Fire Island. He found his father's house deserted. He walked up toward the Half-Moon cottage on the dunes and there was an oil lamp burning in the window. Peggy had already moved in with the baby. They opened a bottle of muscatel, then another, and celebrated until dawn. With the first light, Dana went out and found some driftwood. He made a frame out of it, and they packed it with seaweed, and put a few blankets over it. Then they picked up little Dana Junior and put him into the best crib any baby ever had. They didn't even need to crank up the old army stove to heat the milk for his cereal; the sun was caroming in off the water through the southern window, making a hothouse out of the little Half-Moon cottage on the dunes. The island had begun to give him a bountiful life.

In the warm weather they got oysters from the bay bottom, in the fall they hunted ducks until they were tired of eating them, in the winter they went ice fishing. If they needed oil, Dana would drive a Model A Ford across the frozen bay and haul a hundred-pound drum back from the mainland.

The child photography took off, enough for Dana to pick up more real estate on the dunes near the Half-Moon cottage. America and Fire Island entered the fifties, and the postwar leisure class spilled out to the barrier beach with money to spend. The island was booming, and the navy photographer was flush.

"Dana!"

Wallace snaps out of his reverie. He squints down the long wooden walkway and makes out the rumpled figure of Alan Halstead. For an instant, Wallace is startled by the coincidence.

—

Halstead may as well have been walking out of his own thoughts, for no living person so completely symbolizes this era of Dana Wallace's life, the bounty of a young marriage and the prosperity of the fifties, than amiable Alan. But now, as Halstead walks in and plops down on the ragged sofa facing the sea, the coincidence begins to make great sense to Dana Wallace. When the action gets hot, when the angry sea begins to froth, mystical things begin to happen.

"Hear about the blow?" says Halstead.

"May not even get it," Wallace replies.

True, once these hurricanes got to the Caribbean, they often took a left instead of a right, and pounded the Gulf of Mexico. No action at all for the North Atlantic.

"May not," says Halstead, pouring himself a cup of coffee without asking.

The two men sit and face the sea in silence, as they have many times over many years.

"If we do get it," says Wallace, "you know where I'll be."

Halstead smiles slightly. Where else? Through the long history of the men's friendship, where else had Wallace ever placed himself but right in the middle of the intensity?

Watching Halstead's profile against the sea, Wallace is remembering the days before the flesh hung as heavily off his friend's face. He calls up an image from forty years ago, from the days of the little Half-Moon cottage on the dunes. Postwar hotshots with their new brides, Alan and Dana would pull their chairs up to the big porch mosquito screen with their cocktails and just sit there until they couldn't see the ocean anymore, until they just shut their mouths and listened to it.

Hell, the four of them not only drank together, they lived together! Halstead and his wife were building their dream house a couple of hundred yards inland, and sleeping on Wallace's screened-in porch during the construction. Dana remembers climbing into bed with Peggy every night, the young bride terrified, mortified that the sounds of their love would penetrate the outer walls to the sleeping Halsteads. And it was lying in bed that

—

Peggy told Dana the premonition he's never forgotten. He can still see her lips forming the words, faintly, by starlight off the water.

"No other woman will ever live here," she said to her husband. She had dreamt it.

Did that mean they would live forever? Dana wanted to know. Or that the cottage would one day be a monastery or a fraternity house?

It was no joke, she said. She repeated the prophecy once more, then never again. Wallace forgot about it, and didn't remember it until a few years later . . . when Peggy got sick.

At first it seemed impossible, an absolute betrayal; the war had been won; the boys were home; wasn't everyone entitled to a happy ending? But Peggy Wallace was sick and not getting better, and when the diagnosis came, neither of them could believe it. She had cancer of the stomach, and she was going to die from it. Wallace sank. The bullish, ebullient man lost all interest in life. It drained right out of him. When he visited her in the hospital, he kept up a game face, but alone he wept inconsolably. His freckled little girl from the house called The Shells, the mother of his child, the light of his life was wasting away. When she was finally gone, he sank like a stone.

He kept plodding through life because he had to; his son had to be raised. But his insides had been hollowed out and he took no pleasure, or pain, in anything. Money was no problem; nor was it any solution. There was no mother to the boy and no woman in his life. Nor did he want one. His thoughts remained stuck on Peggy, and at nights, weeping under the starry sky, casting his surf rod into the ocean again and again, he felt, after many hours, that somehow she heard him . . . and then he would wander up to the desolate Half-Moon cottage and somehow fall asleep.

Years passed; bright, freckled young Dana Junior entered college at sixteen, and Dana Senior remained alone.

Then one day a woman from down the walkway, a summer

person, took notice of him. There is something about a man like Wallace that always appeals to city women, whose lives (or husbands) have none of Wallace's rugged textures about them. One night the woman snuck into the forlorn Half-Moon cottage on the dunes while Dana was surf casting in the sea below and began cooking a meal for him. Totally unnerved by the domestic smells emanating from the house, he raced up the dunes and confronted her, bellowing. She settled him down with a few cocktails and served him dinner.

A week later, a storm washed the cottage into the sea.

He recalled his wife's strange dream. *No other woman will ever live here,* she had said. Was Peggy reaching from beyond the grave to fulfill it? He shuddered, quaked at the strange occurrence. Vulnerable and unnerved, he left the island. But the woman down the street followed him, pressing her suit. He couldn't be alone forever, she insisted. After a back-and-forth, on-again-off-again courtship, he gave in and married her on the condition that they take to the road. Dana Wallace wanted to fly as far away from Fire Island as he could. They went to the Far East, to Mali, to Casablanca, to just about every exotic place he could think of.

But the road, ultimately, puts a lot of pressure on a relationship and finally theirs collapsed. After the divorce, Wallace traveled a bit himself but soon grew weary of it, and his heart pulled him back to his spiritual home, Fire Island.

One morning shortly after he got back, he was walking through the surf and felt something strike his foot. He bent to examine it and almost collapsed into the foamy water when he realized what it was—a large wooden object with a half-moon carved into it. *It was the door of the Half-Moon cottage on the dunes!* It had been years since the ocean had swallowed the house to fulfill Peggy's prophecy. Now the door was floating back to him!

Never a man to believe in the occult, he now became totally obsessed with it. The next morning he rose at dawn and walked to the dunes with his tool chest and a few pieces of lumber. Years earlier, he had driven four long, strong poles into the sand for no

—

apparent reason. Now he laid four joists across them. He was beginning the most devout labor of his life, the building of his beachcomber's shack. A month later it would be finished and curious passersby would wonder about it. Some would say it was a mausoleum to his first wife; others would say it was just the ornery man's way of irritating the Law. But more than anything else, it was for Dana Wallace a talisman to the angry sea, an acknowledgment of its unknowable mysteries. When it was done, he hung the sorcerer's Half-Moon door in the entranceway.

Beyond that door, within the confines of those driftwood walls and the sound of the huge breakers, he has sought refuge ever since. When the complexities and distortions of dry land have vexed him, he has wandered down here from his opulent new seaside ranch house to think, to feel, to see with new eyes.

"Dana . . ."

Wallace's head snaps around to the radio, where Alan Halstead is fiddling with the dial. More news is coming in about the storm. Sometimes, these days, Dana Wallace had trouble figuring out where his languid, ancient daydreams end and reality begins.

But this is reality.

Both men sit still and pay attention; this might after all be the vital piece of news. So far, Gloria has given no indication which way she will go . . . toward the Gulf of Mexico or up the Atlantic seaboard. Still impossible to predict even with space-age meteorological techniques, the "decision" seems capricious and arbitrary, despite its life-or-death significance. It has been desperately awaited in a hundred sticky little towns along the Gulf of Mexico, where the graveyards are already full of hurricane victims. It has had town officials trembling along the South Carolina coast, on the little islands in Charleston harbor where Gershwin placed the mythical Porgy and Bess, in the little towns a bit farther north where the Wright brothers conducted their experiments because a little wind went a long way, and in all the coastal villages from Maryland to Maine.

But now the announcement comes and though it does indeed

include a projection of the storm's path, that is only half the news. The lesser half. The big news is the nature of Gloria herself.

Even an ordinary hurricane, according to Owlie Skywarn, the cartoon character who appears in government manuals that issue weather warnings to children, has the force of forty atom bombs going off each second. In fact, says Owlie in a balloon above his head, "No force we know can stop it." But Hurricane Gloria, as it stands at its point of decision near Eleuthra, has a barometric pressure of 27.74. In other words, there is no top on the sky. The winds are now being clocked at 150 miles an hour. The old-timers at the Weather Service, men who generally enjoy a good blow, can feel the bad air in their arteries. In sobriety and silence they thumb through the ticker tape as the numbers feed in. This appears to be the worst hurricane anyone has ever seen.

It is worse than the hurricane of 1938, and it is worse than the hurricane at the turn of the century that littered the streets of Galveston, Texas, with a couple of thousand corpses in half an hour. If the current readings hold, there may be death and damage on an unprecedented scale, the kind that Americans think happens only in the Third World.

The radio goes dead for about five seconds, an eternity in broadcasting, as if to acknowledge the significance of the news. This is the Apocalypse.

Now the radio crisps and crackles with the second part of the report. The mayor of Galveston can mix himself a drink and relax. The news, for him and his Gulf Coast neighbors, is very, very good. Hurricane Gloria, for reasons incomprehensible to and unpredictable by science, has decided to take a Right.

A shudder runs up and down the Atlantic Coast. Someone along that thousand-mile stretch is going to lose, and lose big.

In Dana Wallace's living room, the air is full of a thousand thoughts, but neither man talks. These two have sat on this very spot through hurricanes before and have witnessed wildness beyond the picture window that neither has ever found the words to describe to anyone else. Now the radio is telling them that

—

they haven't seen anything yet. It's telling them that the worst storm ever has been saved for their old age and might at this moment be hurtling toward them.

"Should I mix a pitcherful of margaritas for the show tomorrow?" Wallace says finally, smiling slyly at Alan Halstead.

Halstead shifts on the ragged sofa and absorbs the remark. These seem to be the perennial dynamics of the relationship; Wallace suggests something that makes Halstead uncomfortable; he feels a tightness around his chest . . . but somehow, eventually, winds up giving in. "A pitcher?" repeats Halstead, his forehead creasing into a fist. How stupid, he thinks privately. The greatest force in nature about to be unleashed, we have to augment it with cocktails?

"I'm not sure, Dana . . ."

"Well, pick up the limes anyway, will you, Big Al?"

Now Halstead feels a grabbing at his throat, the beginning of anger. First of all, when did he ever say he even *was* sticking around? When did he agree to it? Sure, Dana Wallace, with no woman pleading with him to leave, will gladly sit here and drink margaritas through Hurricane Gloria. But Alan Halstead has a loving family, and the pressure to behave responsibly and get his own ass off Fire Island will be intense. So why should he feel guilty about leaving? What the hell did he have to prove to Dana Wallace, anyway?

It's not as if he wasn't willing to put his life on the line if the situation warranted it, Halstead thinks to himself. Hadn't he been an Ocean Beach volunteer fireman for most of his adult life? That was no small thing. The island has no greater enemy than fire, not even the angry sea. In clear weather, it takes no time at all for the bleached, bone-dry wood to burn. In '84, in WASP Point O' Woods, a couple of magnificent wood-shingled old Cape houses had gone up like paper. By the time the fire engines had slogged through the sand and the chain-link fence and the maze of tiny walkways, a few people were dead. It had been frightening in its speed and intensity, and whatever you thought about the aristocrats and their fences, it was a tragedy the whole island shared. And the old-timers could remember worse fires, when there wasn't even any real equipment to combat them.

When Alan Halstead was just a kid and old Rufus Hines had just started the fire department, they used to wheel a pail of chemicals around on a wagon! That was the equipment! Now, of course, there were modern hook-and-ladder jobs that could suck the water right out of the bay if they had to, but the name of the game, and the odds, hadn't changed.

Once a dry wind got ahold of them, these blazes couldn't be stopped. The most you could do was wet down a few roofs around the fires and keep them from spreading. That was enough, though, if you could save a life or even just a house that you or somebody's grandfather built with his two hands. Life and property were sacred things to the men of the Ocean Beach Fire Department, and behind them was a long and proud tradition of putting their asses on the line for somebody else; someone who might not even be there, but back in Manhattan somewhere.

All that proved something about Alan Halstead's willingness to put himself in a tight spot, didn't it? Hell, he was just about the king of the Limp Hoses, as they were laughingly, lovingly called—the old guys who no longer went out and fought fires, but sat around the firehouse remembering the early days, when victory depended more on the agility of the men than on the sophistication of the equipment. Like Indian braves, the firemen had competitions to sharpen their skills. They climbed for speed to the top of the tower that Bob Stretch's father built to sound the alarm bell from. They passed buckets of water to see which team could fill up a drum first. They even had contests to see who could get into uniform the fastest. Who would be the Fireman of the Year, the flower of island manhood, the hottest young stud at the Fireman's Ball?

Now, of course, many of the firemen have jobs off the island in the winter, and the spirit of the corps is more fragmented than it once was. But still, when they stage their drills and sit down to a banquet afterward in the Firehall, there is between them the warmth of warriors, and after a belt or two of Firehall scotch, the

—

noble gaiety of men ready to die for a higher cause. And no one is more revered at such gatherings than Limp Hoses like Alan Halstead. *So why the hell should he feel intimidated by Dana Wallace?* What did he have to prove?

"I'll get the limes if I can, Dana," he hears himself saying to Wallace.

"Don't put yourself out," says Wallace with a grin.

". . . I won't," says Halstead with an edge as he closes the screen door behind him and ambles off.

The bastard probably won't even show up, Wallace is thinking.

Fire Island, Thursday, September 26, 1985; 2:45 p.m.

Within an hour of the startling news of the magnitude of Gloria, the world has started running for cover. The Weather Service people are issuing rapid-fire bulletins, each more frightening than the one before. Though the experts still make the storm's chances of getting all the way up to the Northeast a long 8 to 1 (probably it will maul Cape Hatteras, or some other midcoastal spot), they are taking no chances.

In 1938 the world complained it had been given no warning. It laid the blame for the thousand deaths at the feet of the Weather Service, and it was an emotional blow the timid, remote profession of meteorology was unable to take. Sure, the world jostled them and kidded them when they blew a forecast, when somebody canceled a picnic or a golf game only to find the sky blue all day. That the meteorologists could take, but not much more. It wouldn't be unfair to say that many of them chose the profession for its distant, theoretical quality. They were more comfortable with air masses and satellite pictures than with people. They were scientists. Even today, for every glib TV weatherman, there are ten bashful others truly at their ease with only their instruments.

But in 1938, there were no instruments, at least none with today's sophistication. The only way to get readings from a storm

—

at sea was to fly out into it, or to already be there, and those readings, along with the readers, didn't always get home. So the surprise hurricane of 1938 was nobody's fault but whoever put that little spin on the globe and skewed those trade winds. But the loss of lives was so stunning that somebody had to take the heat. It was either shake your fist at a God whose existence was questionable, as Hitler marched into Poland, or blame the Weather Service.

Why weren't we warned? the people demanded to know.

It was the last time the profession would ever hear that awful question from a widow's lips. Every subsequent hurricane of any size got the advance billing of Michael Jackson playing Des Moines. And as for Gloria, with her breath-catching barometers and horrifying winds, well, everyone on earth was going to know about this one. It was time to pick up the trumpet of Gabriel and blow it.

Yes, the thing was probably headed for Cape Hatteras, North Carolina, thought the weathermen. But every man, woman, and child for a thousand miles in either direction along the water was being begged, cajoled, or threatened to leave. And anyone with a brain was doing it. Within an hour, the islands off the East Coast looked like Dunkirk, fishing boats riding low with refugees.

FIRE ISLAND, THURSDAY, SEPTEMBER 26, 1985; 3:45 P.M.

If there were any skeptics about Gloria, any wiseacres who didn't really believe there was a swirl of death a thousand miles across out there on the water, they might now be convinced by the rapid departure from Fire Island of the United States Coast Guard.

The cutter *Point Heron*, its full complement of twelve aboard, putt-putts out of its slip at the end of the Western Kingdom, bound for Tarrytown on the Hudson River, where it will wait out the storm. A few men remain behind to haul the files upstairs, in case the ocean comes through the first floor of the modern brick post building but not the second (although no one really expects it to have that fine a touch). By the time things get dangerous, these men, too, will be gone, on the last government jeep across the Robert Moses Bridge to the mainland.

As Lt. Richard Kassler supervises them, lean and tan in his whites, he looks every inch the modern military man. In his soft, firm, clear commands there is no trace of the troubles, the rugged heroics, and ultimately the compromise and the disgrace of the Coast Guard on Fire Island.

The Coast Guard is descended from the Life Saving Service, a hardy, gristled band of men who roamed the thirty-mile stretch of beach in the nineteenth century, looking for ships foundering on reefs offshore. There were plenty, sailing ships that had slipped and slid along the coast from Montauk looking for a way into New York Harbor, but were betrayed by the tides, by an inlet that no longer existed, or by a false fire lit along the beach.

And even though the pirates were long gone, there was no shortage of ruthless scavengers waiting to pick the wrecks clean. One of them, the notorious Jeremiah Smith, would lure frozen, shipwrecked men into his shack with a cozy light in the window, then cut their throats, steal their booty, and toss them back into the water on the ebb tide. The Life Saving Service had to discipline devils like these, but more often, and worse, they simply had to fight the winter ocean with thick hemp cutting into their waists as they made their way out to rescue some poor soul clinging to a frozen spar. Frostbite, exposure, and pneumonia were the name of the game—usually to rescue people who were already dead, or cargo that was already ruined or lost. The Life Savers were rugged men who lived their lives out in the open, on the flat barrier beach. On their rare days off they would hunt ducks or deer or comb the murky bay bottom for clams.

At the turn of the century, there was a civilizing influence on them. The government decided to merge them with the revenue cutters, the sleek police sloops that patroled the coast for smugglers. The modern Coast Guard was born. The barnacle-butted Life Saving Servicemen were issued uniforms. Their toughness and purity did not dim so much as be absorbed by the military code. The newest branch of the Armed Forces had a more subdued kind of pride; hometown heros who protected the coastline from whatever threats, man-made or natural, came at it.

Then came Prohibition. Creaking old cargo ships began crossing the ocean with illegal bellyfuls of booze, and Fire Island was a natural drop-off point. The Coast Guard was told to close it off. But their government-issue skiffs were no match for the rumrunners' quick, powerful little speedboats, often piloted by local fishermen who knew the tricky waters well. The big ships came with the booze and left with American dollars and frequently with guns for the Irish Republican Army. It was a serious operation, fueled by greed and deep political passion. The rumrunners saw themselves as little different from early-American patriots defying the Stamp Act. You didn't want to be a raw Coast Guard recruit staring into the barrel of a water-cooled .50 calibre machine gun, a trained, impassioned killer's finger on the trigger.

Slowly the Coast Guard gave up. Then, finally, they collaborated.

At the beginning of Prohibition the rumrunners rode the beach on horseback, signaling furtively to sea and dragging cases of whiskey behind the dunes one at a time. By the end, farm trailers with huge loads were crawling along the beach while the Coast Guard looked the other way. When federal agents finally had to be called in from the Midwest to clean things up, it was the most scandalous blow a service organization had ever endured . . . and one from which it still hasn't fully recovered.

But the years since then have been placid ones. Except for the occasional bizarre incident, like a Nazi submarine turning up in a net, the Fire Island Coast Guard has been pretty serene duty to pull. Perched on the western edge of the Western Kingdom, the post today has the appearance of a prosperous, tidy village, full of pregnant women, dogs, and kids. Seamen hang from spars with rags and polishes, making the brass gleam on the government boats while the radio plays old rock-and-roll.

It's true that in recent years drug smuggling has been on the rise, and Coast Guardsmen have once again had to address themselves to techniques of law enforcement, calling up disturbing echoes of the Jazz Age. But by and large this is a problem for their southern colleagues. There are no Colombians moving cocaine ashore on Fire Island, and the Coast Guard, to a man, hopes it will stay that way. They are happy in their placidity, preferring to see themselves as the friendly local deputy rather than the federal law, and softspoken Lieutenant Kassler—likeable, intelligent, agreeably in command—is their leader and their perfect reflection.

And there is no question about the Coast Guard's position vis-à-vis the worst hurricane of the twentieth century. If the storm lives up to half its publicity, there will be no rescues to be made and no property to be recovered; so rather than take a false-heroic stance the men might pay for with their lives, the Coast Guard will discreetly withdraw. The decision was taken at the officer's club on Governor's Island, the civilized eastern command post in the river off Manhattan.

Oh, in the old days one of those yahoos from the Life Saving Service might have stuck around to watch the big blow and probably gotten himself blown away by it, but not the modern Coast Guard.

Coincidentally, Dana Wallace is running an errand at the western end of the Island as the *Heron* putts by on its way to its safe harbor in the Hudson. Observing the confident young servicemen lining the deck, Wallace recalls James Lindsey's childhood image from the hurricane of '38: the lone Coast Guardsman, terror in his eyes, in retreat. A wide, knowing smile breaks across Wallace's face; nothing has changed . . . the bastards are turning tail again!

—

Fire Island Pines, Thursday, September 26, 1985; 4 p.m.

Martin Quartararo has not visited the Belvedere Hotel for coffee today. For one thing, they don't allow dogs. And since Martin has volunteered to take care of Hercules, his friend's Doberman pinscher, for the weekend, he has instead come here for his recreation, to the harbor of Fire Island Pines. Here, both man and beast can stretch out.

But there is another, far more urgent reason for this rare visit of Martin's to the Pines. A hurricane is coming, and in about half an hour a boat will enter this harbor to evacuate anyone who wants to leave. Whether or not to be on it is the question Martin must now consider.

—

Scratching the animal's belly, the small, stocky man contemplates death. Or to be more accurate, he contemplates destruction, at the moment the destruction of Spirits of the Pines, the liquor store fifty yards to his left. The only game in town, "Spirits" virtually fueled the great party era of Fire Island Pines. What a hurricane will do to its phenomenal inventory of liquor, Martin shudders to think. He watches Mario, the owner, in the window taping the legions of rainbow-colored bottles together, though for what reason Martin cannot fathom. If this storm is anything like it's supposed to be, Spirits of the Pines will be a hundred-proof wading pool, or even more likely, a memory.

Not that Martin will shed any tears for the destruction of the store, or the booze, or all of Fire Island Pines, for that matter. When he first got to Fire Island he tried the Pines and was seduced for awhile by the color-coordinated hors d'oeuvres and the nude surfers rolling in on cue. The parties were well stage-managed. What they lacked was sheer human heat, shoulder to shoulder and butt to butt. That Martin found, and continues to find, in his beloved Cherry Grove.

Once a year an "armada" from Cherry Grove raids the harbor in Fire Island Pines. It is a collection of small boats arrayed like floats in a parade, all of them outrageously festooned, none so much as the one that carries Miss Fire Island on his elevated throne, tossing rose petals into the bay. One year it was Truman Capote, in a blue velvet gown. Last year the honor went to a three-hundred-pound black man dressed as Mary, Queen of Scots.

For the "invasion" the Pinesmen spread themselves around this very harbor, relaxing in Bermuda shorts with coffee in hand. When the outlandish flotilla appears, the audience onshore smiles and applauds, remembering their own youthful excesses, perhaps wishing they could still afford the indiscretion of participating themselves. All in good fun, but where you are on invasion day is a pretty good indicator of where you stand in the gay community. Are you on the boats, plastered at noon in exotic drag, or are you onshore in beachwear with coffee?

Martin Quartararo is always on the boat. They will bury him

at sea. And at this moment, as Hercules the Doberman pinscher stretches, yawns, and growls, Martin is remembering his first boat ride to this island, the day Marilyn Monroe died. It was long ago, and it was very shortly after another significant day in his life, a day that the imminence of Hurricane Gloria seems to be calling up out of memory.

He was in New Orleans, still carrying on the prolonged charade for his fundamentalist Christian parents; that he was straight and that he was carrying a torch not for a traveling salesman, but for a blond, winsome Louisiana girl named Grace. The situation at the family home on St. Peter's Street was getting worse, however. His mother's matchmaking attempts to find a replacement for Grace were repeated, dismal failures. So who was Martin staying out all night with? What was going on? One morning the answer came in the form of a vitriolic-poison pen letter written to Martin's mother by one of his spurned ex-lovers.

Martin remembers the moment clearly. He was standing in the bathroom shaving. She came in and sat on the edge of the tub with the letter in her hand.

"Martin, I see a thing here, a thing that if I heard from the angels themselves I wouldn't believe." The razor fell out of his hands and clattered in the sink.

"A thing, Martin," she went on, "that if I thought was true I would kill myself. End it right now."

He couldn't tell her. He should, but he couldn't. He had to deny it. This simple religious woman had no framework to comprehend it, and neither did her brittle, pious husband. Martin wasn't going to cram the truth down their throats for any self-righteous reason of his own. They would have to live with their suspicions. But one thing was for sure: He was getting the hell out of there.

Moslems go to Mecca, monarch butterflies to Mexico, opera lovers to Milan, and homosexuals to New York. Martin was one of the vast tribe that came from everywhere to get lost in the city, where he would have to answer to no one.

Behind him was a dark, stifled childhood and the pain of

—

unrequited love. Yes, a promiscuous floozy of a traveling saleman had caused Martin to weep bitter tears. But never again. Never again, vowed the little man. He washed his hair with Johnson's Baby Shampoo and adopted its motto, "No more tears." No one would dance harder or dress more exotically than the man from New Orleans. Let the music be loud enough to drown out the dark thoughts, let the makeup be thick enough to hide any furrows, let the gaiety never end. All this Martin found in the village of Cherry Grove, where there was no such thing as tomorrow. He was the pixie dynamo of a sex-fueled party machine that never wound down. He snorted poppers and sweated with a truck driver on the dance floor all night, and made love to him with ruined mascara all the next day. If his neighbors heard his love sounds through the paper-thin walls, so what? He wanted love, he needed it, and he had the guts to go out and get it. That's what the Grove was all about. Nobody was pretending anything else.

No, Martin Quartararo had no use for the cool, spread-out chic of Fire Island Pines, and didn't care if the whole place fell into the sea.

At this moment, though, on this desolate Thursday afternoon, he is enjoying its very spaciousness. The harbor, usually ringed with sleek, costly yachts, is empty. It allows his thoughts to grow expansive, which is appropriate given the issue at hand . . . his own life or death. Already the desolate afternoon has only two sounds, the bay lapping the pilings and the air-raid sirens sweeping the empty walkways. And in about twenty minutes the final boat will be entering the harbor he now stares at. It will be decision time for Martin Quartararo.

But what decision is there? he asks himself. What reason *can* there be to endure the Apocalypse and risk death on Fire Island? Only one comes to mind right away; better to be here than over in Sayville on the mainland, looking for a place to stay with a big dog. The fact that Sayville hated gays was something everyone knew who ever passed through it, and that included everyone who'd ever taken the ferry to the Grove or the Pines. Sayville was a community of straight, middle-class people who resented being the gateway to the Eastern Kingdom of Fire Island. Why should their children have to watch this collection of freaks gallivanting through town all summer? Especially when the freaks were on their way to catch offshore breezes that would never reach Sayville. These were the same straight people, Martin tells himself, that were bought off during the Battle of the Pines and they've bitterly regretted it ever since.

No. Under disaster conditions, Martin did not want to be walking around that town with a big dog on a leash and no place to stay. Was that, then, the only reason he might remain on the island? Because it would be uncomfortable and inconvenient to cross the water to safety? Was it a good enough reason? No, it wasn't, not to court the kind of hell this monster storm was going to be dishing out. Martin's mind was made up; he was getting the hell out.

He clambers to his feet and yanks taut the leash, snapping Hercules to attention. As if to confirm his judgment, Mario emerges from his liquor store at the same moment, jangling his key ring and turning out the lights. That settles it, thinks Martin. It was well known on the island that Mario was a child in Paris when the Nazis marched in, and a young man in Cuba on the New Year's Eve when Castro led the rebels into the capital. In other words he was no stranger to the shit hitting the fan. So if he was getting out, the getting was good.

As Mario prepares to turn the key in the lock of Spirits of the Pines, and Martin watches him do it, both men are startled by the arrival of a third. So empty is the afternoon that company is unexpected. Even more shocking is the particular man who ambles toward them—lean, leathery old Bob Tyson!

"What the hell are you closing for? It's four o'clock," growls Tyson.

"Bob, this isn't an ordinary day," replies Mario.

"That's what the guy in the Cherry Grove store said. What the hell am I supposed to do for a cocktail tonight?"

Martin and Mario exchange stunned looks.

"Bob, the last boat leaves in half an hour. Most of us are planning to be on it," says Martin.

"Bon voyage. Can I get a fifth of Cutty Sark?"

As Mario reopens the shop and leads Tyson in among the darkened racks of booze, Martin is confused and immobile. That somebody should be sticking around for this monstrous storm is surprising enough. That it should be Bob Tyson is shocking. The man was eighty years old. *Eighty!* And not only that, thinks Martin, Tyson wasn't making this decision for himself alone. Another human being would be paying the price for it. The man had a wife.

A wife. That was a notion startling enough to Martin Quartararo. But yes, Bob and Allys Tyson were just about the only straight couple in Cherry Grove. In fact the history of their romance *was* the history of that fabled little village, though they remained its oddest residents. Just about the *Only straight couple in Cherry Grove,* for God's sake! They were as middle-class as Ozzie and Harriet and they'd held their ground in the center ring of the most decadent circus on earth.

Bless them! They were a curiosity and an inspiration. But there was a time, Martin remembers, when Allys got so fed up, she wanted to leave. Then it passed. It was all part of the story of their fabulous romance, and for some reason it fills Martin's thoughts as the minutes tick away and the last boat to safety noses its way into the harbor. *They were sticking around for the Hurricane?* What the hell could they be thinking of?

Martin recalls the history, familiar to just about everyone in the Eastern Kingdom; after the hurricane of '38, as Antoine the hairdresser and W. H. Auden the poet wandered about the rubble of Cherry Grove with deeds and surveying instruments, the straight population was in the process of fleeing to Saltaire. The Grove was going to be rebuilt into a freak show, so the middle class was getting out. But the Tysons, who had just fallen in love with the place, had different ideas. They had just drawn up plans for a home of their own in Cherry Grove, and saw no reason to back out. They breathed a sigh of relief that they had waited until after the storm to build, felt in fact that the near-miss confirmed the wisdom of their judgment.

Through the 1940s, as they settled in and started a family, the great gay immigration to the Eastern Kingdom went on around them. One by one, the remaining straight couples saw the handwriting on the wall and pulled out. One morning the Tysons woke up and discovered they were about the only ones left. Entreaties began to come from their friends; what kind of a place was this, people argued, to raise a child?

The Tysons held their ground. Bob made his living being reasonable and the reasonable choice was to stay put, not to be panicked out of a place where you, and even the homosexuals for that matter, had a Constitutional right to privacy and happiness. In this his firebrand liberal wife backed up his cool judgment with her hot one. Over someone's dead body was she leaving her home. She was dug in by the fingernails.

So the Tysons' judgment was not frivolous. And once they made a decision, they committed themselves to it. That meant something, didn't it, Martin Quartararo asks himself?

The boat has tied up in the Pines harbor and begun to load its exotic refugees. The moment of decision is about five minutes away for Martin and Hercules.

The door of Spirits of the Pines swings open and Bob Tyson emerges with his booze, the fifth of Cutty Sark and several other exotic items: a tangerine liqueur for Allys and a couple of chocolates for a treat.

"Bob . . ."

Tyson turns to Martin and the panting dog.

"Bob, I don't know if . . . you're sure you . . . understand about the storm?"

"Understand what?"

"How . . . big it's supposed to be."

"The bigger the better," says Tyson, straining to be on his way.

—

"And Allys?"

"Looking forward to it, too," says Tyson brusquely, disappearing into the shadbush.

Watching him go, Martin tries desperately to understand the old man's thinking. First of all, Bob Tyson was an old lawyer and operated just about 100 percent out of his head. He figured things out. Passions were an impediment and a distraction. He believed there was no human problem, even a problem of the heart, that wouldn't yield to the power of reason. So that was a good sign; maybe Bob had figured out the storm wasn't going to be so bad, after all.

On the other hand, Bob Tyson had always been a little *too much* of a thinker for Martin's taste. It was an occupational hazard. Coal miners get black lung, lawyers get stuck up in their heads. Both were diseases, in Martin's opinion. But his wife, on the other hand! Well, Allys was just about the *opposite* kind of human being. Volatile, profoundly *un*reasonable, and still, at eighty, wild.

So what did it all mean?

It's true that the Tysons will have a fabulous seat for the show, he thinks. The Tyson house was perched on a little knoll right across from the ocean. But maybe it was *too* good a seat. Martin remembers watching the Indianapolis 500 car race on TV earlier in the season, on Memorial Day. A group of picnickers found a great spot on a little knoll near one of the banked turns. Then one of the cars went over the wall and killed them all.

Now the sound of the ferry idling at the dock fills Martin's ears. Roughly two minutes, he figures. If he's going to make a move, it has to be now. He watches Tyson disappear up the tiny road choked with shadbush, and tries to remain calm, and keep his thinking clear, despite the agitated, steady growl of Hercules.

Bob Tyson was not a capricious man. He wasn't quirky, flaky, or eccentric. He wasn't an artist or a designer. And he wasn't senile. Not quite. He had a head on his shoulders and he played the percentages. Such a man was not bent on suicide, at least not in such a headlong way as sticking around for the worst storm of the century. Was he? No. Tyson had made some kind of a clear-headed judgment, based either on the percentages, or on some kind of inside information.

But even more to the point, thinks Martin, with about a minute left to think, where did his *own* philosophy of life come into play here? Was it not Martin Quartararo's credo to wring life absolutely dry of every possibility? You only got seventy-odd years. Wasn't each moment to be tightly embraced? Wouldn't that include a hurricane, which promised to be the most fabulous thrill of all?

And even *more* to the point, he thinks (rapidly and clearly now), what was the extent of his loyalty to his home, to this place that has given him, the sexual refugee, a safe harbor at last?

He has his answer. It has to do with loyalty, a quality that has always thrilled Martin in books and movies. Martin Quartararo has found peace in the bosom of this thin island, and he will repay it with what he has to give: his love and his loyalty.

The little man steps onto the walkway and watches the ferry, now loaded to the gunwales, pull out of the harbor. As it disappears, and the din of the chattering magpie-passengers recedes, a peace comes over him quite unlike anything he's ever known. The squirming is over. He has delivered himself over to some higher order, which will do with him as it pleases.

It's a sublime feeling, really, without responsibility or ego, much like Martin has always heard the Buddhist sects are supposed to make you feel. Car keys, invoices, the minor details of life—hell, even the major ones, mortgages, medical problems—all of these things are being gently brushed away by the huge hands that hold him now, and within a few hours will either crush him or set him back down.

Relax, Martin, a voice seems to be saying.

He's made the right decision. He feels it in his bones. He feels it paying dividends already, not just in the elevated mood he is enjoying, but in the lovely emptiness of Fire Island Pines. Here at the height of Indian summer, the most heavenly time, he has the place all to himself.

But what will he do? That's the problem. How to spend these few hours, how to pass the time so that the waiting will not become torturous. He is by nature a gregarious fellow, but with no one around but Tyson and his eighty-year-old bride, there's no one to talk to. Calling Hercules to heel, he heads home, back through the Meatrack to Cherry Grove.

The walk is beautiful but lonely. The sky is pale blue except for a few scudding clouds. The weather hardly seems threatening. Martin arrives at his cottage, lets himself in, and flops on the sofa. What now?

He picks up a movie magazine . . . last month's. Meryl Streep is having a baby and Barbra Streisand is having an affair with a parking attendant at Ciro's. Big deal. Who in the universe didn't already know that? He puts the magazine down and his small hazel eyes roam the room. There, sitting on the counter, is the solution to his problem, the answer to his prayers. The telephone!

Why not? He'll call everyone he knows and tell them . . . well, what *will* he tell them? Well, thinks Martin, why not let *them* tell *me*, if they're really my friends or not.

He dials the first number in his address book.

"Hello?"

"Hi Jimmy, it's Martin."

"Martin? Where are you?"

"On the island."

"You're still on the island? You better get the hell off!"

"I missed the last boat."

"You missed the—Jesus . . ."

"Listen, baby, that's why I'm calling. I need you to come and get me."

"Come and get you?"

"I hate to ask you, Jimmy, but I got no choice. Listen, you just drive over the bridge, you take a left, and you come down the beach until you get here. You got four-wheel drive?"

"Four-wheel? No . . ."

"That's okay; you don't need it. If you start to slide, you just go with it, just like on ice. You got snow tires?"

"I . . . somewhere . . ."

"Good. Can you be here in an hour? Otherwise I've had it."

"Listen, Martin, . . . don't get me wrong—you know how much our friendship means to me . . . it's just that tonight I'm committed to this dinner thing—it's a stupid thing, really, I don't even want to go—but the reservation is in my name."

"I understand."

"If there was any way I could get out of it . . ."

"I understand."

"And who knows, this hurricane might not even come! These guys have been wrong before."

"Yes, they have."

"So look, Martin, if there's anything else I can do, I mean *anything*, you have my number."

"Yes I do. Thank you. Good-bye."

"Good luck, buddy."

"Thank you."

Martin hangs up, smiles, and crosses the man's name off his list of friends. Then he dials another number. The next man, who doesn't have a car, says he'll rent one and be right over. Then Martin says he's had a sudden change of heart and declines the offer, saying thanks, anyway.

Then he dials the next number.

And in this fashion Martin Quartararo passes the time as Hurricane Gloria creeps north along the Atlantic. Putting little plusses or minuses next to the names in his address book.

Fire Island, Thursday, September 26, 1985; sundown

The Weather Service, obsessed with avoiding a repeat of the tragedy of 1938, is now issuing blanket evacuation orders along the entire East Coast. Privately, though, they're beginning to feel fairly certain of Gloria's target; like many of her predecessors that chose the northern route, she looks like she's heading for Cape Hatteras, which juts invitingly off the coast of North Carolina.

And although they certainly aren't smug about it (that's the *last* word to describe the mood in weather stations up and down the coast), and although they certainly aren't going public with the feeling (hurricanes have embarrassed them once too often for that), the weathermen are starting to sense, as night falls, what the outcome of all this might be.

The thing will hit North Carolina, and batter it pretty badly. But it won't be as bad as it might be, for two reasons. First of all, the barometer has actually, blessedly been creeping *upward* for about an hour; someone is trying to put the top back onto the sky! Second, a cold front (high pressure, stability, motherhood!) over Missouri is hastening eastward, and might well arrive in time to collide with Gloria before she does any real damage.

Fingers of weathermen relax away from dials and fish in pockets for cigarettes. For the first time in hours, people are starting to think about getting away from the instruments for a while, maybe even getting a little shut-eye.

But now the tickers begin to jerk and crackle with the seven o'clock feed, and the information is shocking. The cold front over Missouri isn't coming after all! The damn thing is *so* stable it isn't even moving! No help can be expected from Sam Houston; the Alamo will have to stand alone.

The ticker won't stop. More bad news. Whoever's trying to wrestle the lid back onto the sky is losing. The barometer, which everyone thought was finally on its way back up, is on its way back down! And now the final, unnerving piece of news: The storm is changing directions! Instead of heading for the fat Carolina coast, it's veering off to the northeast. It's making monkeys of the weathermen again, vexing them right to the end. Landfall at Hatteras, a certainty an hour ago, is now barely a possibility. Who's in control of this thing? And if it isn't coming ashore at Hatteras, the weathermen ask themselves, what *is* it doing?

There are only two possibilities—three, really, if you count going out to sea and dying a benign death, but it's now clear to the weathermen, who are beginning to understand her personality, who have quit pretending she doesn't have one, that Gloria is too evil and has come too far to disappear whimpering into the ocean.

No. She'll either skim the coast going north, ripping away the guts of a few dozen cities and towns until sheer friction dissipates her, or she'll exercise her most terrifying option of all: Loop out to sea, refresh herself, and explode headlong into Long Island, which sticks out into the Atlantic like a sitting Long Island duck. And whatever she does she's going to do quickly. The colder water south of Bermuda has forced her to pick up speed to keep her torrid steam engine revved. She's traveling at twenty miles an hour and that will get faster during the night.

So the cities of the Northeast, and particularly Long Island, will have to be given the revised forecast. It's the kind of news that, in person, you'd deliver shuffling your feet and looking at the ground. The chances of the storm hitting the New York area are no longer 8 to 1. The private assurances that have been given the day before now, regrettably, have to be withdrawn. The chances are . . . well, put it this way: If you live on Long Island and you have any real interest in life, you'd better get your ass away from the water.

Commuters straggling home on the Long Island Expressway get the bad news first, from their car radios. This was no longer some kind of a general warning; it looked as if the worst hurricane in history might be coming tomorrow . . . here!

From Massapequa to Montauk, disaster strategies that have been yellowing in handbooks for years are jolted into action. High schools are thrown open as refugee camps. Lazy, bitter high school janitors have new purpose in life; they're part of the disaster team. There's something bracing about the Apocalypse.

One Long Island public high school is designated for Fire Island refugees. The slim barrier beach, a vulnerable finger out in the Atlantic, is being completely evacuated. In the school's cavernous modern gymnasium, hundreds of Red Cross cots and standard issue blankets are laid out for the tired, poor, and hungry. A percolator the size of a corn silo simmers with enough coffee for a regiment. You could thread the Atlantic cable through the doughnuts. At a long table sit a registered nurse, several prim bureaucrats whose dour miens identify them as "disaster officials," and a phalanx of volunteers ... most of them predisposed to disliking the privileged, decadent refugees they are waiting to help.

But the place is empty. Whoever has made the decision to throw open a high school gym for bereft Fire Islanders has made a miscalculation, based no doubt on ignorance of the social makeup of that peculiar little sandspit, with its Eastern and Western Kingdoms and its vast social gaps, from clam diggers to choreographers.

The native islanders virtually all have family roots in eastern Long Island and have merely crossed the bay to the waiting arms and hearths of their cousins and aunts. And the summer people? The Manhattanites? Red Cross blankets and doughnuts! Are you kidding? The summer people, the ones who aren't crazy enough to still be out there, have already fled on the wings of the Long Island Railroad or their own sports cars. Most of them are in cozy East Side bistros sipping dry martinis by the time the Red Cross coffee is perking.

As night falls and the volunteers doze or dribble basketballs around the huge, empty, spotless gym, a yellow bus pulls up from the ferry dock, having met the last boat from Fire Island. Now, for the first time all day, the bus disgorges a passenger! A customer at last! A refugee! Is he hungry, is he cold, is he disoriented, displaced or traumatized, the Red Cross people clustering around him want to know?

Just tired, he says. An unemployed actor from Manhattan, he has been evacuated with his two cats. He turns the cats loose in homeroom 102, wolfs down fifteen doughnuts, and dives onto a cot from which he doesn't budge for twelve hours. The volunteers look around at each other. Two of them dig up some sand and put it in a cardboard box for cat litter. Another gingerly adjusts the harsh lighting in the gym, so the refugee might sleep peacefully. Still another replaces the doughnuts he has eaten with fifteen more, sponging off the crumbs he has trailed across the table and the floor. Then, like everyone else east of the Mississippi, they wait.

FIRE ISLAND, THURSDAY, SEPTEMBER 26, 1985; 7:30 P.M.

There are a hundred people left on Fire Island, and they've made a conscious decision to be there. They've all been warned sternly, ominously, repeatedly. Martin Quartararo, for example, has just been visited by the police and asked for the names of his next-of-kin.

But either these steadfast islanders think the authorities with their prophecies of doom are bluffing or they think the ocean is bluffing; that the storm will wind up scaring a few sea gulls in the middle of nowhere and barely disturb brunch plans for the weekend. Or they think the worst storm of the century is indeed coming and they want to be in it, in order to survive it, or in order not to.

For most of these people, the seven o'clock weather feed is grim news indeed. The chances of a direct hit on Long Island have gone from a longshot to a distinct possibility. They appear to have made a serious misjudgment.

But it will be dawn, at least, before the stakes are truly known. The hurricane still retains the option of dying at sea or it still might jaggedly rip north along the coast, stripping its gears, and arrive tomorrow, impotent. Until Gloria makes this, the last of her decisions, there is nothing for the hundred people to do but entertain the possibility, however small, that this is their last night on earth.

There are many ways to entertain such a possibility, such a guest in your mind. You can put him in a back bedroom where you can't see him. You can give him the run of the house and let him drive you crazy. You can sit him down and have a heart-to-

———

heart. You can throw a fabulous party, with him as the guest of honor. On Fire Island in the hours before Gloria, all these options will be explored.

Invisible through the clouds rises a full moon that doubles the stakes of tomorrow's adventure. Low tide will be lower than low, and high tide higher than high. If the storm arrives then, on the equinox full moon high tide, it will mean death for all of God's children on whom the blanket of night now settles.

Across the great expanse of Fire Island Pines, the fantastic houses that peek through the woods are dark; sober monuments to the American devotion to style, which has paid for them. In the desolate Meatrack, only the brown fox tumbles and writhes in the bramble. In the winding walkways of Cherry Grove, the little gingerbread sex cottages are mute and still. In all of the Eastern Kingdom only a light or two twinkles, like headlights in the desert.

Though the vast Sunken Forest is darker still, with no lights at all, it is now, as ever, the center of life on the island. The white-tailed deer are converging far in advance of their winter yarding time. The red fox have abandoned their burrows in the swale and moved to the heart of the woods. The rabbits are everywhere beneath the catbrier understory. The toads hold council in the hollow logs where they will hibernate in the winter. From either end they send out toxic wafts to discourage their enemy the racer snake, who also slithers about the hollies and swamp maples in confusion. Without the benefit of radio reports from the National Weather Service, the Animal Kingdom has gotten the message, by the way things look and feel and smell, that the heavens are in disarray somewhere close by.

Nowhere is there more agitation than high in the sassafras trees, where the American redstarts brood over a decision. These are Ferron Bell's favorites; the moody poets of birdland, renegades from the cheerful warbler family. Tonight they have a vexing problem, apart from their perennial melancholy. Nature is sending them two signals at once.

On the one hand, the feeling in their hollow bones is unmistakable; the air is getting lighter. Soon it will have no weight at all. This means that nothing can be counted on. The sky will be sucking things up, and soon there will be water rushing out of it, and then the air will rise and swoop six ways at once, and they won't be able to fly. And if they're out over the water, they won't be able to land. They'll be at the mercy of the wind. That's what the light air means, as their mothers know and their mother's mother knew, just by being born a bird.

And yet the insects that they've feasted on all summer are disappearing, the victims of the cold September nights. All this together with the steadily dying light, the fact that every day the sun rises an instant later and sets an instant sooner, all of this suggests something very different.

It's time to go.

People used to think that when birds disappeared in the winter, they were hibernating in the mud or had flown to the moon. When the truth was learned, it was no less wondrous.

The Arctic tern, to maintain its exotic diet of cold-water shellfish, was flying from the North Pole to the South Pole. In two days! Hardly did the amazing bird ever witness the dark of night, flying from one midnight sun to another. The tiny golden plover would be nibbling on cranberries in Nova Scotia one day and skimming the Argentinean Pampas the next! Squadrons of snow geese were flying at thirty thousand feet, practically reading the magazines on the laps of airline passengers!

And no less amazing than the distances they covered were the ways they navigated them. When the clouds were above them, they read the coastlines of the continents. When the clouds were below them, they read the sun and the stars. When the clouds were everywhere . . . who knew? But they got there. Birds from a little Polish square got to their wintering spots all over Africa, and birds from all over America got to a single rooftop in San Miguel, Mexico, year after year after year. On time!

Put a bird in a cage and decrease its daylight, or project a

September roof of stars onto the ceiling, and it will beat relentlessly against the south side of the cage. How? Why? Nature just takes care of it. But what happens when the instinct, deep as it is, is challenged by another one just as deep?

All over the Sunken Forest, councils of the anxious songbirds squat on branches to weigh the question. Death in a storm is awful, but so is death by starvation. Nothing is worse than flying south late and being a few days behind your food supply. You arrive somewhere just as the bugs have gone a little farther below the ground than your bill can reach. Without the food, you're too weak to continue, and while you wait for your strength to recoup, the nights get colder. It's a desperate way to die, worse even than the violent death of being whipped out of the sky by a big wind.

Across the forest the tangerine hoods and black shafts bob and flutter. The decision is taken. Tonight is the night, the dangerous light air notwithstanding. The sound in the forest is a giant *whooooosh*. A thousand branches spring and quiver, shooting their live arrows into the sky.

The redstart is gone.

Up through the night goes the dark mass, stretching, pulling and elongating, wildly changing shape as it reaches for the bright high nimbus. In the dark western sky, the constellation of the archer shows the way.

In the Atlantic, the fluke are heading out early. Usually October sends them from the shallow, cold island shelf to deeper, warmer waters. Even in the sea they can feel the weight of the sky, and they know that the light air means the bottom gets all kicked up and silt gets in your gills, so you'd better be deep.

Offshore of the Eastern Kingdom, the redstart and the fluke move together, reflections through the looking glass of sea level. The landmass is dark and the hour is late, but one light burns.

A man sits reading beyond a curtain of sassafras trees, a curtain impenetrable to moonlight and to the gaze of passersby on the walkways of Fire Island Pines. On this night, though, no one is passing by. Ivan Bekoff, the Daniel Boone of Fire Island

Pines, is quite, quite alone. Nonetheless, he senses the presence of the moon, so he peers out, acknowledges it, and returns to his novel.

Ivan briefly considered evacuation earlier in the day when news of the storm began to filter through the shadbush from transistor radios along the walkway, from urgent conversations echoing through the trees, even from the behavior of the birds and the fox, who seemed to feel the low pressure in their bones. Right then and there, Ivan made his decision to stay. He had a cold. Besides, the last time he evacuated for one of these things he dragged himself to some motel near the McArthur Airport on Long Island only to flip on the radio and be told, "The storm now appears to be headed for the McArthur Airport."

So what did it matter? And if it was such a pain in the ass to pack up and go, and it really didn't make any difference anyhow, why bother?

Because, argued one of his neighbors who dared stick his head in to check on the irascible man, this storm was not simply an inconvenience, a little zephyr that was going to dump a few inches of rain and be gone. This was the worst storm of the century.

Yes, but his sinuses were acting up and it was so comfortable here, replied Ivan.

But didn't he understand that death was a real possibility? said the neighbor.

Yes, but his cats were such terrible travelers, said Ivan.

So Ivan Bekoff had become a man for whom the value of life could be weighed against the inconvenience of traveling a few miles to preserve it. And on this gray Thursday he has puttered around his cabin, going resolutely about his usual business as the walkways swayed and trembled with baggage and refugees. And now, with the island empty and dark, he is reading a book.

In midsentence he's startled by a noise on the walkway. Voices punctuate the stillness. Briefly cocking an ear, Ivan concludes that a couple of wild young people have decided to miss the last boat and stick around for the storm. Or maybe they hadn't decided anything, but just had one Quaalude or Manhattan too many and forgot about it, or never even knew about it. Idiots, thinks Ivan. Complete incarnations of what the gay male has become: vapid and glamorous to the point of unconsciousness.

Now he recognizes one of the voices. It's Mitchell, Calvin Klein's beautiful houseboy. Paternal and lecherous feelings competing within his breast, Ivan steps outside his curtain of shadbush to greet the men, the other of whom turns out to be an unemployed chauffeur named Timothy.

What are they doing? Ivan asks.

Just carousing around, they explain, exploring the empty wonderland and the abandoned pleasure palaces. Immediately, Ivan begins to feel out of place, a little too old and too plain to relax with the chattering Adonises.

Would he like to join them? he is asked.

His chest tightens. Although he's not so old that he can't remember his own resentment of these gaudy houses, he is frankly scared of breaking into them. Criminal Trespassing is a serious crime in this community.

"Ordinarily, I would . . ." he says.

"Then why don't you?" says the houseboy, with the casual tone of youth, fixing a stare into Ivan's dark, hooded eyes.

Taken aback, Ivan tries to interpret the glance. It may be a sexual invitation. It may not be. Either way, it has struck a nerve in the older man. Why don't I, indeed? he is thinking. Or was my boldness only a product of youth. Am I now an old maid? Will I pass the night with a cup of tea and my lonely novel? Will I do the comfortable thing or the daring thing? Will I get laid? Or will I only be humiliated, disappointed, rejected?

The argument rages in the older man's head as the youths strain to be on their way. Finally out of patience, they disappear into a forest of juniper. Ivan thinks intensely for another minute, then hurls himself into the dark green thicket after them. After a breathless run he catches up to them at a large iron gate—separated from a palatial home by a moat.

A moat!

The young men are stymied. Not just the usual electronic and wrought-iron barriers, but a moat.

They turn to go, but Ivan does not move. A *moat*, for Christ's sake! Something inside him snaps. Startling his companions, he rips the expensive wood facade off the gate post and lays it across the brackish water. In the darkness, he leads the young men over into private property, aglow with the vague thrill of revolution.

They grope around for a while in the darkness. Suddenly, Ivan's foot strikes concrete. His eyes focus in the moon shadows, and a vast, flat clearing comes into view. It is a pool deck, perhaps the most spacious he has ever seen. The darkness notwithstanding, the water is china blue. The house, though even darker, though barely visible through taped windows, is a wormwood palace. And the bar, which sits just beyond a sliding stained-glass door, looks *very* well stocked. If the door is open . . . It is!!

Instantly, it's a party. It's one thing to face death alone, and quite another to do it with a little company and a little booze. It brings out the pluck in you, especially when it's on someone else's tab. Suddenly there's nothing grim about the Grim Reaper. You just mix him a drink and tell him to join the party. The event reaches dizzying heights almost immediately. The sound system is cranked up to a fierce level. The sexual vibrations are pert and crackling, and the conversation far-ranging and incredibly important. The high is jet-fueled. Ivan feels twenty years younger.

Then, in the next instant, the conversation stops cold. The moon, which has presided over the party like a gleaming pearl in the bosom of the hostess, disappears. It's as if someone has dumped ink into a pan of water. The faint romantic light is out. Suddenly, the men can no longer see into each other's eyes. It's positively Biblical.

They began to mix themselves doubles, but no amount of booze can stave off the feeling: The pitch black of night, which is usually so fabulous and mysterious, is suddenly full of dread. As giddy and manic as the pool party began, it now unravels. The sexual tension goes limp, the flawless faces turn hideous. Then it occurs to them. The clouds are the beginning of the storm. The darkness is a preview of their own tombs. They're going to die.

The two younger men begin to fall apart. They drift off to different corners of the pool deck, staring dully into the gloom.

Only Ivan Bekoff retains his equilibrium. He is by nature a dour man, and has not as great a height of giddiness to fall from. And he has a little age on him. But more than anything else, Ivan knows the land. To him Fire Island is not simply a "fabulous" place, but a specific natural arena. He understands the power of the sea, the habits of the wind and the dunes, of the fox and the holly tree. His expectations of survival and his sense of danger may be just as grim, but at least they are real, something more than a nightmare spun by youth out of drugs, alcohol, and radio reports.

His first instinct is to take off and leave the young men to their hysteria.

His resentment is surfacing.

Ivan Bekoff, pioneer of the Pines and veteran of its brutal land wars, is a disillusioned man.

He first came here, and made his sacrifices, because the twenty-four-hour sexual bazaar of Cherry Grove left him cold. The unsettled Pines gave the promise of an almost Grecian purity—Whitmanesque, almost, celebrating the beauty of the body and the beauty of nature simultaneously.

And indeed it was a vision that was actually realized on a balmy summer night in the swale, sometime in Ivan's youth. He doesn't even recall how the word spread, probably from man to man, like songbirds passing a note along a fence. Men began pouring over the dunes in small groups. Before long there were a thousand of them. They began to touch. Ivan remembers being passed from one pair of strong arms to another, the power and perfection of the young bodies, the sheer starry beauty of the night. It was not many acts of love that were taking place, but one, one heart beating, and one giant breath heaving under the high dome of the sky.

In his dreams, Ivan has never let go of that moment. Of

course there is still sex to be had there, in the Times Square of nature, and it can still be done in groups, rudely and quickly, with equipment. But that balmy night of Ivan's youth, with the swale now rechristened the Meatrack, is merely an ironic memory and a bad joke.

Opulent, splendid, and spacious, the Pines became for Ivan Bekoff, as it did for Martin Quartararo, as cold as a Cartier pin. People arrived in private boats and made love without sweating. And when people did get together, one of them had a famous name you'd see on a shampoo bottle or on the back of a pair of jeans. He'd be accompanied by a few vacant, gorgeous young men, and they'd be amusing themselves with someone from "under the bridge"—a "troll." It was a way the beautiful had of describing the ugly. A desperate little man would be on his knees in front of the entourage, unzipping one fashionable fly after another.

It was the last, sorry development that completed Ivan's journey from idealist to cynic. And his disillusionment has no more perfect and potent symbol than the "moat" over which he has just led the houseboy and the chauffeur.

Staring into the darkened pool, he remembers his acts of rebellion in the old days. For a while he and his pioneer friends took pleasure in screwing under the pool decks of the elite (decks like the one he is currently standing on) and disrupting the posh parties taking place above them. But it was little satisfaction indeed. What else could he do? Kick over the hors d'oeuvres?

Unlike Martin Quartararo, who resolved to paint his face and dance until the music died, Ivan Bekoff turned his disappointment inward. He secluded himself in his rough cabin, a stark contrast to the temples of opulence that surrounded him. But unlike Ferron Bell, whose reclusiveness had the spiritual underpinnings of the Order of St. Basil, Ivan was merely . . . alone. A curtain of sassafras protected him from the babbling boulevards and from his neighbors. In his little forest he sat as presidents were shot and ridden out of office, as men traveled in space, and as he himself grew to middle age. His only allies were the white-tailed deer and the mourning dove.

And now, on the eve of a hurricane, he finds himself with two classic Pinesmen of the eighties. Calvin Klein's *houseboy*, for Christ's sake! An unemployed chauffeur who looked like a Greek statue! They're getting hysterical? Well, let them fend for themselves, Ivan is thinking. They think Fire Island is a *fabulous* place? Let them find out just how fabulous tomorrow morning. Meanwhile, thinks crafty old Ivan Bekoff, I'll be dug in somewhere like a fox.

Aaaaaahhhhh! The agonized wail of the houseboy pierces the night. Utterly helpless, thinks Ivan. He'll as likely drown in his own tears as in the raging ocean. Ivan takes a step or two toward the new bridge over the moat, looking to disappear.

Aaaaaargghhhhhh!

Ivan takes another step, and can go no farther. The simpering bastards haven't got a chance without me, he is thinking. Giving in to the Jewish guilt that is his birthright, he turns and looks at them. What do they need? First of all a little rough talk, which he gives them. Now what? Food, firewood, and (for spiritual reasons) champagne. He gives out the assignments, and the chauffeur and the houseboy fan numbly out across the Pines to execute them. Ivan reclines back into a chaise lounge and watches the sky turn from black to eerie shades of purple. Now he is alone with his own brand of terror.

Looking down, the Man in the Moon sees the bulging North American coast shrouded in silver clouds. Halfway up the coast a piece of land juts like a hook on a hatrack. Nearby, the clouds are a dense concentric swirl; the hat about to be hung.

This is the storm.

At the stroke of midnight, she will finally show herself to Man. For days Gloria has moved across the water like some dark idea, a phantom known only in numbers and decimal points. Now, at last, she will make an appearance. The hook of land, Cape Hatteras, will feel her western edge as she passes at sea.

The weathermen sit erect at their dials, poised for their first real look at her. They are expecting the numbers to be mild.

The western edge is the least ferocious part of the storm; the counterclockwise winds and the hurricane's forward speed collide, almost neutralizing each other. The dreaded eastern edge, that slice of hell where the two forces augment each other, remains out over the water.

Nevertheless, the trembling Carolina coast braces itself. Reassured, terrified, then reassured again, it trusts nothing and no one. Bustling Nags Head, the Coney Island of the South, is desolate and boarded up. The Wilbur and Orville Wright Memorial, usually crawling with tourists in Indian summer, is a tomb. The brothers chose this spot for their experiments because there was always a wind, even when the rest of the coast was becalmed. Now a wind was coming that would have blown them and their eccentric machine into the next life. Up in Norfolk harbor the pride of the American navy is lashed together, gray warships clinging to each other like a litter of kittens. Anything human is gone. The southeastern coast is emptier than the day the English settlers arrived three hundred years ago.

The first figures begin to register on the dials. Obviously, they are mistaken. The wind could not be blowing at 150 miles an hour. Not on the mild western edge of the storm!

The first observations come in from the field. Who's sending them? A drunk? A madman? Roofs being blown off and tumbling end-over-end down the empty streets? Livestock being blown around? Huge cows being lifted off the ground and pulverized against buildings? Impossible. Not on the *western* edge of a hurricane! What's happening here? Has the capricious storm, now thought to be headed north, reversed directions *again*, spun suddenly on its axis and decided to attack Carolina full force after all? Is this, in fact, the teeth of the storm?

The terrifying answer is no, it isn't. This is, in fact, the mild western edge, and this is the worst hurricane of the twentieth century.

And then, just as quickly, it's gone. Within half an hour you can stand on Main Street and light a cigar. The weathermen read the tearsheets with white faces. The brush with Carolina has not diminished the winds, which even on the "mild" western edge are steady at an average of 145 miles an hour. Nor has it buoyed the barometer, which is still well below a frightening twenty-eight inches of mercury.

What kind of a storm is this, that can show this kind of power without losing any of it? Usually, traveling over land rips these things apart with friction. But this evil, insatiable . . . no, it's a mistake, the weathermen keep telling themselves, to attribute human qualities to this natural event.

After all, they were state-of-the-art meteorologists, not a bunch of Africans trembling and supplicating before the dreaded Harmattan wind, or some other nonsense. Hurricane Gloria was nothing more than an eminently understandable and measurable compendium of convectional, torsional . . . well, what had happened was this: The bitch only dangled a flirtatious petticoat to let the boys up north know what kind of a date this is going to be. Sometime tomorrow morning, boys. Right now she was going back out on the water to put on her makeup and slip a dagger into her garter belt.

———

E I G H T

FIRE ISLAND, FRIDAY, SEPTEMBER 27, 1985; MORNING

Autumn . . . New York's most glittering season. The chilly nights
have put a bite in the air and the Big City Beast, so long languid
in the dead, wet summer air, is stretching and waking. People rush
where a month before they ambled. The air smells of perfume,
not sweat. Women wear crisp tweeds, not the lime summer dresses
we loved but of which we've grown tired. Though elsewhere on
the earth the falling leaves are a sort of death, here in New York,
the Capital of Perversity, they are quite the opposite.

A fresh start. A new season.

But on this particular September morning, the Fifth Avenue
stores, customarily poised to unveil to the world the goods it will

soon thirst to own, are closed. The goods themselves are obscured by crude "X"s of masking tape across the famous windows. There is no one to ogle them, anyhow. Manhattan is empty. Oddly, eerily, unbelievably empty, like some papier-mâché rendition of itself on a Paramount back lot. Elevator operators are taking people to the top floors of buildings only with stiff warnings. But there aren't many people to warn, because most of them have stayed home. The ordinarily listless commutes from New Jersey and Westchester and Long Island are today something nobody cares to risk.

And the tourists? Forget about it. People stopped flying into the Big Town twenty-four hours ago. Hotel managers are wringing their hands.

What's happening here?

New York is cowering. The swaggering Big Town, which is supposed to *make you afraid*, is itself scared shitless—of weather.

Weather? Weather doesn't even *exist* here, usually. Whether the narrow band of sky between the buildings is blue or gray or even black or goddamn pink, what difference does it make? These aren't farmers here; these are fast, important people making big deals, faxing each other memos, shipping each other goods on trucks and taxis and trains and planes that barrel through rain or sleet or the darkest night of hell to get there on time. Sure, a big pain-in-the-ass snowfall might snarl traffic on a couple of winter mornings, but that's about it. Basically, Nature was beaten a long time ago.

But on Friday, September 27, she is calling the shots again. For many city-bred people, it's a new experience. How powerful can this phenomenon, Nature, actually get? Could Manhattan, built on rock out of rock, actually be threatened by it? Since the hurricane of '38, dozens of gleaming skyscrapers, many of them spindly and architecturally ill-advised, have reached for the sky. Might Gloria snap them off?

It's the sort of thing New Yorkers love to speculate about, and with the help of their several hundred TV and radio stations and periodicals, they are doing just that. Gloria is the newest, hottest starlet in town.

Out on Long Island, however, it is not an amusement or an intellectual parlor game. At dawn, the Suffolk County Police announce the evacuation of the entire South Shore of Long Island—population: 100,000. A new piece of information has come in, the final piece of information.

The storm has committed herself, at last.

After endless measurements, projections, revisions, apologies, reassurances, new projections, and wild guesses, the National Weather Service has finally fixed the precise point of landfall of Hurricane Gloria. After her own series of whimsies and furies and uncertainties and demonic pirouettes, she has chosen her mark. The evacuations of St. Croix, St. Thomas, Ponce, Antigua, Eleuthra, Abaco, the Northern Leeward Islands, Nassau, Jacksonville, Savannah, Charleston, Myrtle Beach, Edisto Beach, Cape Romain, Cape Lookout, Little River Inlet, Cape Henry, Albemarle Sound, Pamlico Sound, Ocean City, the Delmarva Peninsula, Merrimack River, Newport, and Eastport have all been unnecessary.

Hurricane Gloria has indeed exercised the option the weather people most deeply feared: looping out to sea after the brush with Hatteras, fortifying herself with a final dose of steaming ocean, and pointing for the next body of land in her path—Long Island. And now that the storm is only a couple of hours away, its point of landfall can be finally fixed with laserlike precision by the instruments of the Weather Service, which have until now been so impotent.

Hurricane Gloria has chosen for her target a thirty-mile strip of sand called Fire Island.

The dark journey across the sea has not been a frivolous one. There is a drop-off point, a destination for this twenty-megaton natural bomb, and that point is this tiny island, this Sodom infamous for its promiscuity and homosexuality. To moralists and Biblical Fundamentalists across the country, it all makes sense. God sometimes makes his feelings very clear.

Dana Wallace's friend Alan Halstead, the king of the Limp Hoses, is one of the hundred people left on Fire Island. Upon awakening, he gets the news via his kitchen radio.

He is going to die. Never again, not even once more, will he watch the late-afternoon sun crawl across the twisted Pines behind his house. There is nothing in his ice box but margarine and a couple of bagels, and this means that never again will he taste a thing so simple and joyous as a spoonful—a soft, chilling spoonful—of ice cream. Or a velvety swallow of milk. Or even the tart sting of a lemon. Never again will he sit in the Firehall with the other Limp Hoses and hoist a glass of that dreadful cheap scotch. Nor will he ever again hear the old recordings of the Dorsey brothers, at this moment sitting on his mainland mantelpiece, that have given him so much peace so often. And more important, far more important, never will he hold in his hands again the face of his wife, the woman he loves; nor will he feel the smooth downy nape of her neck or the small scar it hides, or smell her faint lilac scent.

Curse Dana Wallace! Curse whatever inside of me allows him to bully me! No, the ocean was not bluffing after all. The reward for the whimsical, daring decision to "experience" the hurricane now appears to be a violent, horrible end. The penalty for not being able to say no, for not being willing, at the age of sixty-eight, to be thought unmanly, the penalty for this, apparently, will be death for Alan Halstead.

For about an hour, he has lived with this thought in silence.

He flicks on the radio again. Let me track the progress of death, he thinks morbidly. Let me see how quickly it hurtles toward me.

This self-indulgent instinct saves his life.

The radio is crackling with a new piece of news. In light of the most recent (and the last) predictions of Gloria's landfall, the authorities have decided to take mercy on the "Fire Island 100," as the broadcasters have begun to call them. Last night's "last boat" was not the last boat after all. Two more are being sent, one to the Eastern Kingdom and one to the Western Kingdom. They will leave Fire Island at 8 A.M., which is about as late as anyone wants to be out on the water. After that, any mercy will have to come from God himself.

YAAAAGGGHHHOOOOO! A scream of joy that begins in Alan Halstead's belly rushes up through his larynx and explodes out his mouth. He hurls some things in a suitcase and races out without shutting the door.

Five miles to the east, the morning boat, the boat of Salvation, is already idling in the harbor of Fire Island Pines. It looks like a party cruiser to heaven. Redemption has been offered to the fifty or so daredevils left in the Eastern Kingdom, and they seem to be grabbing for it. The boat is packed to the gills.

Standing on the dock, immobile, is Ralph Cain. Certain people have been spoken of as "chiefs" and "priests" of the Eastern and Western Kingdoms. Every Kingdom must have its exchequer, and somebody has to keep an eye on it. Ralph Cain is the accountant of the Eastern Kingdom. His profession is to make sense of numbers. It is something he does well and is comfortable doing. It is not in his nature to take on wild adventures or to put himself at risk.

On the rare occasions that he has done so, however, he has found the rewards to be substantial. He took a boat down the Amazon once and had the time of his life.

Sticking around for Hurricane Gloria did not at first seem even as great a risk as that. He had endured terrible storms in Texas as a child and he knew that even though they scared the hell out of you, they eventually passed; at least they did in Texas. But as Ralph Cain observed the numbers Gloria was putting on the board, he began to understand that this was a different kind of storm. It might be his last one.

He was not a man for whom even small decisions came lightly or easily, and he very carefully weighed his options. He had no direct dependents. His life had been a long and a full one, with not many things left undone or loose ends untied. These considerations, together with the bracing thought of witnessing something outside the pathetic arena in which men (and accountants) usually operate—something wild and free and jolting and alive—all of this tipped the balance sheet against his customarily dowdy nature and he had decided to stay. "The world is sick to its thin blood," he loved to quote a great modern philosopher whose name he always forgot, "for want of elemental things."

But his resolve was not made out of steel. When at dusk on Thursday the authorities came around getting the names of next-of-kin, Ralph turned off the lights and pretended he wasn't there; he didn't know if he could stand up under that kind of pressure. All night, in the dark, he agonized. Were the authorities right? Had he thrown his life away? Had he, the master accountant, added up the numbers wrong? But with the last boat gone, it seemed an academic question. Mercifully, a fitful sleep took him, and anesthetized his agony.

Then he was awakened at dawn with radio confirmation of his nightmares. The storm was headed *directly for Fire Island*. His immediate instinct was to take a hundred sleeping pills and get it over with. But then, after the news sank in, it gave him a curious peace. The issue was going to be quickly resolved one way or another. The agonies and the ambiguities would soon be over. The sooner the better.

Then he flicked on the radio again and heard there was going to be another boat.

"One more boat," said the devil.

At first, like any reasonably sane man, like Alan Halstead in the Western Kingdom, Ralph Cain threw some things in a suitcase and bolted out the door, opting for life. But now, suitcase literally in hand, standing halfway between the dock and the tiny cottage where a good friend prepares to wait out the storm, he is paralyzed. He cannot move a muscle in either direction.

Decisions, even tiny ones, are his bugaboo. He might, for

example, suffer a moment of anxiety over whether to eat Chinese or Mexican, about whether to spend a hot Manhattan night in an air-conditioned movie, or laze it away in a bar. Now, having made an agonizing decision once, he is being asked to make it again. There in front of him, engine idling, is the boat. It is a large police launch full of wild men and women who have already decided to throw their lives away once. Even Lady B, the notoriously wild lesbian, is there popping open champagne under the noses of the outraged Suffolk County Police. Surely there's no disgrace in throwing in the towel now, Cain is thinking. Not if this mad-woman is allowing herself to be taken away from the action for the first time in her life. Surely by this point, thinks Ralph Cain, I've absolved myself of the bad rap laid on all accountants, Timid-ity, and shown I'm capable of throwing caution to the winds. Surely there is no disgrace in leaving now.

On the other hand—the awful phrase, the one that people who have trouble with decisions hate to see forming in their brains.

On the other hand—four words that tie your intestines into a double knot, thread them through your brain, and yank.

On the other hand, a few yards away in a small cottage, his old friend Ferron Bell prepared to wait out the storm. The food and drink would be sublime, the camaraderie rare and warm, the experience bracing and unforgettable, the reception in the com-munity afterward heroic. Life! Life itself was calling, as it rarely did, to Ralph Cain. And above all, he thinks, how intense to share the moment with Ferron Bell. It would be like flying with Lindbergh.

Bell's influence over Cain is enormous. If middle-aged men can experience hero-worship, then Cain feels it for Bell. And it's nothing sexual, or at least, thinks Cain, it doesn't seem to be. It's more . . . spiritual. Ferron Bell really *is* the high priest of Fire Island Pines, Cain has always felt. It isn't some bullshit fey accolade, and it isn't just his old monk's cassock that barely fits him now. It has to do with the fact that the man has been the soul of this place through every one of its storied phases. Now, when the Pines has become so insufferably chic, he has the good sense to spend most of his time talking to birds.

Cain admired that deeply. He admired the artist in Bell that dared to take chances and endure frozen days to paint winter landscapes. He admired the goodness and unselfishness and, yes, wisdom of the man. In fact, maybe Ferron was the very one to consult about the current, paralyzing dilemma! What else were high priests for, if not to help with impossible decisions?

Cain gets his feet to move in the direction of the cottage, from which the smells of a potentially magnificent breakfast emanate. Ferron Bell is visible in the kitchen window, mincing onions on a cutting board.

"Hi, Ralph," he calls out. "About ready to eat without you."

Cain stands mutely at the window, his vocal cords taut and dry.

"What's the matter?" says Bell.

"Ferron, I just don't know what to do about . . . the boat."

"The boat?"

"The police launch. It's leaving in ten minutes. Everybody's on it: Lady B, Trudy, Raoul, Gustave, Bobbi, Rudi. Apparently the storm is going to be worse than anyone thought, so I thought maybe it would be smarter . . . I don't know . . ."

Ferron has stopped listening to him. Another boat? Ten minutes? This is new information. Ferron Bell lives without a radio and has heard nothing about any boat. He digests the news over and over, like a cow.

Until now, the question of whether to weather the storm hasn't even been a question for Ferron Bell. Yes, the whisperings of gloom and doom have unnerved him; but without the island, Ferron's life has no meaning. It was here that he came to manhood, here that he defined manhood for himself. Here, through hot, decadent summer nights and grim, ascetic winters that both he and his art were formed. All his images, on canvases or planks of wood or stretched sharkskin, are images of this place: birds, fish, lighthouse. Simple. Clean. Inseparable from his very soul.

True, during the late sixties he wintered in Puerto Rico and was lushly influenced by the tropics. The sea greens and the sky reds and the fat dripping leaves and the monstrous bugs opened up a new chamber of his soul. But he had brought all that back to Fire Island. In his North Atlantic seascapes were the luminous blues of the Caribbean, all filtered through the Egg Tempera genius of the Sisters of St. Basil. This was the resonance of his stuff. This was why he was the foremost visual interpreter of Fire Island. This was his life's work, and it was just hitting its major stride. No, anything that was going to wash this place away may as well take him too.

But there is another boat in ten minutes.

Into Ferron Bell's considerable serenity dark confusions now intrude. Having achieved such a deep inner peace, having nurtured yourself and your art through heaven and hell, you did have the right to *preserve* all of it, didn't you? If life had become so precious, why pitch it away?

Why *not* pitch it away? After all, it wasn't flesh and bones that really mattered, but something much more elusive and enduring, something that all the hurricanes of hell couldn't ruffle. Perhaps, in fact, this was a *test* of that faith. Or was all that just a pile of crap, and shouldn't one get while the getting was good? After all, there was a difference between real spirituality and mindless, pious martyrdom, wasn't there? But which was which in this case?

On the other hand . . .

Ralph Cain watches the sentence form behind his friend's eyes. Ferron Bell doesn't know what to do.

Now in the white-hot moment of decision, Bell is pitched back into the past, back to his youthful wanderings away from his California home, back to his arrival at the Hermitage of the Orders of St. Basil. He sees himself walking up the long clay driveway, he hears the voices of two hundred Russian monks singing. What if he had stayed behind the walls? What would such a life have held for him? What would it have been like to go a step further; to wind up in a place like Gethsemane, the grim Cistercian monastery in Kentucky that monks everywhere whispered and wondered about?

First, you'd shuffle through the dank dawn to vespers. Then, in the afternoon, you'd be out in a cotton field sweating beside your fellow monks in absolute silence. You'd be struggling for a little elbow room in your cowl so you could wield that hoe, you'd break free, you'd take a huge backswing and you'd conk another monk on his shaved noggin. You'd turn and find yourself staring into the face, already smiling benignly, of Thomas Merton.

Merton! A warm smile breaks across Ferron Bell's face just mouthing the name. If Ralph Cain can be said to idolize Ferron Bell, then Bell prostrates himself before the memory of Thomas Merton. Merton led ten thousand men into the Church, and his life story reads like Scripture to the burly, red-haired artist.

Born to privilege and sent to all the best schools, Thomas Merton quickly was disabused of the high life, which seemed to him a "gray slop of movies and nicotine." Neither intellectualizing in his classrooms at Columbia University nor prowling sensually through the nightclubs of Harlem could he find any meaning, or any relief. His frustration took a physical form. He felt as if he couldn't breathe. He fell ill. He saw that illness later as a gift from God.

He began kneeling and praying on the marble floors of the Catholic Church. To the shock and amusement of his sophisti-cated friends, his faith grew and his focus intensified until his soul and his sinuses were rainwater clear. Finally, the only step left was the spareness of the monastery, the rough smells and the hard work and devout prayer taken through a pure instrument. At Gethsemane he wrote crystalline poetry and radical theology and issued it to a waiting world. To Merton's life the sensitive young men of postwar America said yes yes *yes*!

To impressionable Ferron Bell, Merton was like an arrow shot into heaven. Frenzied with inspiration, Ferron hurled himself into the life of the Order of St. Basil. The litany of Christ was so real to him he wept inconsolably on Good Fridays and leapt to the rafters kicking his heels on Easter Sundays. But as every monk and every priest knows, youthful zeal is one thing and staying power another, the difference between a sprint and a marathon.

Ferron couldn't go the distance. There were too many questions, not enough patience, too many youthful hormones zinging, pushing, stretching in too many directions. Of course, he didn't so much leave St. Basil's as he took it with him. He turned his world into a monastery, no small trick given the world he was to inhabit—gay New York, perhaps the most decadent environment on earth.

Fire Island, though, was more than a sexual hothouse; it was also a spare, rich natural expression of God's handiwork. Even during the great party era of the Pines, Ferron Bell frequently absented himself from the very gaiety he had created, in order to take a long walk. These days, while his friends screw in the Meatrack, he searches for blackberries in the wild bramble. While everyone else dances in the Ice Palace, Ferron may be outside with a bag lady he'd found on the mainland, washing her feet and feeding her grapes. Ferron Bell had, indeed, joined an order, but his monastic brothers were not men, they were birds, the strangest birds in the sky, the American redstarts—truly serious clerics whose vows of silence were broken only by wild, gloomy bursts of song.

So now, in the fall of 1985, with a life-or-death-decision in front of him, with the redstarts gone yesterday on their fall migration, Ferron Bell asks himself . . . what would Thomas Merton have done? In this instant, the question posed and poised, an amazing and potent thing happens.

The lights go out. The power company has turned off the juice. It's a common precaution during hurricanes; who wants loose wires flapping around with their sting of death? For Ferron Bell, the event comes as a direct communication from Merton. The room is as dark and quiet as an abbey, Ralph Cain's agitated form barely discernible. Ferron's mouth closes, pursed around an *m* sound, then speaks a silent word. Cain reads his lips, but cannot understand them.

"Memento Mori." It was the first thing young Ferron Bell had seen in the Hermitage of St. Basil, the evening of his arrival. It was written over the front door. "Remember death," it meant. Indeed, death could not in that place be forgotten. Old monks were buried in open holes, covered by shrouds. The smell of them was everywhere. And yet "Memento Mori" was not harsh or morbid. It was divine. As the old men decomposed, the young men knelt beside them in the weak predawn light and sang their souls, now free at last, to heaven.

Patiently, lovingly, Bell explains the concept to his friend.

Death? Decomposing? Cain is horrified. But Ferron Bell pushes ahead. He explains that they probably will not die, that they do not expect to die, but that the *acceptance* of it—as an event as natural and inevitable as a sunrise—will give them a serenity for all time.

At any other moment, despite his deep regard for Bell, this would seem a preposterous and infuriating argument to Ralph Cain. But he is at this moment having his own flashback. Last week he was in Cincinnati attending to one of his major accounts, Proctor and Gamble. As usual, the tax team from New York was getting the red-carpet treatment, a lavish buffet in the executive dining room, silver service, linen tableclothes, the works. Then they were all led inexplicably into a spotless bathroom and each man was given a brand new toothbrush and a tube of Colgate toothpaste! It was unbelievable, more in its implications than anything else; that there was no human function that would not be well-served by being immediately sanitized by a Proctor and Gamble product. Jesus! If Ralph had taken a crap, would someone have immediately followed him into the stall with a spongeful of Comet!?

The experience bobs to the surface of Ralph Cain's mind about the same time that Ferron Bell is repeating a phrase from one of Thomas Merton's books, a phrase Bell has never forgotten. "The soul is an athlete," Merton once said, "that needs opponents worthy of it." Ralph Cain hears the words clearly. First they soothe him, then they embolden him, then they transport him. The valise is set down. As the sound of the police launch revs up, fades, and then disappears, a peaceful feeling radiates through the two men.

Several miles to the west, the last boat out of the Western Kingdom idles in the harbor of Ocean Beach. Sitting behind the wheel is Captain Jack, who has run this route across the Great South Bay longer than anybody can remember. It's only fitting, think the grateful mob clambering on board, that it be in the end old Jack standing between life and death.

Jack fidgets up in the cabin, watching the boat load: about fifty souls, he figures. He's glad now that he's come for them, though earlier in the morning he thought twice about it. The storm wasn't due until the afternoon sometime, but the bay had already whipped itself into a froth.

There was a story among boatmen about the guy who piloted the last boat out in '38. At least he *thought* he was on his way out, until the first big blast of wind blew him, the boat, and the passengers ten miles down-island in about a minute. They wound up on top of a sand dune and were still there ten hours later, miraculously not among the debris or the corpses that floated in the bay.

Jack revs the engine. Even thinking about '38 makes him want to get moving. The people who'd stuck on the island even this long were damn fools and he wasn't about to wait around for anyone else.

As he gives the order to cast off, another figure tears breathlessly around the corner. It's Alan Halstead, who's just completed the run from his house, his sprint reduced to a haggard trot. The squat, white ferry is the most exalted vision of his life. He drags his suitcase on board, flops down on a seat, and listens to his heart pound.

Now, as Captain Jack's mate throws off the rope, Halstead's thoughts turn to Dana Wallace. Shit, he didn't even call him! Was Wallace sitting up there with the pitcher of margaritas waiting for the limes? Guilt washes over Alan Halstead.

But did he actually, *actually* commit himself to anything yesterday?

No. Not actually. Yes, he'd been tempted by the idea—
sitting at Dana's big picture window with a dozen margaritas and
watching the big blow. A man's weekend, like the ones they used
to have shooting ducks together. But even before the dire morning
announcement of the point of landfall, Halstead had been filled
with second and third thoughts. There *was* family to consider,
wasn't there? It was fine to pitch your own life away, but did you
expect people who loved you to sweat it out with radio reports,
picturing your broken body lying across a bulkhead and being
pecked apart by the gulls?.

No, Alan Halstead did not feel guilty. Wallace was a lunatic
and he was entitled to throw away his own life if he wanted to,
thinks Halstead, but not mine.

But as the boat begins to edge out of the harbor, Halstead's
guilt will not leave him. An old friendship is a sweet, valuable
thing. Over the years Dana Wallace has shown him all the tricks
of an island boyhood—digging clams and oysters, ice-fishing, all
of it. And of course when Alan and his wife were building their
dream house after the war, they lived for a while on Dana and
Peggy's generosity, sleeping on the screened-in porch of the tiny
Half-Moon cottage on the dunes. It was a summer-long double
date! The four of them would tuck little Dana into his driftwood
crib and toast a future that was as bright blue as the sea itself.
Hitler had been licked, the boys were home safe, and God had
set them all in a little paradise, stocked with game and fish and a
big sky full of heaven-sweet air.

Of course, postwar America did not deliver on its promises,
either with jobs or with the moral clarity everyone expected after
the defeat of pure evil. It became a time of confusion and suspicion, new enemies appearing as quickly as the old ones vanished.
But Alan and Dana threaded their way through the hardships and
the ambiguities until the economy boomed and America smiled
again and Fire Island became crowded and commercial.

Then, when Peggy Wallace died and Alan divorced his wife,
grief forged a second deep bond of friendship between the two
men. And years later, when they both lost their hearts to very

young women, their humiliation forged a third bond, maybe the deepest of all. It is this last period that fills Alan Halstead's thoughts as the boat leaves the harbor.

It didn't take Halstead long to come to his senses and stop making a fool of himself over somebody young enough to be his own daughter. But Dana was so deeply in love, or so deeply obsessed, that he continued to carry the torch for Maureen for an agonized five years after she left him. Hell, he was *still* carrying it! Men in their sixties, men with triple bypasses, weren't supposed to be on fire that way. Take the matter of their houses. Even after Dana's cottage was taken into the sea, he built another one on the same goddamn spot! Alan made sure his place was a good distance inland. Why throw money away into the insatiably destructive ocean?

And always, after their drinking bouts in Ocean Beach were through and the two men were reeling home, Dana wanted to stop somewhere to have a nightcap, or bellow "The Cremation of Sam McGee" one more time into the freezing starry night.

It was a matter of degree of . . . civilization.

Dana would not be tamed or restrained the way a modern man had to be to get along. As time went by, the roars got louder, not softer, and it became impossible for Alan to keep up. There was a natural feeling in your bones as you grew older that told you to slow down and *receive* the things of life, rather than to roll up your sleeves and swagger out to get them. That was the great gift of old age, really, that wisdom, that ginger respect for your own delicacy, that deep, many-shaded perspective on mortality.

Bullshit, Dana Wallace would say to that. Never let the fire die.

Alan Halstead sits on the top deck of the *Fire Island Belle* as Dana Wallace waits for him, not really expecting him to come. Captain Jack guns his ten-cylinder engine and the *Belle* accelerates, its passengers clustered in the stern watching the familiar landmarks recede, possibly never to be glimpsed again—the twin cupolas of the Community House, the silvery water tower, and the white steeple of the Catholic church.

* * *

Three miles to the east, wandering along the fringe of the
Sunken Forest of Fire Island, a creature remains oblivious to Hurricane Gloria and all the anxieties that attend it. She has no access
to periodicals and radio news; nor has she the lightness of bone
to feel the radically shifting barometric pressure.

Truly, her world consists of not much more than the creature
who ambles in front of her, nibbling low-hanging beach plums,
straining for high branches, generally cutting a swath through the
foliage for her to follow. These are a pair of white-tailed deer, a
buck and a doe.

The Buck looks not at all like he did last November when
they first met. Then, he had magnificent antlers, a proud ochre-
colored rack with twelve gleaming points. The Doe spotted them
first above a shadbush, deep in the heart of the Sunken Forest.
She had to see what was beneath this amazing rack, so she boldly
stepped through the welter of juniper that separated them. What
a dusky, muscled chest did she behold! What a pair of shining
eyes!

What made them shine, of course, was the Doe herself . . .
particularly the odor coming off of her. It was delicate, fecund,
bloody, and irresistible, the smell of the earth itself.

But it wasn't a smooth courtship. Another buck had been
eying her, sniffing her, making wailing, loonlike sounds from his
chestnut throat. The issue had to be settled in the timeless way
of deer, and so one gray November dusk the two bucks squared
off in a thicket of bayberry, and by the time they were through
ramming and thrashing, the bushes were as flat as farmland, and
the racks of both bucks were jagged and cracked.

It was no clear victory for either, and that meant that the
Doe could choose. She went with the one she fancied, the proud
twelve-point Buck. One starless night shortly afterward, they
mated, but no fawn ever came. Deep in her bones, the Doe knew
why. She was weak from hunger and her slim diet of twigs and
branches was barely enough to keep her insides operating, let
alone summon the energy to produce a fawn. She made this

known to the Buck in the way that deer have of communicating—with swift, angular movements of the head, with low sounds from the throat, and with the eyes.

The Buck understood. In fact all of it, the fight with the other buck, the undernourishment of the Doe, all of it was further proof to the Buck of what he already knew: There were too many deer. When he was a yearling, it seemed like there were half as many. But since then they had so thrived and multiplied that now they were their own worst enemy. Death in this place came often from starvation, not (as it does to their cousins in other places) from the black bear or the barrel of a gun.

The Buck has resolved that this year his Doe will bear a fawn, so they have set off to find new ranges to feed. Already the journey is strange and unsettling. As they stand at the edge of the Sunken Forest, at the threshold of the first small settlement of manmade houses, the smell of humans comes to them and unnerves them. The Buck has heard that there is new bounty here for deer, but he is wary of it. He has seen deer return from here fat and happy, but too bloated and soft to make the crucial adjustment to the food of winter; twigs and branches.

Still, with food so scarce, he must take the gamble. The Doe must somewhere find rich berries and thick, succulent leaves that she can store in her blood for months, well past the time when she will conceive.

Most of the time, in the unchivalrous world of deer, a buck will send a doe into a dangerous situation first, just to look around. Ordinarily this Buck would be no different, but he knows that every meager bit of the Doe's energy is crucial, so he will go first, alone, and hunt out the feeding range to which he will then lead her.

They stop among the low sassafras trees. They are very close now to the houses along the eastern edge of the Western Kingdom. The Buck turns to the Doe and burns a look into her eyes. He is asking her to stay, to remain here at the fringe of the strange human world while he forages through it.

She returns his look. His magnificent rack does not yet exist.

It is a velvet nub, waiting for the hormones of October to harden it with great ebony flourishes. But his eyes still shine. So she says yes. Yes, she will wait for him here.

Standing on his oceanside deck and looking out to sea is lean, eighty-year-old Bob Tyson, renowned as the male half of the only straight couple in Cherry Grove. Inside his brown clapboard house, his wife, Allys, also eighty, chain-smokes Virginia Slims and watches her husband stand there and make up his mind. Yes, there is still a decision to make, even though the police launch left the Eastern Kingdom fifteen minutes ago. If he feels like it, Bob can still get himself and his wife off. He has only to phone the authorities and hitch a ride on one of the emergency vehicles fleeing the beach via the Robert Moses Bridge. Age has its prerogatives, and Bob knows how to use them. He just doesn't know if he wants to.

Watching him, still smoking furiously, fuming in still other ways, the slight, fine-featured woman wonders how she has allowed herself to be put in this position, how she has come to place her life in the hands of this man who, through the applications of pure reason, is now making a life-or-death decision on behalf of both of them. What was the matter with him? What was the matter with *her* that she was letting him do it?

How did she wind up with this man at all, with his maddening cerebral approach to things? Was she not an utterly different sort of person?

It was the dawn of the Jazz Age and no one knew it better than a wild teenager from Queens named Alice. She flaunted all the rules of a starch-collar–stiff America. She ogled the doughboys coming home from the First World War and she read naughty European novels on the street in broad daylight. You couldn't control her!

When she finally fell in love, she fell hard ... with the handsome son of a prominent undertaker. This was an era of opulent funerals, and the boy's prospects were excellent. Unfortunately he was a bit mad. Their love affair was more volatile than even wild young Alice could handle. It ran amuck with adolescent hormones. One minute she'd be weeping behind the library, the next they'd be slugging whiskey together on the newly built subway into Manhattan. What caused the passionate swings was the boy's jealousy. He was a monster. He saw competition in old men and children. Once, after a particularly bad fit had Alice in spasms of tears, her sister decided to show her an alternative. She fixed her up on a blind date with a completely different kind of person.

Indeed, Bob Tyson was the last guy on earth you'd figure Alice would go for. A gangling, conservative prelaw student at Princeton, he was as drab as she was outrageous. While she was swirling about Manhattan in a velvet cape, smoking cigarettes, and attending scandalous theatrical productions like Jeanne Eagles's *Rain*, he was attending lectures by William Jennings Bryan.

On their blind date they went to Coney Island. It was a damp, moonless night in September. Under the boardwalk, horseless carriages sputtered along. She did most of the talking. She was studying at the Parsons School of Design, she said. She was planning a trip to Paris. She had just changed her name from Alice to Allys, trying to "get in touch" with her Lithuanian roots.

He was totally smitten. He had arrived at Princeton as F. Scott Fitzgerald was leaving; the Jazz Age had made its impression on the Ivy League and on all its impressionable young men, even bashful Bob Tyson. He had to know more about this exotic creature named "Allys."

Amazingly, the feeling was mutual. Something about his quiet steadiness appealed to her. She was a wise teenager. The possessive tantrums and the sexy indolence of the undertaker's son, she was beginning to see, were getting her nowhere. The courtship with bashful Bob began and grew. Slowly. This was the America of another time; carnal knowledge was a long way off. Their first Christmas he gave her a book, because he felt that anything else, even clothing and especially perfume, was too intimate a gift. Precocious Allys was getting impatient. Another impediment to their passion was his mother. She was a conservative woman and she was scandalized by the Bohemian hussy her son was courting. "Allys" indeed! What was wrong with plain old "Alice"?

Allys got tired of waiting for the blessing that never came. The day that Babe Ruth hit his sixtieth home run, she dragged Bob off to Manhattan to get married. They had the ceremony in City Hall and told no one. Then, even more defiantly, they checked into the Albert Hotel in wild Greenwich Village and disappeared upstairs with a bottle of champagne. The long wait was over.

The young couple set up housekeeping and had their share of good and bad fortune. Bob's law practice took off and they had prosperity even through the early Depression. But they also had great sadness. Allys lost her first two children in the womb and the intense young lovers became frightened of a barren life.

Then, in 1931, a great blessing. Allys delivered a son! They raised him lovingly, and as America climbed out of hard times, the young family began to look for a summer home. On the advice of friends, they took a place on a remote little barrier beach called Fire Island, in a quaint little town called Cherry Grove. It was strictly a family community, with only one exotic amenity: Old Man Duffy's hotel, a rundown place with a couple of choke-cherry trees out back (hence the town's name) and a pretty good restaurant that lured fishermen and tourists in for Sunday dinners. Yes, there was a homosexual or two who would flamboyantly check into Duffy's from time to time or anonymously rent a cottage in town, but they were so rare as to be an exotic spice on an otherwise-wholesome meal. The Tysons, and scores of other solid families, were happy in Cherry Grove.

Then came the hurricane in 1938, which changed the map of the Northeast, obliterating Cherry Grove to the rubble on which the Gay Nation would one day be built, and reshuffling the frightened straights to Saltaire; more of a family place, as the emigrants were quick to explain.

But the Tysons remained firm. They would not be chased

out by anyone's hysteria, or anyone's unfounded prejudices against these homosexuals, these gentle, misunderstood souls. They *did* raise their only son there, and raised him damn well.

But by the sixties, things had changed. As the couple grew older and dowdier, the gay revolution began to explode around them with loud, abrasive music, with wild, flamboyant, drug-induced behavior, with nudity. This last matter, particularly, of-fended the Tysons. People were screwing on the beach, for God's sake! People of the same sex. Even for the hot-blooded Lithuanian, it was too much. It got so Allys didn't dare go out on her own deck, for fear of what she'd see walking down the street, or writhing around in the bushes. Her husband backed her up. How dare anyone offend his wife on her own property?

The battle lines were drawn.

It turned out to be more of a cold war than a battle. There were unspoken tensions and stark alienation. Joyless summers came and went. The Tysons began to mistrust everyone, and were themselves mistrusted. They lived as strangers in their own town, like people from another race, or another planet.

It almost caused a fatal rupture in the marriage. Bob, with his merciless courtroom logic, concluded that the situation would never change and it was time to get the hell out. Allys, irrevocably in love with her house by the sea and always believing in people and hoping for miracles, begged to stay. Such would be their eternal argument; head versus heart.

But why is it *Bob* who now stands outside making this crucial decision about Hurricane Gloria? Allys asks herself, lighting an-other cigarette. Why am I allowing him to?

God knows the women's movement ought to have been tailor-made for firebrand Allys. She wore her politics on her sleeve and was more than ready to breathe life into them at the drop of a hat. So why was she sitting there like Miss Muffett on a goddamn tuffet?

"Bob?"

"What?"

"Are you ready to go?"

"I'm just trying to think it through."

"Think it through!" rasps Allys. "What the hell is there to think about? There's a goddamn hurricane coming!"

"I know, I know," her husband mutters.

Damn him, she is thinking. Was it love, to indulge this kind of stupidity? Maybe it was. Maybe she just wanted to give him, just once more, the satisfaction of using his mind, that wonderful steel-sharp instrument that the years have blunted. Or maybe, for all her old leftist politics, she was simply stuck in one place forever, condemned by the morés of her generation to have men hold out chairs for her, pick up the dinner tab, and make the life-or-death decisions.

Either way, as the sky grows dark and the time grows short, Allys Tyson is starting to get nervous and angry.

And as Bob Tyson watches the ocean brim up to the dunes, a spectacle that would deeply unnerve the rest of the world, he is well aware that his wife will pay the price for his decision, that she will live or die by it. Based on his experience, however—strolling these fifty years through the harvest-moon tides, surf casting for hours on end, watching a thousand copper moons climb out of the sea—based on all this, it will probably be a more accurate judgment than the Weather Service has ventured in its ten thousand hours of broadcasting on the subject.

Basically, it's about fifty-fifty, he figures.

The tide was pretty high right now, but it was on the way out. If the storm got there in a couple of hours, with the full-moon tide at dead low, it would probably do no more damage than the nasty Northeasters that are the bane of an islander's life, depositing half the bay in your lap and skimming the top of the dunes into the ocean. A pain in the ass, but not death.

If Gloria sauntered in fashionably late, say in about six hours, the tide would be on the rise and the storm surge, the pucker of ocean that the monster wind blows ahead of it, would take out about half the houses on the island. Your chances of survival depended pretty much on your luck. If you were standing in the way of a loose joist when it came by, like a log rushing down a river, or a loose roof, as the wind whipped it through space, you were gone.

If the storm came at high tide, in nine hours . . . Well, only this could be said about it; death would be fast. Instant. The place would be razed and scoured of all life, human and animal, before you even knew you were in the ocean, or you were the ocean, or the ocean was you. However you wanted to put it. It would be an interesting spectacle to watch from a distance—say the moon.

That was about the size of it. Of course, it was all just dead reckoning, but probably not far off the mark. Only one question remained, thought Bob Tyson. Why not just turn on the radio and find out exactly when the storm *is* coming? Surely the information is available by now.

Simple answer. Bob Tyson didn't particularly trust the weather people's instruments to tell him how fast the storm was moving and when it was going to get here. They've been wrong before. Plenty of times.

Fair enough, Bob, he says to himself. But then, acting the devil's advocate (as he loved to do in matters of logic), he asks himself another question. Given the fifty-fifty chance of survival, *What the hell was he doing here?*

Well, it sure would be a romantic way to end the summer, and who knew, at eighty, how many more summers there would be? And it sure would be proof to everyone who'd refused to hire him after he turned seventy that he could still think, and think lucidly in the face of the mountain of hype and hysteria that accompanied this storm. And if he could do that, he could sure as hell outthink most practicing attorneys in New York, no matter how goddamn young they were.

But were these good enough reasons to risk his life and his wife's? This is the question for which Bob Tyson still has no answer, and he knows he doesn't have long to come up with one. In another fifteen minutes even the police vehicles won't be risking a drive on the beach. They'll be long gone, with just about everything else.

Beyond the curtains that adorn the sliding patio door, his

eighty-year-old wife lights another Virginia Slim and waits for him to make up his mind.

Not far down the beach, Ocean Beach Chief of Police Joe Loeffler has indeed closed up shop and is gunning the engine of his Jeep Wagoneer toward the beach. The ocean is up so high now there's only a narrow corridor of sand, and time, to get down-island and over the bridge.

That's what he intends to do, even though in his heart of hearts he would prefer to stick around, as he has for every other storm during his long tenure as Chief of Police. But something about this one was making the main Suffolk County office jumpy. They were evacuating themselves as well as everybody else. The captain wasn't being allowed to go down with the ship. Loeffler had orders to leave.

A Fire Island cop. What a bizarre career that was. For months on end you'd swat flies in your office while the rookies booked ten-year-old kids who were riding their bicycles too fast. Then all of a sudden there'd be some grisly society murder among the summer people that would confound the toughest Manhattan homicide detective.

Through it all, Loeffler has maintained his office with good humor and perspective. From the summer people he keeps his distance, emotionally, as all the natives do. But when the crowds thin out in September, he reemerges as the chief; big, genial, chastening when he has to be, tough once in a while.

The way he sees it, there are two reasons people decide to become cops. The first reason was the wrong reason: to prove something to yourself, or your girlfriend, or the world. These were the bullies, the guys who get their rocks off by polishing medals or pistol-whipping weaklings. Loeffler likes to think he's a second kind of cop: somebody who wants to show his love for people, not his contempt for them. Over the years he's done just that on the island, fashioned a relationship with a small group of people, treated them with goodwill and respect, and had those feelings returned. He's been as much a priest, a lamplighter, a mayor, a wiseman, and a friend as he has a cop. No doubt there was some stiff-necked, uptight, by-the-book jerk in the Suffolk County Police Department who thought Joe Loeffler was too close to the people he was supposed to be controlling, but that would be someone with no idea about island winters and the bonds they create between people.

But Joe Loeffler has orders to leave and so he's leaving. Moving through the notch in the dunes, he swings his Jeep onto the sand and heads west, the ocean licking his left wheels. In his rearview mirror, another police vehicle bursts out of a walkway and weaves up behind him, kicking up a little surf as it struggles for control. Loeffler smiles. Young Officer Charlie Shannon still had a bit to learn about driving the beach. Loeffler's already given him a lot of lessons, about a lot of things.

Once when Shannon was a rookie, a drunk pulled a gun on him. Charlie spent about ten minutes looking down that barrel and pissing in his pants. When it was all over and the drunk had been subdued, it was learned that the guy was an off-duty cop from the mainland who had just been feeling his oats. The Department decided to hush up the matter and deal with it internally. It was Charlie's first taste of compromised justice and his first look down the wrong end of a gun. Loeffler took his rookie into John Palermo's bar and spoon-fed him tequila until he settled down. Loeffler called his wife and said he wouldn't be home for dinner, and spent the rest of the night acquainting Charlie Shannon with some of the ten thousand things you needed to know to get along as a cop and a human being. Not all of them were in the *Police Handbook* and the Pledge of Allegiance to the Flag.

Charlie took the lesson and the love from the chief and never forgot it. Loeffler was the kind of cop Charlie wanted to be. If Joe Loeffler had said, in the face of the storm of the century, "We're staying," Charlie Shannon would have sat right beside him in their tiny shack of an office, and waited for what happened next. But the chief said, "Go," so they were going.

At the western edge of Ocean Beach, Loeffler runs his vehicle through a broad cut in the dunes, turns off his engine, and puts it in gear. He has one more job to do before he hightails it over the bridge, a job at which he figures his chances of success at about zero. He's going to try to talk that madman Dana Wallace into getting off the island.

Shannon parks beside him and the two lawmen walk past the tiny beachcomber's shack, the very existence of which produces an invariable wince from Loeffler. It seems like every couple of weeks he gets a memo from the Main Office to do something about the illegal structure.

As the lawmen move up the long wooden ramp to Wallace's house, two pairs of eyes watch them from the darkness of the makeshift stable a short distance away. The eyes belong to Dana Wallace and his prize colt, Maelstrom, who is being fed a couple of handfuls of grain. Maelstrom is shipping over to Belmont for a six-furlong race next week, and Wallace has a theory about sprints: Stoke that grain in, power him up so he just about busts through the starting gate.

Loeffler and Shannon shuffle on the deck, looking around. Wallace makes no move to reveal himself. He likes Loeffler, but he always enjoys making cops cool their heels while more important things are taken care of. And truly, in the clarity of his old age, nothing is more important to Dana Wallace than these animals— his roan and chocolate colts and fillies, and his two black dogs. And that's about it, he is thinking. With Maureen gone and most of his friends dead and Alan Halstead probably on his way to the mainland, this is his entourage as he enters old age.

He corrects himself. That isn't quite true. There is the little guy, the one who cooed in his driftwood and seaweed crib when Dana and Peggy were starting their lives together in the little Half-Moon cottage on the dunes. There is Dana Wallace Junior.

Young Dana at this point is probably more well known on Fire Island than his father. He picked up where the old man left off in the real estate business and has already made a great success out of it. Whenever a big house goes on the market these days, you're very likely to see "DWjr" on the offering.

The real estate business aside, though, you'd have to say the apple has fallen a good distance from the tree. The son isn't the wildman his father is. Dana Junior is a businessman. He has conservative leanings. When he married a woman even more conservative than he was, the rift with old Dana grew even wider. She was a clear-thinking young person who saw herself as the antidote to her father-in-law, and she would be zealous in keeping her husband away from him. Over her dead body would her marriage dissolve in the alcoholism that seemed to come so naturally to islanders.

The old man and the young woman were enemies. The very fact that she *was* a young woman, given Wallace's recent disaster with Maureen, only fueled the fire.

No, young Dana had more in common with his wife than he did with his father, and that was to be expected.

But where did that leave Dana Wallace Senior?

Out here on the beach facing a hurricane with two dogs and five horses. The odd man out.

Had he been a good father? Was it natural for this . . . remoteness to creep in between father and son? When did it begin?

This last question is the only one he has an answer for. It began when the boy's mother died. God knows Dana had loved Peggy, loved her like life itself, almost gave up on life after she was gone. But after a while, he had to go on, didn't he? Was he supposed to cave in and creep away whimpering just because life dealt him a horrible card? No, there eventually had to be other women. Not to replace Peggy Wallace, but to succeed her, so that an old man's heart wouldn't turn to stone.

He couldn't make the kid see that. Little Dana resented his father's second wife, and all the women who came afterward, but no one did he resent more than Maureen, who was even younger than he was.

Well, maybe the boy was right. Maybe Dana was a fool to let his heart get broken by somebody half his age. He wasn't *trying* to make a fool out of himself. God knows, he'd tried getting interested in women his own age, but the truth was that most old women, and most old men, had lost interest in life the way Dana Wallace thought it should be lived: that is, grabbed by the lapels and shaken for everything it was worth. It wasn't the nubile flesh of young women that interested him as much as their spirit, their yearning. Their explorations of life were just beginning. His were continuing. Why shouldn't they explore together?

Take Maureen, for instance. She applauded the youthful heart that beat within his hoary old breast. She clung adoringly to it. Why shouldn't she? He was still searching for big answers while other men his age were worried about their magazine subscriptions running out. Why shouldn't he win the fair young princess?

They met through horses, naturally. They were both at a yearling auction somewhere, and they found themselves staring through the slats of a fence not at the horseflesh but at each other. They ignited like dry brush. Together they blazed across the sky, they cut great rolling swaths through the landscape of love. With horses like Maelstrom in tow (God, she would have loved this colt!) they drove all over the south, entering local races in tiny fairgrounds on the edge of nowhere. They'd race for money or blue ribbons or jars of peach preserves. They'd swap lies and have a few beers with the local people and wind up in each other's arms in some rose-choked bungalow motel by the side of the road.

They spent the winters in the South, in the Smokeys, breeding horses on the gorgeous Carolina turf. In the spring they'd come north to Fire Island. When the dog days of summer filled the beach with too many tourists, they'd get on their boat, a ramshackle old thing they called the *African Queen*, and take off. They loved to tie up at fancy docks in between society yachts, and let the blue bloods wonder what the cat dragged in. When the first chill of autumn came, they did . . . whatever the hell they wanted! Whatever whimsy presented itself, as they stretched and opened their eyes, propelled them into the new day!

Lovers rule the world.

So what went wrong? For too long he's asked himself the

question and now even *he's* getting sick of it. The question has no answer. Surely Maureen would not answer it, as he begged her to, on the horrible November day six years ago she threw some things in a suitcase and walked out. Where? Where are you going? *Why*? Please . . . !

No. No more. Today, as Dana Wallace prepares for the incredible display of natural power that will unfold in front of him, today, which might be his last day (he has to be honest with himself), he will not get caught up again in the circular bitterness, as he does on all other days, about Maureen, Maureen of the wild sweet-smelling hair and voice like the summer wind off the sea. No! Today was for wider, larger thoughts.

"Dana! Where the hell are you?"

Loeffler! Shit, the poor guy had been standing around for ten minutes, probably pissing in his pants to get off the island.

"In here, Joe," calls Wallace. Much as he was tempted to, he wouldn't make the cops chaperon his date with Gloria.

Chief Loeffler and Charlie Shannon trot down the walkway to the stable, their polished black shoes taking mincing steps through sand and horseshit.

"Better get off now, Dana," huffs Loeffler. "Pretty soon there won't be any beach to drive."

"I guess I'll stick around, Joe."

The two men measure each other. They're about the same age. One is a lawman; the other, emphatically, is not. Half a century ago, in the time of the rumrunners, they would have been on opposite ends of one of those water-cooled machine guns.

"Better get the horses to high ground then," says Loeffler.

"Yah," Wallace mumbles.

Charlie Shannon turns his back and watches the white ocean. He has no place in this ancient grove.

"Hope you ride it out, Dana."

"Thanks, Joe."

The two cops get in their cars, and drive off down the beach toward the bridge. Dana Wallace grabs a rope and climbs to his stand of high pines. As he fashions a rough hemp corral for his horses, the police cars disappear from sight. Nothing else will leave or enter the Western Kingdom until the storm.

Over in the Eastern Kingdom, Ivan Bekoff and his two young friends have secured themselves in a house considerably smaller and more compact than the one in which they had their cocktail party the night before. Like the first house, this one does not belong to them. The men have taken the liberty because of the extreme circumstances, and because the liquor cabinet here, too, is full. Nearby, in Ferron Bell's small bungalow among the pines, Ferron and Ralph Cain are lighting candles as Ferron teaches him barely remembered prayers. Across the Meatrack in Cherry Grove, Martin Quartararo is done with his diabolical phone calls and is giving Hercules, the Doberman, his huge daily feed. And with only a few minutes left to decide whether or not to summon an emergency vehicle to get himself and his elderly wife off Fire Island, Bob Tyson watches the sea and sips a Cutty Sark on the rocks.

Whatever their distractions, the few souls left on Fire Island address themselves now to death and to the circumstances and histories of their lives. Has it all made sense? Has life paid off or disappointed on its early promise? Are there things left undone? Have I stood for anything, really? they want to know.

Who truly loves me? each asks himself. Who pretends to, but doesn't? (And to this question, Martin Quartararo of the scarlet telephone already has his answer.) Is there any real design or meaning to any of it, or are we all day-to-day slugs who eat, sleep, and defecate for seventy years and, poof, are gone? What's the first thing I'll do if I get out of this? What's the second? What *am* I doing out here, really? Do I value life at all? What will death be like? Will there be parties on clouds in heaven, or only hungry worms squirming toward me through the dank, dark earth?

Fire Island, too, faces a kind of death, or at least a demolition, for the science of geology does not include in its lexicon the

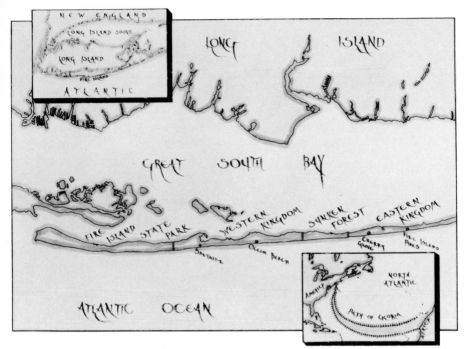

Map of Fire Island and the path of Hurricane Gloria (cartography: Sue Anne Harkey; calligraphy: Mary Lou Wittmer; shading: Roger Yogis).

Maelstrom and Dana Wallace (Chuck Doersam).

Ivan Bekoff (Layne Redmond).

Height of the Eastern Empire (Ferron Bell).

Above: Elders of the Eastern Kingdom (Ferron Bell). *Below:* Elders of the Western Kingdom (Dana Wallace).

Above and left: Hurricane of '38 (courtesy of Ocean Beach Historical Society).

After Chataqua: Fire Island sunbathers, turn of the century (courtesy of the Fire Island National Seashore).

Bob and Allys Tyson (Layne Redmond).

Fire Island flapper (courtesy of Isabel Frazer Adler Collection).

Above left: American Redstart (illustration by J. J. Audobon). *Above:* Ferron Bell, circa 1970 (courtesy of Ferron Bell). *Left:* white-tailed deer (Ferron Bell).

James Lindsey, right, with his father and grandfather, circa 1950 (courtesy of Mrs. Virginia Lindsey).

Martin Quartararo, in front of one of his paintings of Fire Island (Marty Heitner).

Ferron Bell (Layne Redmond).

Wayne Duclos (Layne Redmond).

Dana Wallace (Chuck Doersam).

concept of death . . . at least not with the tones of drama and sentimentality that human beings bring to it.

Past hurricanes, though they exacted a dreadful toll in human, animal, and plant life, were often a renewal of life. The storm of '38 rearranged Fire Island socially, with its razing of Cherry Grove and Saltaire, and naturally. There is a theory that "Fire Island" is really a misreading of an old map; that the place was really called Five Islands, though that might have been Four or Six depending on how many notches the most recent hurricane had cut through the thin barrier beach.

But when new inlets are carved, floodwaters that carry corpses also carry fresh water into stagnant bays, seeds of life for colonies of shellfish that will feed future generations. Fishermen suddenly have a wonderful new access to the open sea.

Of course, it takes time for nature's design to reveal itself and until it does, many doleful widows' wails sound in the night. Hurricane Gloria, with her unprecedented power, might do much more than pierce the island with a few new inlets. At her worst, she might obliterate this thin ridge of sand that has existed, after all, for only a moment in the planet's history. Since a piece of land cannot contemplate its own mortality, we will act for a moment as its soul and its memory.

Every so often (every few millennia, say) too much ice accumulates at the North and South Poles, as it does when a freezer needs defrosting. The planet simply becomes topheavy with it, and like the nasty childhood prank of breaking an egg on your friend's head and watching it slide down his face, the ice slides down from the poles and spreads itself out more comfortably on the earth's surface.

Of course, when it gets too near the scorching equator, it stops and melts. The last glacier stopped on Long Island fifteen thousand years ago. When the mile-high wall of ice melted, it released all the trash it had accumulated during its long journey down from the pole.

In the case of the Long Island glacier, the debris was a lot of the Northern Appalachian mountains, through which the ice had gouged huge valleys, and from which it took as souvenirs the sediment of the Cretaceous Age; dead plants, sharks' teeth, and giant extinct lizards. As the wall of ice lumbered southward, it ground up the Cretaceous crap inside itself and compressed it. When the glacier finally stopped on Long Island, it included all manner of rocks, from huge boulders to tiny grains of sand.

The boulders it gratefully plunked down on the spot, and they can still be found in all the towns of Long Island, as numerous as Burger Kings or high school football fields. The smaller stuff, the tiny red, white, and black crystals we call sand, traveled much farther. Like dice thrown from the hand of a huge crapshooter, the crystals tumbled down the long slope to the sea, which was much lower and farther away than it is now, since much of the world's water was tied up in the glaciers.

Down the long tilt to the sea the crystals rolled, forming a huge, sloping beach many miles long. Had nature's design been symmetrical, the water level would have risen inexorably with the melting of the ice, slowly climbing the hill of sand, and the ocean would today lap the shore of Long Island.

But something happened.

A ridge formed along the sloping beach. Perhaps a dead bird on top of the ridge trapped a wedge of sand against itself. Perhaps the bird's mate, come to mourn it, excreted a seed of beach grass that germinated, grew, and stabilized the tiny burial dune. The wind off the sea pushed more sand against it, and the beach grass sank its tenacious roots into that, too, and the ridge lengthened and widened and grew. When sea level finally reached it, the water went around it, not over it, filling in what we now call the Great South Bay. Fire Island had been formed.

A thousand generations of beach grass died and made an inch of soil. A beach plum seed from the rear end of a passing bird now had a place to sprout. A pair of deer swam across the glistening new bay and ate the beach plums and dropped their own, richer kind of feces, enough to sprout a juniper seed blown in on a wind from the north. Soon there were many kinds of plants, and the strong, lacy network of their roots kept the ridge of sand together in the stiffest of winds. The island was here to stay.

Now, thousands of years after that, the wind threatens to take back what it has given. Along the ridge, inhabiting it and defending it, are two tribes of men separated by a great forest. The preliminary winds have shorn the tribes of all but their rarest and purest examples.

To the west of the forest is Dana Wallace, an ox of a man who has served the race by reproducing himself and by building things. What he has done he has done with his strength, and with the force of his will, by daring to unravel mysteries that have stood forever and by moving with his body stones that would not be moved. When the big wind comes, he will stand his ground and defy it to move him.

To the east of the forest are men who do not reproduce but who serve the race (and bequeath their legacies) in different ways, who draw their power from the clarity of a thought or a drawn line or a note of music. By giving out the music and the color within them, they strengthen the hearts of all people and give us a reason to do our work and live our lives when we are otherwise too sad and weary. These Eastern Kingdom men will not stiffen against the big wind, but will try to become a part of it, dance gracefully with it, and hope that its patterns are benevolent.

Between the tribes, in the forest, are an array of animals who don't know exactly what's coming but will react to it by instinct when it comes.

Now all God's creatures face the sea and wait.

PART II:
ROARS

Whe does good weather end and bad
weather begin? The last hazy sigh of a summer dusk is sometimes
an overture to the moist bedlam of low pressure. Later, the darkest
thunderclouds part to reveal the sun.

Friday morning, September 27, is nature at her most unnerving.

Nothing.

No weather.

The air is still enough to build a house of cards. Everyone
knows that the most violent force of nature is careening across
the water at them, but it has chosen to introduce itself not with
a Northeaster, or a breeze, or even a puff, but with nothing at all.
The lid is not going to be wrestled clumsily off the steel gray sky.

Instead, a thousand little craftsmen with the skills of a Willie Sutton are quietly, ever so quietly working on the hinges. Then, before you know it . . . SHHHHWWWAANNGGG!!! The top will be off, and every blessed thing on earth will be sucked up into it.

The handful of people left on Fire Island understand this habit of nature's, either by hearsay or experience, so for them there is no peace in the "calm before the storm."

Rather, it's the stillness of their own tombs.

Hercules the Doberman is burrowing into Martin Quartararo's armpit, seriously interfering with Martin's ability to smoke the joint of marijuana smouldering between his fingers.

Now the dog lumbers to the door and begins to paw and pummel it. He wants out. But Martin is wary of taking him on any long walks. The storm may arrive suddenly, capriciously, he has been led to believe. You don't want to be caught far from home.

Besides, Martin Quartararo's fortifications are already in place and he doesn't want to mess with them. Basically, his strategy is to barricade his senses. He will not hear the storm because a Sony Walkman is blasting both his ears with rock and roll. He won't see it because the powerful Jamaican marijuana that bloats the areoles of his lungs and the capillaries of his brain is giving the simple textures of the room extraordinary dimension and he is seeing other things; some of them for the first time. He is seeing the acorn from which the tree grew that was cut down to make the kitchen table, and all of it is lit by the intense glow off the coat of Hercules, which he is also seeing, in a sense, for the first time. Nor does Martin intend to feel the fear of death in the pit of his stomach, because his stomach is full of freshly popped popcorn, swimming in rivers of just-melted butter with a pinch of Worcestershire sauce.

The phone rings. Despite the Rolling Stones' "Sympathy for the Devil" pounding in his skull, Martin hears the ring, sets down his headphones, and answers it.

———

"Martin? It's Cecil."

Martin groans inwardly. Cecil is a British army officer with whom Martin's been having an affair for some time. The romance was amusing at first, full of military regalia, weekends in Devonshire, Beefeater hats, and all the rest of it. But it simply went too far. Cecil fell too hard, became possessive and overbearing, and the whole thing became a big drag. And last month Cecil made the fatal mistake: offering to resign his commission in the British army and come across the sea to live with Martin. You don't show your cards like that, Martin believes. He found out the hard way, courtesy of the heartless traveling salesman in New Orleans.

"Martin? Are you there?"

"Yes, Cecil."

"I was trying to ring you for hours yesterday."

"I had a lot of calls to make," says Martin, recalling his diabolical telephone game, the one that resulted in the plusses and minusses in his phone book.

"What about the hurricane?"

"How do you know about the hurricane?"

"The whole world knows about it, for Christ's sake. They're getting it on the bloody instruments *here!*"

"So?"

"So you better get the hell off!"

"It's too late for that, Cecil."

"Too late! What do you mean?"

"I mean the last boat is gone."

"What? But how can . . . I'll call someone! I have connections in the American navy!"

"Forget it, Cecil."

Martin was almost enjoying the man's hysteria. No, that wasn't quite right. Not *enjoying* it exactly, but certainly enjoying the fact that it was Cecil feeling that way, and not Martin. Really, the sheer desperation of it! No, truthfully, there was nothing to enjoy about it. It was pathetic. And for Martin, it was suffocating.

The thought of suffocation reminds Martin that he owes his

father in New Orleans a phone call. It probably wasn't going to be a very comfortable call and that might be why it's slipped his mind.

The last time they were together was in the kitchen of the old man's retirement home, a shotgun-style house in St. Bernard Parish. It was their first meeting since Martin had informed him (by mail) that he was gay. It was quite a scene. They thrashed and hollered and argued for hours, each quoting the Scriptures to his own advantage. At the end of it the old man gave up and his face went into his hands and he cried softly, and wondered where he went wrong so that his only son should be a homosexual. Martin tried to reassure him that he had done nothing wrong, that in fact his father's strength and simplicity and honesty were lessons for a lifetime. It was a moving scene, BUT, CHRIST, WHAT A STRAITJACKET ALL THAT WAS!

Martin's dad lived life by the book, the book of Christ to be specific, and he was paying the price for it. Yes, it was comforting to have all the rules written down for you, but it also had a downside; you couldn't think for yourself when the shit hit the fan. Martin had that figured out when he was a kid, even before he knew he was gay, when they tried to lay all that Fundamentalist crap on him. You couldn't depend on anyone else to do your thinking for you, not even God himself.

"Martin are you there?"

"What, oh yes, Cecil. Sorry."

"Jesus, I thought the wind had blown the line dead . . ."

"It didn't."

"Or blown the roof off . . ."

"It didn't."

"All right! You don't have to be so short with me."

"I wasn't being short."

"You sounded short."

"I'm sorry, Cecil. I have to get off."

"Martin, I . . ."

"What?"

"You know that I . . . how I . . . how much I . . ."

"I'll get back to you in a couple of days."

"I'll be praying for you. As hard as I can. Tonight in the regiment chapel, when they have the moment of silence, I'm going to ask everyone to give special thoughts to a special friend of mine. I can't tell them exactly who it is, of course."

"Of course."

"But I'm going to ask them to sing your navy hymn. 'For Those in Peril on the Sea.' "

"Thank you, Cecil. Good-bye."

"Oh, and Martin . . ."

Enough! Martin lays the receiver in its cradle. Rude? Not necessarily. Conceivably, the line *could* have been blown dead at this moment. He sucks hard on the nub of his joint, scorching his fingertips. Someday . . . someday he would find the perfect lover, he truly believed. Someone who would challenge him, not make things too easy for him. Of course, he didn't want someone breaking his balls, either, like the traveling salesman. Something in between the two extremes would be fine. So far, that has eluded Martin Quartararo.

Stubbing out the joint in an ashtray, he moves to the front door. No sooner does he put his hand on the knob than the hulking Hercules begins to skitter around like a Chihuahua on amphetamines. The dog can't wait. The dog *has* to go.

Martin cracks the door and peers outside. Nothing. Absolutely nothing. Not a whiff, not a hint of a zephyr. It was eerie. Was the thing coming or not? He takes the dog's leash off a nail on the wall. Maybe taking a walk would be a good thing, a way to cut the tension. Hercules trembles with anticipation.

But on the other hand, thinks Martin, the prudent thing to do is probably to smoke another joint and just sit tight. He chooses the latter course of action. He hangs the leash back up and closes the door. The dog sinks into a low squat, his eyes trained on the small man from New Orleans, his snout quivering into a snarl.

* * *

Vooosh. In the Sunken Forest a toad, mucking around in a swamp, sees a ripple across a cranberry bog. A snake? Maybe. All is quiet again. Snap. A branch is suddenly dangling off a beach plum bush. The weight of the fruit?

The wind. Out of the west, a warm, cottony puff tumbles across Fire Island. A minute goes by and then another one comes, bigger, warmer, sweet and benign, a hint of the tropics. Soon pockets of it billow across the island from east to west like a series of huge caresses. The toad in the swamp looks up in amazement. He is being strafed by big warm shadows.

For the human beings, the torture is over. The verdict will shortly be in. In a few hours the sky and the earth will be as clean as only a hurricane can scrub it. Then the Fire Islanders will either dance in the rare clean air (air that ordinary, cautious people never breathe), or they will be part of the debris.

The wind gets warmer and stronger. Gusts of balmy air slam home from offshore. As Martin Quartararo, Dana Wallace, Ivan Bekoff and company, and Ferron Bell and Ralph Cain batten the hatches, break out emergency rations, pour drinks, take their drugs, or say a prayer, a single figure leaves his cottage in the Eastern Kingdom. As the erratic blasts buffet him, he heads for the ocean. Who is this daredevil?

As he steadies himself along a driftwood fence, we do not recognize him. He has not been visible during the prelude to the storm, beating his breast or searching his soul. His decision to stay came placidly, as most things in his life now do. From his usual perch, lying beside the eastern window of his hundred-year-old cottage, the growth of his summer garden has been lush and slow. The stringbeans and snow peas have climbed, the strawberries have crept out, the radishes have poked through, the wild grapes have draped the arbor . . . unspectacularly.

Not that he takes it for granted. The greening of his garden has never been more miraculous. Each pert new knob on a vine is a revelation, each berry a sweet exultation. All of life—the garden's growth, his lover's smile, a showgirl's kick, a fawn's birth, a bird's droppings—all of it brings tears of joy and wonder to his wide, brown eyes.

Why does a man who so loves life now so abuse it? Why does he amble so casually into this turbulent air, wilder now by the minute? Has he no fear of death? Not from the wind and the sea. Wayne Duclos has already gotten his death sentence from a Manhattan doctor.

He has AIDS.

The slightest head cold, a mere irritant to millions of unhealthy Americans who slouch in armchairs with cigarettes and potato chips, gallops unmolested through Wayne. He lies supine while common germs feast on his muscled, chiseled body, and will do so until nothing is left but a gaunt corpse. Where is the justice in it? Right where it belongs, say the moralists. God uses AIDS to punish homosexuals the same way He will momentarily use Gloria to smite the licentious Fire Island. If this is so, His punishment is an awful one. The most beautiful and gifted specimens of the race are being cut down in their prime by the tens of thousands.

The disease has eaten through the Eastern Kingdom like worms. Every house is a tombstone. The only real parties now are medical fundraisers or funerals; the only decorations are black crepe. The flowering of this oppressed people, so brilliant and creative and intense, is over. The agonizing road to freedom that led finally through these happy gardens has led back out again. Once more they are the pariahs, the outcasts. Their contagious disease is now not only moral; it is physical. A modern-day Dr. Mengele, unveiling plans to lobotomize, castrate, sterilize, or even execute them, might have greater support than ever.

All of this seems an unfair weight for the slim shoulders of the sandy-haired young man who now climbs the last few feet to the dunes by the Atlantic. Breathless and spent, he barely makes it.

Wayne Duclos hardly fits the mold of the Eastern tribe. For

one thing, he is the salt of the earth. He is not beautiful, prodigiously talented, or notorious. He is no Adonis with an instant fortune. The world does not wait for his fall collections, or for the newest eau de cologne with his name stamped on it. Nor is the home from which he has emerged a split-level fantasy made out of three acres of glass and a shipload of cured wood from Sumatra. It is a cottage. For entertainment, though his Manhattan apartment is only a block from Lincoln Center, he does not stroll to the opera or the ballet. He watches wrestling on television. He earns his daily bread by cleaning houses and taking in some laundry on the side.

He totters on top of a dune and looks out over the ocean, which presents him with a picture no one else can see. The water is beginning to boil like a witch's cauldron a thousand miles wide and it is white. Rockets of spume shoot past his face. As far as he can see, arching whitecaps slice in, kicking spray as high as clouds. The roar is so loud it is like no sound at all, only a harmonic that vibrates to the center of the earth and back out again. People in good health cower in houses. Wayne, alone, is here. He feels a purity that has eluded him since childhood.

He was born in Concord, New Hampshire, one of nine sons and daughters of an immigrant French Canadian couple who came to work in the shoe factory during the Depression. Wayne got a job in that cold factory himself when he was fourteen, worked his tail off every day, and prayed to God in the Catholic church every night, which he still does. When he came of age, he had a terrible secret to reveal to the French Fathers in the dark confession booth. He was not going to contribute to his mother's tribe of grandchildren, of which there are now fifty. He was in love with another man.

When his mother found out, she wanted to have him committed to a mental institution. She didn't have the heart and stood by, with shame, as he left her home, and the shoe factory, to move in with his boyfriend above the pizza parlor. It was like leaving a dark German winter to go and live and love and sing in sunny Florence—except that it all happened within the narrow town limits of Concord.

The mortification of his family was intense. His brothers no longer acknowledged him on the street. It was the time in a gay man's life, traditionally, when he flees to the Big City. But Wayne was a small-town boy who loved Concord both for and in spite of its simple souls and its blistering winters. He saw no reason to bail out, especially if the God he prayed to from marble floors every day was really up there. There was no simpler soul in Concord than Wayne, nor, finally, one so reviled.

He stayed on, hoping the love in his own heart would thaw the ice in his family's. It never did. Even now that the doctors have told the little man he's going to die young, only two of his brothers have come to see him. The rest have never left Concord.

Wayne might never have left either, except that his boy-friend jilted him. One night he got home to their little flat above the pizza place and found it empty—not only of the boyfriend, but of all the antiques they had collected together on their week-end expeditions to dusty little New England mill towns.

Wayne was devastated. And he was unable to cope with the icy glares of Concord by himself. In stages, the hometown boy left home. In the evenings, he began drifting over to Manchester, to the only gay bar in the Green Mountains. There, one night, he met a most exotic creature from Manhattan named Jacques, a man considerably older than himself who had come north to visit his mother. The two men had a small dalliance, nothing unusual for the city man, but monumental to vulnerable Wayne.

Jacques returned to New York, thinking nothing more about it. A week later there was a knock on the door. Big, rangy Jacques opened it, cast his eyes left, right, then downward. There was tiny Wayne with a suitcase, his eyes shining like a puppy who'd tracked his owner a thousand miles. Jacques didn't have the heart to throw him out. An unlikely love affair bloomed between the urbane opera afficionado, creature of the night, and hairdresser to the famous, and the plain, little guy from a freezing little town in the middle of nowhere who walked around the Big City agape at the rare air, even on the #7 train out to the wrestling at Sunnyside Gardens.

But the love affair was made out of stuff that lasted. Jacques was patient with him, even when Wayne did things that broke the older man's heart, when he stayed too long at the Meatrack and when he took another lover for a while, a handsome Canadian. Jacques held back the tears and the demands because he knew that youth will be served, and that for Wayne, sex was just the outgrowth of a sunny disposition. Taking Will Rogers to the limit, Wayne Duclos never screwed a man he didn't like. Every part of the little guy was wide open: his smile, his tough North Country heart, and, fatally, his rear end.

This is not the first plague to visit Fire Island. A hundred years ago, when fish oil was still a greater industry here than tourism, a cholera epidemic broke out on an ocean liner bound for New York. The state took over the newly opened Surf Hotel on Fire Island to receive and quarantine the victims. Angry fishermen mobbed the deck, refusing to let the boat unload. Militia men had to intervene, reminding the islanders to have a little compassion.

No one has had to shove compassion down the throat of the Eastern Kingdom. When Wayne came back to Cherry Grove after the diagnosis in June, the citizens were indeed lining the docks . . . not howling with grappling hooks, but throwing kisses and flowers. These men have been to many funerals lately and broad channels of compassion are carved through them. Jacques was asked to show the grace of a saint and forgive the transgressions that had not only broken his heart, but were now casting a shadow over his own health. He hemmed and hawed and mewled and screamed and accused and pouted and wept and threw up, but he finally forgave Wayne. The handsome Canadian, on the other hand, heard the diagnosis and took off.

Jacques spends his life nursing Wayne. All his salary and most of his savings have gone into the treatments. Apart from the medications and the doctor bills and the round-the-clock nursing, he has just heard about a machine that may help, but will cost ten thousand dollars for two weeks. A side effect of the machine is that it attacks the bone marrow, and medication to combat that will cost another several hundred dollars a week, for a much longer time.

How do you say no to your dying lover when it's only money? Jacques asks himself.

When the weather is good, he undergoes the complicated, careful process of hauling Wayne out to Fire Island. Once there, when he's not nursing him, Jacques tries to keep Wayne's laundry business alive by washing the Eastern Kingdom's sheets and underwear while Wayne sleeps and everyone is out drinking and dancing.

But on this week in September, Wayne has been blessedly free of symptoms, and was allowed to remain alone on the island while Jacques worked in the city. Yesterday, when the evacuation was announced, Jacques began making arrangements to come and get him.

"I'd rather you didn't," said Wayne.

"What are you talking about?" demanded the older man in a frenzy.

Wayne explained that for a fatally ill man, a hurricane warning is a slight thing. Maybe the storm would give him a vision to take through eternity with him.

Jacques had a fit. But as usual he gave in to the little guy, the love of his life, and Wayne is here alone.

The roar of the ocean has chased every thought out of Wayne Duclos's head. For as far as he can see, it is white fire, crackling, frothing, aching to boil up and devour the land. The water roils up to his feet, and back down, like licking flames. The wind-driven sand stings him like buckshot. The wind forces itself into his mouth. It flattens his flesh against his bones.

He fights to hold his ground and keep the amazing picture in focus. Now he starts to reel and quiver. He digs his feet into the sand. The wind and the swirling tide are trying to move him and devour him, but that is not his only problem. Something is coming at him not from outside but from inside. All week long he's been sweating through sleepless nights, as if something has been trying to break through, and now it's coming. Some kind of paralysis is setting in along the back of his neck and his jaw. He tries to form a word, but can't, not that anyone could hear him, if anyone were around, in the thunderous symphony of earth and sky. He turns inland, pivoting on his short, gaunt legs, but the tide bubbles up around his ankles and recedes, taking him back with it, sucking him into the ocean. On all fours, soaked to the skin, he tries to crawl out of the foam. It does not release him. He grabs what is left of a snow fence, but it dislodges under his touch and joins him in the tumbling surf.

A wave sucks him up and throws him down, so deeply into the carpet of foam that the tide recedes above him. He surfaces soaked and shaken and sees a window of two or three seconds before the water will come back for him again. He crawls wildly through the wet sand toward the dune, feeling the ocean right behind him, feeling the imminent crash on his back of the last killing wave.

It never comes. He reaches the crest of the dune and pitches himself over it and begins to tumble down the other side, gathering speed like a rock. His bones are too brittle for this, for the crash at the bottom, he is thinking. Suddenly he is not tumbling but sliding. The sand is wet and slick. The ocean has brimmed up over the dune, and is cascading down the landward side. The immediate effect is to slow Wayne's descent, and save him some broken bones at the bottom of the dune. But if he lingers there too long, it will fill with water, and as he flails about, the next wave will crush him or drown him. The ocean is chasing him.

He lurches inland, a pain in his head like some kind of numb fire. The wind shifts slightly to the south, and the big warm gusts are rolling him like tumbleweed across a swale away from the ocean. This is the direction he wants to go in, but unless he can grab something solid and slow himself, he'll go right off the narrow island into the bay.

A lamppost looms up. He grabs and misses. He is on a

wooden walkway now, careening down it end over end, arms and legs catching splinters, beginning to bleed with them. THWANNG. Something catches and holds him. He is upside down in his neighbor's rosebush, ten feet from home. His system is a circus of disease and adrenaline and he doesn't even feel the thorns as he extricates himself. Between gusts, he hobbles to his front door and lurches through it. A transistor radio, which he had left on, announces that the storm is expected shortly. Expected shortly? What the hell was going on out there now?!

He picks up the phone to call Jacques, but the strange paralysis that he felt up at the beach is sabotaging his fingers and his brain. Remembering the number and then dialing it is an impossible coordination. Wet to the bone, he gets himself up on his divan, the one he can see his garden from. Through closing eyelids he watches the silver-gray sky.

Farther down the walkway the bay boils in the harbor, contained only by the wind blowing parallel to the shore. Between the bulkheads, sea gulls cower. Once in a while one of them ventures out, and the wind whips it against the dock, cracking its neck and killing it instantly.

The noises of the growing storm blend into a low harmonic that acts as a lullaby for Wayne Duclos, and soon he is sleeping deeply.

Salt paste has covered Dana Wallace's oceanfront window and obscured the arrival of Hurricane Gloria. His frustration is intense. He is ready for the show to begin, for the curtain to go up. His first margarita sits before him, exquisitely mixed. He's ready for the far-ranging universal visions he has been anticipating. But although he can hear the storm mounting, although its moaning overture fills his ears, he can't see a thing.

He grabs a bottle of Windex and opens the front door. Immediately, it blows shut. Of course. Wallace feels chastised. A bottle of Windex? In a hurricane? No, he will simply sit and wait for nature herself to clean the window, and in the meantime he will drink and think about something else.

Instantly his eyes fix on a photograph in a gilt frame. It is his father, long dead. Numbed by the first hit of booze and the drone of the storm, Wallace is drawn into a meditation on the pomaded hair, the high brow, the pale eyes that glare at him across time.

Dana Wallace always hated to take anything from his father. When circumstances forced him to spend that first postwar winter in his father's summer house, he took the favor but resented it. A psychologist would have no trouble figuring out why, Wallace will tell you now. His father was a man of great accomplishment, and the tension between generations was natural. The old man was a trial lawyer, one of the best of his time. He made his reputation as counsel for the defense, winning cases that no one else would touch. His flamboyance in the courtroom was legendary: He read Keats and Shelley to juries, he wept in front of them, he broke his collarbone once and his spectacles many times acting out crimes in front of them. He was famous not only for his theatricality but for his humanity. He embraced the lowliest pickpocket, whom he would not only defend but bring home to entertain little Dana with his sleight of hand.

What a father! Dana remembers the day the old man gave him the surprise of his life. His father knew how much Dana loved horses, knew how much time the kid spent around the old Jamaica racetrack, begging to be allowed to exercise a horse at dawn, or hell, just to walk one around the paddock. He was a wily kid and he knew the negro grooms loved frogs' legs, so he'd catch a few frogs and use them to bribe his way onto the backstretch.

The old man thought that was a little unseemly, and so one day young Dana got home from school and there, nibbling grass in the backyard, was a beautiful bay pony! It was a gift from his dad. Young Dana finally had a horse of his own! He called the pony Peter Piper and spent hours with him every day, riding him, washing him, brushing him, talking to him.

Dana's father was a giant at home, in the courtroom, and in the eyes of God. His honesty could not be compromised. He would take a case at any price if it was just, and refuse it at any price if it wasn't. The great man was soon tapped for public service and elevated to the position of district attorney. He brought the same passion to prosecuting the guilty as he had to defending the innocent. One of the first bastards he really wanted to nail was Augie Pisano, a vicious small-time racketeer. Among his other sleazy operations, Pisano owned a couple of racehorses and was always squirming out of charges about race-fixing and beating up jockeys who refused to obey his orders.

Dana's father just about had the goods on him when a nosy reporter turned something up; Pisano's horses were occasionally exercised in the morning by a kid named Dana Wallace, *the son of the district attorney*. What was going on here?

Young Dana was still sneaking over and exercising an occasional horse just for a lark.

The district attorney was mortified. The one thing his personal largess could not digest was humiliation. The next day, when Dana got home from school, Peter Piper was gone. The boy ran to his father. Where was his horse?

The district attorney continued reading the paper, as if he did not hear the question.

Please, Dad, WHERE IS MY HORSE?!

No reply.

For weeks afterward, Dana traveled the city, checking every stable, every riding academy, every nag with a bonnet pulling a carriage through Central Park. To this day, he doesn't know what became of Peter Piper.

CRACK!

The wind blows out the picture window facing the sea, and a hail of glass flies past Dana Wallace. Nature has just cleaned his window. Wallace is frozen by the suddenness of it. The glass misses him but slices one of the dogs, whose howl is barely audible in the wind. Wallace jumps to his feet, grabs the collars of both dogs and leads them down the back stairs. The wind whips a chair after them, splintering it against the kitchen wall. Wallace tumbles into the basement, only to find the ocean has beaten him there. It has already invaded the concrete foundation, and has started to chunk it up and carry it away. All of it has happened in less than thirty seconds. He lurches out the door, trying to think what to do next. The schoolhouse! He remembers a tequila-sodden memo to himself the night before. Schoolhouse . . . emergency center . . . something like that!

He moves away from the house and the wind slaps him to the ground. Even the dogs must keep low, or be lifted up and blown away. He hears a wild whinny in the din. The horses! What will happen if the water gets up into that corral? He'll find their bloated, floating corpses when the water goes back down. He's got to cut them loose. Cut them loose? Thoroughbreds? That's a hundred thousand dollars' worth of horseflesh! No choice.

He unsheathes his knife and moves toward the corral. In front of him now the gusts of warm wind are bending his pines almost to the ground. They sway like underwater plants, which they will soon be if the ocean gets any higher.

Maelstrom stands underneath the trees with four other horses, only their bulk keeping them from being blown away. Wallace crawls up to the leeward side of the corral, wind-driven sand stinging his face. He grabs one of the thick, bending pines with a hammerlock, to keep from being blown away himself. With his free arm he cuts the burly hemp, all six rows, until the horses are free.

Three of them take off, but Maelstrom and an unnamed two-year-old don't move. Christ, they're stupid animals, he is thinking. All that speed and beauty, and they didn't even have the smarts of the mangy black labs, who were cowering and whimpering under the house.

"Get moving, goddamnit!"

Now the wind starts to move them. Broadside, it is stinging them and lifting them. They turn their backs to it. They swivel, amble a step or two inland, then stop again. *Move, you idiots!* He has to get them out of there. If they wait until the water comes in they'll tangle their feet in the rope fence and drown like mice in a toilet. Still clinging to a pine with one arm, Wallace picks up a piece of two-by-four and throws it at Maelstrom's head.

It jerks the colt back. His knees buckle and a cut squirts blood out of the white star on his forehead. He still isn't moving. The little filly, who's even stupider, is even more immobile.

Wallace will have to crawl right up to them and whip them out. No choice. On his belly he squirms through the wet sand, foam off the water slapping him hard. He gets up to the horses and gets to his feet holding on to both halters for dear life. He looks up at Maelstrom's face to check the wound. The colt's eyes, wet and black, are twice their normal size. The lids are pulled back so far that half his face is eye whites. It's like a death mask. Loose feces are pouring out of him and he's frothing like he's just galloped five miles. He's scared witless.

Wallace puts his arms around his neck and hugs him and whispers something in his ear. Then, with his open hand, he hits him on the rump as hard as he can, and both horses take off and disappear.

Now Wallace has nothing to hold on to. A gust starts to pick him up, but he kicks his hands and feet into the wet sand just in time, and saves himself. He has to get out of here. He's a huge target on this little open mesa. He curls, bolts out of the sand, and sprints inland, but his heart starts to pound hard and he has to stop and lie down. He knows what it looks like, this heart of his. The doctors have showed him pictures—waiting to explode, like an overripe tomato.

He lies still, stinging sand flying over his head like rifle shot. He feels something warm and wet in his ear. It's the tongue of a dog. The Labs are there, trying to get him moving. They're right. The gully he finds himself in is going to fill with ocean in about one minute. He gets into a crouch, and the wind does the rest. It starts to roll him down the hill to the schoolhouse, on concrete. He screams wildly for it to stop, like you would to a drunken Ferris wheel operator who's goosing the controls. The dogs pull him to a stop, one grabbing his shirt with its teeth, the other getting in front of him, like a wedge, and stopping his roll.

How do the dogs, light as they are, even manage to keep themselves from being blown across the bay?

Only by lying flat; and now Wallace does the same. In front of them is his destination of five minutes ago—which now seems like five centuries ago—the public school. Wallace denounced it as an eyesore when it replaced the little red schoolhouse of his youth. Now he's glad for the squat, drab building, which is built like a brick shithouse. The dogs move off the walkway and anchor their paws into the wet sand as Wallace edges to the door. The wind is blasting his eardrums.

Who will he have to face? Which smirking, pale-livered town official will greet his retreat from the ocean with dull, pig-slitted eyes that say, "Couldn't take it, huh?"

Wallace raps on the door, then tries the handle. Locked! Open up, you bastards! What the hell kind of game was this? Some kind of ass-backwards protocol or penance? Were they making him beg to get in?! He pounds furiously on the metal door. Nothing. Where was everybody? Ahhh. Of course. On the mainland, keeping their pale livers and unctuous smirks and paperwork dry. *Officious bastards!* He's probably the only one left on the whole bloody island, he's thinking.

The wind rocks him on his heels, but he anchors himself to the door handle. Should he break in?

Never! And give the bastards the satisfaction of finding his corpse floating with textbooks and basketballs? Or worse, if he survives, to answer a knock at his door next week to find one of the unctuous ones, inquiring, just for the clarification of disbursement records, if that had been Mr. Wallace's hairy mitt that had smashed the nursery school window? Never! He wasn't enduring this nightmare to cower among the artifacts of children.

"Let's go," bellows the sixty-eight-year-old wildman. The dogs, already burrowing under the school, are stunned. They can't believe they're expected to head back to the ocean, back into the wind. Wallace screams at them again, but his voice is lost in a roar that pulverizes the air some distance to the east.

The ocean has broken through.

In Robbins Rest, a mile away, the Atlantic Ocean and the Great South Bay are no longer two bodies of water. A gash of rushing sea has joined them together across the football-field width of Fire Island. It's a phenomenal display of the storm's power. If she wants to, Gloria has revealed, she can change the shape of the land. In '38 the storm made an inlet in five seconds at Moriches that the army had spent months trying to engineer. It's still there.

Wallace knows what else the roar means. Going back to the ocean is suicide. But it's either that or break into the school, or into some inland pleasure palace built by a pasty Manhattan garment king for July and August weekends, or dig a foxhole or lash himself to a tree.

No! What for? He has a house of his own, goddamnit! He'd make his stand there, where he originally intended to, staring the ocean right in the face.

He gets down on all fours and he and the miserable dogs face south. The wind has shifted around, and is blowing right off the water, right at them. They are crawling into hell. As they inch forward, wooden shingles, ripped off oceanfront houses, fly past them like demented razor-winged birds. The wind is shearing everything that isn't bolted with steel. Wallace raises his head to see what's in front of them, but the wind gets underneath him and almost carries him away. Again, but for the dogs digging their teeth into his pants and shoes, he'd be in the bay. Goddamn old age. There's a will inside me made out of pure licking fire, he is thinking, but the flaccid shitty equipment I have to work with isn't doing the job.

The dogs are totally flat on the ground now, like living rugs. Wallace is between them and they are a crawling wedge. The debris in the air is larger; actual pieces of driftwood the size and weight of table radios dance like butterflies in the wind. The sand whips the corneas of man and dogs, forcing them shut. They have reached the wooden part of the walkway now, and they hold their course by feeling along it with white knuckles and blood-engorged paws, grateful for the splinters as proof that they're still alive.

"How ghastly she looks through her rouge, the lady that's

known as Lou!" screams Wallace. They are single file now, and he is bellowing "The Cremation of Sam McGee" into the rear end of the dog in front of him. It is an epic poem about men trying to keep their sanity in the dark, violent, frozen nights of the Yukon. He knows the whole thing. He recites it, uninvited, in the bars of Ocean Beach. It is about creatures he feels he knows, poor stumps of men who spend their lives scratching gold out of rock and wind up with frostbite of the brain and crotch.

He finishes the two dozen verses and he and the dogs have barely moved up the screaming slope of wind. He feels the strength leaving him. He can hardly stay even and soon he will start losing ground to the wind, first an inch or two, then, soon, it will feel like the surging bay behind him is pulling him like a magnet, and then it will devour him.

In the distance, barely visible through the salt-caked slots that are his eyes, a dark object, like a cloud, blocks out part of the sky. It is not a cloud. As it comes closer, Dana Wallace recognizes the object, but his rational mind will not allow that it is flying through the air.

At the head on every walkway on Fire Island there is a large wooden staircase leading down to the beach. Together with the platform it abuts, the unit weighs a thousand pounds.

It's tumbling through space toward Wallace and the dogs.

That the wind could move such a thing is a frightening idea; that it can *fling* it is ridiculous, an insult to physics. Wallace laughs out loud, roars as it flies toward him, instant death. It misses them, passing over their flattened forms with a clearance of about a foot. Wallace turns to watch it go, but the wind almost snaps his neck off, and he must face back into it.

In that instant he sees a chance for himself. There's about a few feet of crawlspace *under* the wooden walkway. If he can get himself and the dogs down there, without getting lacerated on the wooden slats, he's got a shot. He's got to take it. The wind is about to blow him away. He crawls to the edge of the walkway and hangs off. Bless his bulk! The miles of pasta and gallons of booze are anchoring him. He drops to the sand and rolls underneath the walkway.

But the dogs are too light. As they dangle over the side, the wind slams them against the wooden slats. It's the same action that's killing sea gulls down by the bay. The smallest dog, the one that was sliced by the flying glass, is impaled. Wallace reaches around and pries him off. His haunch is half-severed. Wallace tears off his sleeve and knots it around the dog's leg. The other one is whimpering above, afraid to let herself down.

"Get down here, you dumb bitch!" yells Wallace, banging the underside of the wooden slats with his bleeding palms. The dog jumps off and dives under, faster than the wind can scoop her up. The three of them are in the dark world under the walkway. The wind is above them now. They hear it, but don't feel it. They are in a wet, eerie place. Wallace feels an instant of peace, but it is instantly replaced in his brain by another kind of threat.

Water.

Death has a color, and the color is green. If the ocean gets up into here, it will be the worst imaginable end. They'll be trapped by the wooden boards above them. It will be the nightmare of diving into a pool and trying to resurface only to find a metal grill at water level. He's actually had dreams like that, and he wants out of this place in a hurry. He moves the dogs ahead of him through the darkness under the walkway. He feels around like a blind man for something that will tell him where the hell he is.

He's got it. A smooth wooden spruce pole. They don't sink these babies into the sand anymore (the bastards don't know how to build a house anymore!). This is a support of an old building. That's a good sign; this is a place that's stood up in a lot of big winds. He leads the dogs up a wet sandy embankment to a crack of gray light. They peer out.

He owns this house! It's part of his seaside empire! This summer it was rented to an orthopedic surgeon and his alcoholic wife. They sat around all season cooing about the "quality of light." Where were they now? Cowering in Manhattan, of course! The house was as empty as the day it was built. He's lived in this house! He knows its every warped joist!

He tears off what's left of his shirt, wraps up his hand, and breaks the only window he can reach. With the last of his strength he throws the big black dogs inside, and clambers after them.

In a small house well protected from the bay and the ocean, Ivan Bekoff, Calvin Klein's houseboy, and Timothy, the chauffeur, squint at each other through the darkness. Ivan chose the place for its thick, secure walls. The glass and wormwood palace where they held their manic-depressive cocktail party last night was too vulnerable, in his opinion. So here they are, the guests of another absent host, in a bungalow. What Ivan didn't account for was the darkness. The place is well-fortified, but almost without windows.

The dim light has intensified the dynamics of the relationship. Ivan can barely see the young men, but that makes their shrill chatter even more unnerving. They are like wild owls somewhere in a forest.

And although the men can't see the storm, the sound of it has them on the edge of hysteria. The high, wailing wind seems to build to some frenzy, some terrible thing-about-to-happen, and then, teasingly subside . . . only to do it again. At the moment, though, they are blessed with silence—a silence they neither like nor trust. Though the storm is only a quarter-hour old, they are already intimate with its evil habits; if it's quiet now, that's only because it's preparing to do something else to scare them witless.

But now the silence is interrupted by a sound more jarring than the wind—a human scream. They race to the small cut-glass window in the door. There on the walkway is a starkly terrified man on his knees next to a suitcase. They crack the door and motion wildly to him, finally topping his screams with their own. "Get in here!" they are telling him. They watch him get to his feet and weave precipitously toward them, the wind blasting him along the narrow tunnel of walkway like a billiard ball between cushions. When he is finally close enough, they pull him inside.

They dull his nerves with a glass of whiskey and piece his story together from his babbling. He was intending to leave. He missed the last boat by a minute. He didn't want to stay. *He didn't want to be here!* The reality of this nearly drove him to hysteria even before the first puff of wind. For the last fifteen minutes he has been a lunatic, curled up in a ball and letting the wind roll him around as he screamed his head off.

It's a profoundly disturbing tale, but before they can absorb it, the men must first absorb something else. A last boat? A morning boat? Why were *they* not told? It takes a moment for them to comprehend the implications. They could have gotten the hell out. *This morning!*

For Ivan, the moment is particularly bitter. No doubt the wealthy homeowners, the fabulous ones, were advised about the boat. Had the houseboy remained up at Calvin Klein's house, *he* would have been advised about the boat—personally—by the Chief of Police. But as for Ivan, the gaunt, impoverished eccentric who lives in the woods, nobody bothered to make the effort.

Slowly it sinks in to everyone. There was another boat. They could have been on it. They could be on the mainland now, laughing about the whole thing in one of those horrible little coffee shops in Sayville! *They could have gotten out!* It was too much. With this new information, and with the catalyst of the hysterical young man, the others now fall apart, utterly. Emotions already frayed bare by the wind and the sleepless night now unravel. The evil wind chooses this moment to come up again, and even Ivan feels himself coming unglued.

As the frame of the tiny bungalow begins to rattle with the new gusts, he moves away from the young men, suddenly unable to deal with their hysteria. Yes, for a while now, Ivan thinks, he's behaved admirably. He's taught them things they never learned in Manhattan: things about trees, wood, fire, and herbs. And he's been a mature presence in the face of death.

But what has he gotten in return? Respect? No. Gossip about musical comedy! Newsflashes about who down the street eats Quaaludes like candy and once slept with a prince. The idiots!

They seem to glide through life effortlessly, like greased surf-boards . . . with about as much intelligence. To them, Ivan was merely an oddity, a strange bearded man who lived alone in a house he'd built himself. In Fire Island Pines? He was like a Hasidic Jew at an amusement park.

Now the wind is back full again, actually starting to rock the tiny cottage, but Ivan holds on to the thought. What really pissed him off about the younger generation was that he felt they owed him something; not just for last night, or this morning, but for the last thirty years, for Christ's sake! For getting beaten up in alleys and for slinking through much of life masquerading as a "confirmed bachelor," fighting through his own darkness every step of the way. As Kerouac's twisted sufferings had paved the way for the hippies to dance in the sunlight, so had Ivan, in his persecutions, been a shock troop for the green-eyed house-boys. They had him to thank for carving out a small slice of the world where they could be themselves, without suffering or humiliation. As America owed Lewis and Clark, these kids owed Ivan Bekoff . . . a statue in a public square if nothing more.

No, Ivan was through wet-nursing them. Leaving their manic wails behind, he moves off into the kitchen. He is greeted immediately by the wind, which shatters the window into a thousand pieces, soaks him with cold wet air, and flings him brutally into the door, knocking him unconscious.

The dank, sturdy old house . . . Bless it! It feels to Dana Wallace like a cathedral during a war. For an instant there is peace. He hears a pipe drip. He hears the breath of a dog. He imagines the ocean flat and calm under a sky full of stars. It is the first night he ever made love to Maureen. She blows out the kerosene lamp in the shack by the water and the only light is in her small gray eyes, and the only sound is her voice, singing him a song, "If I were the only girl in the world, and you were the only boy . . ."

Aaaaarooooooo! What? What interrupts the beautiful turn-of-the-century melody? The demented wind? No, the injured dog, wailing. Shit! At some point, he'd have to dress her wounds.

Later. What about his own, for Christ's sake? Even at rest, his sixty-eight-year-old heart, swollen and surgically altered, protests. Forget Maureen, forget the dog, what about me, his heart asks him? What are we doing here? Why aren't you playing gin on a pool deck in Boca Raton, like any ordinary old bastard, growing old gracefully? You've got the dough for it. You like horses? Fine. Pad about your breeding farm in North Carolina, making decisions, letting a yearling schmooze a handful of grain from you every once in a while. A real country gentleman, elbow patches, fireplaces, a brandy after dinner. Surely the doctors would allow . . .

No! Fuck the doctors! Fuck the elbow patches! Dana Wallace knew just what kind of trap "aging gracefully" was. Death tapped you on the shoulder and you smiled politely and said, "Yes, certainly, I'll be right along. Just let me pack a few things."

The correct response was *NO NO NO NO NO . . . NEVER! GET AWAY FROM ME YOU SON OF A BITCH!* And if Death did finally begin to drag you away, you made goddamn sure your screams were heard in the next county, and in the next world.

As if in response to his arrogance, the ocean now lifts up the house.

A universe of yellow muck—half-sand, half-water—pushes through the floorboards. As the water swirls around his ankles, Wallace pushes the dogs up the stairs to the top floor.

Truly, that's about it, he figures. The Alamo has fallen. Once the water gets under a house like this it scours out the foundation and takes the whole thing away. That was how '38 wiped out Saltaire; got under those beach houses, knocked the posts down like bowling pins and swallowed the little bungalows up. A cubic yard of water weighs a ton. An ocean roaming across an island weighs . . .

You could feel the deadly action. First the tide boils in and surrounds the place, and then the receding tide takes all the water back, and a little something more. A little percentage of the land. The house percentage, like the westward tide that shaves a foot off the island both in calm seas and rough. Only this is faster. Now you're not merely a hapless crapshooter waiting to go broke, you're an aristocrat with his neck on the guillotine.

Any second now.

Deep in his bones, Wallace feels the sand coming away from the piles. He remembers driving them forty years ago, sinking that beautiful straight spruce into the wet sand like making love to a movie star.

Forget it. There isn't much time left, so he has to think fast and clearly. This is hard because here on the second floor the sound of the storm, the high, keening wail, is rattling the walls. He feels the shingles ripping off the house like his own flesh tearing. He scans the room, the scene of so many of his youthful excesses . . . the old soggy sofa that the dogs array themselves on, shivering . . . the old bar that has so faithfully dispensed passion and illusion for so long . . . the telephone. Hah! How useless *that* invention seemed at the moment. For a macabre laugh, he picks up the receiver. A dial tone! Incredible! The power has been off for a couple of hours, the whole universe is plunged into a primal fury, and he was getting a fucking dial tone! The cable at the bottom of the bay slumbered, undisturbed by the carnage above it. If he felt like it, he could call up some old biddy having a cup of tea in Cleveland and compare notes on the violence and/or the placidity of existence.

The amusing thought does not stay long in his head. The house is lurching now; the piles are utterly naked to the elements. He feels them shiver, spindly and delicate like a thoroughbred's legs. The next blow will be the last.

Where will they find me? he wonders. Under a ton of collapsed wood? Will the fishes find me first? Or will sediments of sand cover me, as they do in the desert, overnight. Will the obituary be in the *New York Times*? How will the news be received by the community, who snipe and gossip about my excesses? Oh, ghost of Christmas Still to Come, whisk me to my own funeral!

Let me study the faces in the pews. Let me scrutinize them for the hint of a smirk at the corner of a mouth . . . . *The bastards!*

Who will weep? What about the ones who love me? Is there anyone, besides Dana Junior? Will he be allright? He's a sensitive kid, underneath it all. What about Maureen? Will the bitch shed a tear? Can one form in that cold cavity of mascara that is her eye? Where is she now? What stranger is she buying a drink for with my alimony?

Bitter? Why not. The last months together were hell. How was Dana Wallace expected to learn about Women's Liberation? Open the door for her and she complained about being patronized. Don't open it and she fumed all night. Pick up a restaurant check and she's insulted. Don't pick it up and you might spend the rest of the night washing dishes, because she never had two nickels to rub together.

How was an old-world guy supposed to change? Did she really want him to? Wasn't that who she'd fallen for, the rough-hewn gentleman in an era of smooth-faced bullshitters?

"I have some growing to do," she said, leaving. What can you say to that? Don't grow? Grow here? "I can't grow here," she would say. You couldn't win. Of course, what you really wanted to say was, "Forget about that crap. Yes, ideals are important, but I *haven't time for that.* I haven't time for you to work through that. I'm an old man. Take my word that you'll get over it, and come lie in my arms eventually anyway, so please, *come do it now.*"

But you couldn't say that. If you were in love with somebody, you were supposed to let them go, and let them "grow." Bullshit. Dana Wallace's brand of love was here and now, in a shack by the ocean's edge, every moment white hot, fused together, moans of lovemaking, screams of anger, all of it here together now. You "grew" in each other's arms.

CRASH!

The sound beyond the eastern window pulverizes his thoughts. Wallace knows what it means, even before he turns his head to look. The game is over. Two streets away, John Lardner's roof has blown off. The wind has lifted it up and flung it like a huge, razor-sharp Frisbee, lopping off a couple of ancient trees and buckling the walls of a house farther down the street. Wallace probably has only a few minutes now. He picks up the phone.

"Operator?"

"Yes sir."

"My name is Dana Wallace; I'm in the middle of the hurricane on Fire Island. I think I'm about to die. I want to tell you where my body can be found, and where my son can be reached."

He hears her pencil scratch down the information. "I'm very sorry, Mr. Wallace."

"Thank you." He drains his cocktail. Dragging the long phone cord behind him, he goes to mix another.

"I hope you don't die," the operator says. "You may not. I hope you don't."

"Thank you."

Her voice is the richest, sweetest, most compassionate instrument he has ever heard on this earth. As he listens to it, the lunatic wind now peppering his eastern wall with sand and wood and birds and Christ-knows-what, tears fill his eyes. Perhaps if he had found a woman like this earlier, the course of things might have been different.

"Who are you?" he asks her in the din. "Where do you live? There is a silence.

"I live in Bellmore," she says at last.

Wallace calls up the image of the dull little Long Island village. Perhaps in the right house, in the coziest little nook of town, on a clear winter night, it could be lovely.

"What do you dream of at night?" he presses her. "What makes your heart pound?"

An even longer, flushed pause through the cable under the raging bay. The bashful thing. "I go to the dog show in New York every year," she says finally.

An animal lover!! He looks triumphantly to the wet, matted Labs, their chests heaving in unison on the sofa.

"I like to walk," she says. Walk with me until one of us drops, he is thinking.

———

Enormous mad gusts now rattle the rafters, naked under the deshingled roof. The dogs howl throatily . . . and an image of Maureen comes uninvited to Wallace's head.

No! No, he does not want this thought now! Anything but this! But here it is anyway—a memory of the last time he saw her. He has not been able to bear thinking of the moment since it happened.

It was about a year after she walked out on him. He was puttering disconsolately in the barn, as usual, when someone came in with a message—Maureen was calling from Massachusetts! He ran to the phone, breathless, tracking horseshit into the house.

She wanted to see him, she said. Immediately.

In an hour he was on a plane. By nightfall he was on the tiny island of Martha's Vineyard, sitting beside her in her favorite restaurant, a little nautical nook. In the dying light she was lovelier than he'd ever seen her.

"St. Emilion '76," he said to the young waiter, remembering her favorite wine.

"Are you Dana Wallace?" the young man said.

". . . Yes . . ."

"Here."

He handed Dana a legal document. It was something to do with the divorce and the alimony. It was the serving of a paper. Maureen had set up the whole thing. She stood to leave. "I'm sorry it had to be this way, Dana," she said. And then she left.

Dana stared at the paper. Tears of disbelief froze along his face. The process-server looked down at his shoes. He was just a college kid with a part-time job. The treachery of it was incomprehensible. She had gotten him up there, pumped up the foolish hopes of an old man, just to serve him *a fucking legal paper!* Could God really have made such a creature as this?

"Mr. Wallace?"

It was the operator, his beloved operator, summoning him back.

"Is there anything you want me to say to your son?"

"Thank you, operator, let me see . . ."

What he saw was a tragic fool, an impotent Lear raging out here by the water because he hadn't mastered the simple thing: to love and be loved. Here he sat, with a stomach full of bitterness about women, about half the human race. What a pathetic way to go out. Maybe, he thinks, that's why God has sent this angel of mercy, this Bernadette of the Switchboard; so I can make peace with them, these scented, lithe, bleeding, childbearing creatures who I have so loved, and who have so confused me.

He conjures up a vision of the operator's naked bosom, and he lays his head upon it. Through the singing wires and the barnacled cables, he feels love and redemption coursing to him. Something within him begins to yield. A steel infrastructure that for sixty-eight years has carried the weight of his head and shoulders over his torso gives way, and in its place is an open channel, through which great salty tears gush up from his guts and out through his eyes.

"I'm sorry," he blubbers into the receiver.

"That's all right, Mr. Wallace. It's good to cry sometimes."

"I love you," he blurts.

There is a short, deep silence. Finally the operator says, "I love you too, Mr. Wallace."

He feels warmth all over his sodden shivering skin. Every part of his heart—gristle and aorta, plastic and screws—clanks and heaves. It is the moment of grace he thought would never come.

Suddenly the tears on his fat red cheeks fill with bright light, blinding him. He races to the window, dragging the phone.

"The sun is out!" he cries.

"Then you're going to be all right!?" she says breathlessly.

No, not by a longshot. Because he loves her, he will explain to her patiently (he never had any patience with Maureen) about the eye of a storm: how at the very center of wild torsion and suction, Nature leaves a thin cylinder of peace—a sunny sky as blue as a robin's egg, here and there a wispy cloud.

Having endured the nerve-and-bone-jarring wind for an hour, you want to believe it's all over, and you want to let these warm zephyrs caress your face. But when you stand still enough to feel the set of your bones in your flesh, and hear the sound of the blood rushing through your big arteries and trickling through your little ones, you know something is wrong. There's nothing over your head. This is the very pinpoint where the devil's workmen have removed the lid from the sky. Through the grace of centrifugal force, you stand in a square mile of peace in a thousand miles of chaos; the eye of the storm.

Dana Wallace knows he's in the beautifully appointed waiting room of hell. Shortly, he is going to be led out of it and into hell itself. Everyone who lived to tell about '38 agreed on one thing; the first half sets up the pins, the second half knocks them down. It was after the eye that the Wall of Water came, the huge pucker of hell ocean that ripped away roofs that had been unhinged, toppled wooden piles that had been revealed, and washed away souls that were cowering in closets.

But for now, the eerie light air is soft and peaceful. It may be the last peace Dana Wallace will have on this earth. In his mind, he pushes a wisp of hair out of the telephone operator's eye, takes her face in his hands, and kisses her on the mouth in the sunlight.

T E N

Under the false sun, only one creature walks the walkways of the Western Kingdom: a white-tailed deer, the big twelve-point Buck who only this morning, in the calm before the storm, bid farewell to his Doe at the edge of the Sunken Forest. Now he emerges from a thicket after an hour of hell.

The sun is warm and dry and sweet, but he doesn't trust it. His bones ache slightly and tell him they're not sitting right. Everything is strange, as it has been since his mission began.

At first, after leaving his Doe, he moved easily through the carpet of rolling swale that lies to the west of the forest. Then, farther to the west, he encountered the first large dark structures, built by humans and full of their disquieting smells. No sooner did that happen when, as if to confirm his discomfort, the sky did something it's never done before. It opened up. It howled at him, it stung him, it tried to lift him up and blow him away, it made him cower in a thicket of juniper trees, gray powdered berries pelting him endlessly.

Now this, thin light air that just doesn't feel right. But he moves out into it anyway because he's desperate. Unless he can find a feeding range for himself and his Doe, unless he can lead her to the hotly rumored bounty of this strange place—juicy leaves and berries unknown in the dense thickets and wide woods of the Sunken Forest—never will her blood be rich enough to guarantee a fawn.

By now he knows the large structures well, having seen many of them, and he warily sidles up to one. He sniffs a container spilled open on its side. He pokes through its contents, his olfactory system rioting at their richness. He balks at some of the shiney wrappings. His wet probing nose is sliced by other things—sharp things—but still he is intrigued and keeps poking.

He's tempted, but he won't take any of it. On his journey he's seen other deer with their faces in this mess, and these are the deer that return to the deep winter woods with the bloated, glazed look that the big Buck now knows to be dangerous. They live through the first leafless months off their own syrupy blood . . . but then when they must forage, and take their meals from twigs and bark, they've grown too soft. After a bad winter, the spring ground is littered with their corpses.

The Buck raises his head and sees something more to his liking. Fat red fruits, things he's never seen before, hang gleaming from thick vines. They're irresistible. He chomps one. Its pulpy insides escape from both sides of his jaw and carry tiny seeds in rivulets down his chest. The taste makes his haunches quiver with delight. Yes! Here is one place he will bring the Doe.

Flushed with his first success, the Buck moves to the north, to where a small clump of houses sit beside the bay. A ribbon of something slick and dark green lies on the sand beside the water, water that is calm by comparison to the roaring braying sea over the sandy hill. Deeply, he feels a pang of hunger. Tasting the fat

187

red round things has stirred his appetite after all. Now, with the slick green stuff, he will really indulge it. Like his ancestors, who emerged wet and starving from the bay after their swim from the mainland, he will have a meal of seaweed.

As he extends his long neck, his eye catches something downrange along the slick belt of food, indistinguishable from it in color except for a white chest that heaves violently.

It's a bird. Rarely, thinks the Buck, do they lie like that in seaweed.

But this is a tired bird that cares not where it lies. Three days ago and a thousand miles away, she made the mistake of flying up into the same peaceful air that is now seducing the Buck. Then the peaceful air *began to move*, and for days the bird fought to stay aloof over the water . . . compelled to travel at the same speed as the eye of the storm, or be slapped down into the sea by the surrounding winds. At last the little band of fine weather passed over land again, and the bird dropped gratefully to the ground. Panting and thin, she takes in her new surroundings through violet eyes.

Large dead white birds float in the brackish water. Nowhere are the great swaying palms and lush undergrowth of her homeland. Nowhere are the thin houses with reed roofs where the two-legged creatures with the shiny black skin live. Most important, nowhere are the fat juicy bugs the bird must eat to live.

Now, to make matters worse, a huge brown-horned creature is staring at her a short distance away! Never has the bird seen such a thing. With no strength to fly, she rolls over, protecting herself by showing her iridescent back against the seaweed—by disappearing.

The Buck is not fooled, nor is he interested. Deer stopped eating birds long before the last glacier got to Long Island. Nor is there anything unique about this bird. The Buck has seen thousands just like her all over the island.

Not *just* like her. True, the bird has close relations in the swallow family here. The chimney swifts and the purple martins and the barn swallows all bear a certain resemblance to the stranger. In fact these Fire Island birds will soon be making their winter trek to places not far from the sable beach where she was, a few days ago, sucked up into a bad dream.

But the Bahamas Swallow, who lies cowering and shivering in her bed of seaweed, may be going nowhere. When the sun sets on this island tonight (if there is an island left), this bird will experience something new: cold. She will not be able to relax in the chilly, black air; nor will she find anything to eat. Back where she comes from, the bugs fill every balmy night sky. Unbeknownst to her, her cousins here make do with little, even in the hot months. Now, every last precious meal is fuel for the trip south. The Bahamas Swallow, exhausted, must find the strength to compete for the few bugs that are left, bugs she has never seen, bugs with a whole new bag of tricks. And the nights will only get colder. She closes her eyes and dreams of little red scarabs, the fat ones that crawl in and out of guavas.

The Buck pokes along the ribbon of seaweed, and finally abandons it, leaving the desolate bird alone. Everything about this day—the fierce winds and the strange sunshine, the empty walkways and the dead gulls—all of it gives the Buck an uneasy feeling. He has found bounty for his Doe, perhaps not the paradise he had heard of and hoped for, but good enough. The fat red round things alone will be a feast for her mangy, ribbed body. The Buck has located the spot with deer precision, and he will bring her back here . . . another time. Now he wants only to be with her and he breaks into an eastward trot back toward the Sunken Forest.

First he must negotiate the town of Point O' Woods, through which he passed on his westward journey. The storm has blown down a section of the fence that is such a pregnant symbol to islanders, so rather than bypass it up by the ocean, as he did earlier, the Buck steps gingerly over the flattened wire mesh and continues on his way.

Destruction is everywhere in the WASP bastion. Its spaciousness has been its undoing. Across the great lawns the wind has gathered, and ripped apart huge sections of the old dormered houses. Turrets and widow's walks lie about, crushed and splintered. Porches are collapsed, never again to host birthday toasts with glasses of Glenfiddich. Wooden and slate shingles have been shorn off and flung willy-nilly, murdering birds and slicing electrical wires. Bushes are flattened, having surrendered their fruit to the wind.

Though the Buck knows little of the normal look of men's affairs, he senses they are in disarray and moves on. Soon he is in the last outpost of humans before the dark Sunken Forest. This is Oakleyville, once famous as a vacation spot of the reclusive Greta Garbo. Knowing nothing of the cinema, the Buck sees only a cluster of empty structures in a juniper thicket and moves on.

Now he is at the western edge of a small stand of pines. This is the edge of the forest. Though he is still a good distance from home, he draws strength, as all animals do, when he pulls on the cloak of the Sunken Forest. How old are these woods? It takes a thousand years to make an inch of humus. The Buck could stick his hoof and haunch into the black ooze and still not feel the bottom of it.

It all started with the pines. The pitch pine that leans into the dune in front of him pleases him deeply, and not just because it is a landmark on the way home. This tree is deep in the memory of the race of deer. Pines are the guts of this island. They got here when this beach was just about naked to the wind and the stars. They forced their seed into sand, and sucked their sustenance from the quartz and the sun. The ancient deer ate the bark and the cones, and it gave their shit some bulk, enough to lay down a bed for other seeds so that something might happen here, so that the island wouldn't collapse at the first swipe from the back of Mother Nature's hand. The pines are the pioneers, and the survivors.

The Buck pokes among the cones on the ground, baring his teeth to find and snare a seed. Suddenly he bolts erect. Something has unnerved him. He backs away, his eyes widening.

These pines grow two kinds of cones. One kind lies scattered about the ground, dessert for the deer and the fox. The other kind the tree clutches like a mother a child, as tightly as the cone in turn clutches its seeds. Only when the pine feels the heat of a fire will it release these cones, and only into the cool ash afterward will the cone release its seeds. In this way will the race survive any conflagration and endure forever.

But the cone the Buck holds in his snout is as tight as a drum, and this is what disturbs and confuses him. Surely this is not a survival cone, the kind the pine saves for forest fires? If it is, what is it doing on the ground?

The wind.

That the wind may have knocked one of these tenacious cones out of a pine is a more frightening symbol of the storm's power than all the Weather Service's readouts, or even than the staircase that flew over Dana Wallace's head. It is, in fact, the only measure that the Buck understands besides the wind itself. For the first time, he feels the chill of the day. In fact the dark clouds have come in off the water and hidden the sun again. He moves quickly inland, forgetting about seeds, seeking only the darkness of the inner forest and his Doe.

The Buck's Doe is indeed in the heart of the ancient forest, from which she has not moved in an hour. Once the high, awful winds began to blow, she proceeded here immediately. She does not trust the false sunlight any more than she trusts the faint smell of men. So she sits on her haunches and waits, and she simply feels this place.

The peace is thick, immense, dark and quiet. But the Doe knows it is deceptive. Deep within her is a sympathy for all living things, and she shudders as she remembers, through her ancestors, the slow, incredible violence that unfolded here across centuries. It was the battle of trees to rule the inner forest.

First the speckled shadbush, which blooms every year when the shad run, sank its deep roots. Then the wild cherry tree staked its claim, spreading its scarlet leaves everywhere. It wasn't long before the shiny bayberry bush insinuated itself among the cherry branches, strangling them. The squabbling was petty but ruthless.

Each epoch brought a new pretender to the throne. Finally, though, two combatants emerged above all the ambitious flora and forced everything else to the outer edge of the forest. As the wind off the water picks up again, weaving through the woods to find her, the Doe's eye falls upon those dominant, muscular trees, the prince regents of the forest, the Oak and the Sassafras.

The battle these two waged for control of the Sunken Forest is legend among its ghosts and fairies. It was endless, bitter, and brilliant. The majestic warrior Oaks, with their height, drew first blood by blocking out the sky. The wily graceful Sassafras learned to twist and lean into the shafts of light that pierced the oaks' canopy and survived. Then the Oaks sent their roots farther and deeper, trying to monopolize the soil. The Sassafras parried, sending their own roots down into the swamps, learning how to suck nourishment out of water. The Oak shed its bark, sending the famished herds of deer to the sassafras. The Sassafras made their thick bark tough and bitter to the taste, and the deer went back and tore apart the Oak.

As the fierce battle raged, though, the ground itself was changing. The graveyard of the noble, slain giants was becoming too rich for their own blood. The forest floor, growing thicker, mealier, moister, and blacker under a hood of catbrier, was a wildly potent concentrate of life and death. As such, it was ready to host a truly elegant machine of nature, one that would dominate and wither the Oak and the Sassafras both. The kingdom was ready to receive its monarch.

It only waited for the seed.

Indeed, as the Doe peers at them from her vantage point in the center of the woods, the Oak and the Sassafras look as if they've been beaten down. The tough healthy bark of the Sassafras is in tatters. The proud straight Oaks languish and droop. What tree, finally, could dominate them? Above the Doe's head is the answer.

She is in a place of absolute quiet. The wind, raging again through the woods, barely penetrates here. Nor does the gray sky. The top of the forest witnesses the chaos, but so completely absorbs it that the forest floor is only dark and tranquil. Nowhere else is there such space between trees. The Doe can maneuver nimbly and silently on the soft, unlittered earth. But for the moment she remains still. She looks straight up. She can't even see the leaves of these trees; she feels only the high arc of their canopy. What tree is this that rules the Sunken Forest?

Its seed might have come with a bird, perhaps an ancestor of the lonely redstart, on his way north in the spring. Along the Atlantic flyway he may have stopped for the night on one of the small islands off Georgia or the Carolinas, and eaten a red berry off a tree, being careful to avoid the waxy, sharply pointed leaves. As he flew north the next day perhaps he digested the berry, all but the pithy seed, which tumbled out of his rear end and fell to earth in the sandy loam of Fire Island. From then on, the Oak and Sassafras's days were numbered.

The seed sprouted and the young tree soared. The balance of salt water and fresh water, of wind and moisture and warmth (as the island reached east for the Gulf Stream) approximated the conditions of the tree's homeland, and even improved upon them So completely did its leaves intercept the sunlight that even the puggish catbrier had to retreat to the outer woods for light. Everything was banished from the inner forest but the brash victorious trees, and the luxurious space between them.

The Holly tree ruled alone.

It witnessed the dark debaucheries of the pirates and it presided over the powwows of the Secatogues. The Holly was here before the birth of the nation that bestowed upon this island the designation of "National Park." It is an old, dark, moist, exclusive club. The Doe is proud to be among the great, straight trunks. She is at a shrine of Nature. She draws herself up, blowing out her brown chest.

Now she hears a rattling high in the Hollies, among their studded leaves, then a low moan. They are the first sounds she has heard since arriving here in the inner forest. Is it because I stood up? she wonders.

Crack! A sound attacks her ears, the chestnut flaps instinctively close. In front of her a giant Holly has split open. It is one of the oldest in the forest. Underneath it, a Secatogue brave wooed a maiden. The white pulpish marrow, suddenly exposed, sweats and bleeds. The Doe is shocked to glimpse the magnificent creature's inner pathways. She wails. She knows the tree relinquishes its privacy only in death.

It will be a while before the sticky contiguous insides curdle and brown and dry. It will be longer still before the message is received by the leaves, and the roots are informed in their turn of the end of production. But the tree is swooning. It is gone.

Its trunk still erect, it hangs in the network of its neighbors' branches. It will die in their arms. The forest and the world will be different places, with the loss of this tree.

The Doe moves out of the small gully that has been her mother's bosom for an hour. Deeply agitated, she begins to walk, then run back out of the Holly grove, back out past the sad Oak and Sassafras, back through history. By the time she is at the eastern edge of the woods, she is at a full gallop, going she knows not where. At this same moment, the monstrous, final winds of Gloria begin to soar, and the Buck enters the heart of the Sunken Forest looking for his mate.

He just missed her.

ELEVEN

Ferron Bell and Ralph Cain have the look of prizefighters taking a breather in the middle of a savage beating. Soon, they know, the bell will ring again and their handlers will yank their stools from under them and push them back into the ring.

For ten minutes the phony peekaboo blue sky of the eye has mocked them. Now the silver-gray clouds are back, and shortly the two men will hear again the high keen of the wind, and be pitched back into the terror. Soon Bell will be on his knees in monastic prayer, as he was during the storm's first hour. Cain, who is to a monk what a Jacuzzi is to the river Jordan, will begin again his agitated kvetching and pacing.

This time, they know, their tricks may not get them through

it. Despite their differences, both are students of history and they know that in '38 the wall of water came fashionably late; that the low pressure around the eye simply lifted the ocean up, and then the wind slammed it home. As terrifying as Gloria has already been, rocking the house to its moorings and bending the backyard pines to the ground, it is the second half that will bring death, if death is coming. The wall of water will swallow the house whole.

In utter silence, their nerves stretched beyond elasticity, they wait. They are poised for death. Ferron Bell shuts his eyes and tries to kill the thoughts.

He hears the clipped hooves of the Doe pass along the wooden walkway. He manages a meager smile. It's good to know the deer are getting through it. He feels close to them, though he no longer feeds them, as he once did, out of the palm of his hand. A ranger set him straight about giving them "one last big meal" before the winter. All that did was make them soft and vulnerable, their stomachs too flaccid to grind up the twigs and bark that would be winter's main course. Now Bell had contempt for his neighbors that coax the animals onto their decks, give them names, and feed them pâté and Brie. It is that way for him about much of what was once considered "fabulous" about Fire Island Pines. The mists of sentiment and glamour have blown over, Tab Hunter and Bette Midler vacation elsewhere now, and a hideous fatal disease lurks everywhere, the unseen guest dancing madly at every tea dance.

Of course, to a former monk it comes as no surprise when the wages of sin turn out to be death.

He corrects himself. Not "sin" exactly. There's nothing wrong with screwing other men. God knows he's built his life on that principle, and backed it up with a few of his own broken bones. He celebrated the liberation of Stonewall and he mourns with all of his big heart at the funerals of the beautiful young men. It isn't their sins they're paying for so much as their frivolity. Christ, he thinks, I'm becoming as big a misanthrope as old Ivan Bekoff. But it was true. The endless, mindless nights of drooling over Myrna Loy double features at the Regency are no doubt what Merton would have condemned them for.

Merton, Merton, Merton!

How many times, in the journey from the Order of St. Basil through the wild parties of the seventies to this very moment, has he conjured the image of that modern saint when the choices of modern life confused him? It was even Merton who turned out the lights and convinced him to stay for the storm! Worship God, not Myrna Loy, Thomas Merton would surely have told the young men.

"It's starting again," says Ralph Cain.

So it is. Lost in his reverie, Ferron Bell has missed the march of the dark, scudding clouds over his head. He will not miss their anthem. The distant wail of the wind begins again. Both men feel the quickening and heaviness in their chest. Ferron drops back to his knees, amid the candles, incense, and icons of the makeshift altar by the fireplace. His eyes are riveted to a gaunt hermit painted on a wooden board. He begins to pray again; the same low, liturgical mumble that got him through the first hour of the storm, and has by now become a profound irritant to Ralph Cain.

The agitated accountant slinks away, resentful, and contemptuous. "Memento Mori" indeed. "Remember death" indeed! How had he allowed himself to be conned by this solemn, pious crap, and this promise of "inner peace"? The peace of his own grave, perhaps. There was Ferron Bell, the would-be, used-to-be monk, imploring some half-baked saint to keep the chimney from falling on them. And here am I, muses Cain, with nothing more spiritual to call on than a few nightmares out of a Texas boyhood, of cowering in a wet basement through a Gulf storm.

Cain's bitterness has gotten the better of him. He feels like a cigarette. He feels like putting it out in Ferron's incense tray, right under his nose.

Ferron Bell is back into his prayers, and deeply. He is not praying arbitrarily about the chimney. He knows that in '38 more than a few people were buried alive by the bricks from their own hearth. Now, as he chatters away, the wind comes up again. The Second Act, both men feel, is going to proceed quickly to the Curtain. Already there is the dreadful patina of the storm that so terrorized them before; the flying shingles battering the outer walls, the soft constant clitter of thousands of pine needles shaken from trees and landing on the brittle green floor of thousands of others. The trees themselves, proud pioneer pines with boughs you can hang from, are bending again almost to the ground.

This is where they left off. Something new was going to happen now, they felt. It had better. The wind tortures them with its potential power. It was as if they'd been kidnapped by terrorists and sat in a small room watching the door. They knew that at any moment someone might come in and put a bullet in their heads. Try to read a magazine in a situation like that, thinks Ralph Cain, and you have the rough equivalent of praying in a hurricane. At any moment the wind can lift the tiny cottage and fling it away . . . yet it chooses not to; chooses instead to toy with us, to flex and preen its muscles instead of smashing us with them.

Ferron Bell's hooded gray eyes look up at the wooden painting of St. Anthony and the tone of his prayers changes. "Get it over with," he now pleads.

It is no accident that he addresses what may be his last prayer to the gaunt St. Anthony, a Carthusian, a black belt of Christianity. This order takes it hard and straight. The Hermitage of St. Basil, where Ferron Bell had his taste of devotion, was Disneyland next to the grim barren places the Carthusians call home. They are monks who find laboring in silence together far too frivolous and social an activity. They live alone in holes carved out of rockface, and take their food on ropes lowered a thousand feet from the tops of cliffs.

Ferron Bell aspires to this. He has cultivated the deep silent joys of solitude and denial and he wonders what it would be like to climb up into one of those holes. If he gets through this, he hopes to someday visit the cliffside where St. Anthony spent the last forty years of his life without saying a word.

Out the silver-gray window, object fly past with jet power.

The wind is getting under the bungalow and starting to rock it on its feeble, sodden foundation. The deep harmonic sound of the storm, a violent near-silence, swallows all other noise. Bell tries to keep his concentration on the faded oil-on-wood medieval snapshot of the gaunt, bearded Carthusian. Into the eyes of the hermit Ferron pours his own eyes.

What's this? The eyes are looking back at him! They are moist and intense. They are moving! They are alive! No longer are they the dark expressionless eyes of St. Anthony! They are green, and sprightly and inquisitive and huge and sad, and they are moving! Where had he seen these eyes before?

Merton!

The eyes of Thomas Merton, dead these twenty years, are staring at Ferron Bell. Bell turns to the frenetically pacing Ralph Cain. Has he seen the apparition? Fat chance. Cain is oblivious to everything but his own anxiety, even the soul-rattling sound of the wind.

But why does this great man, this spiritual beacon of a generation, visit Ferron Bell at this moment? What does he want? What message does he bear? Bell stares back at him. The eyes are changing their expression. They are not comforting or benevolent. They are accusing. Of what? What has Ferron Bell done to offend the spirit of Thomas Merton? "What am I charged with?" he asks the eyes.

WITH GIVING UP, comes the answer.
WITH GIVING UP THE WORK OF GOD!
WITH LEAVING THE ABBEY.
WITH COPPING OUT.
WITH GOING SOFT.

Ferron Bell topples off his knees. He checks the painting again. The vision is even more intense, the eyes greener, moister, sterner. "Yes," Bell says out loud, "yes, it is true that I lacked the will and the patience to have a vocation in the Order. It is true I have wasted much of my life on frivolities of the flesh. But in my layman's life, in my art, I have put myself at the service of God . . . tried to put myself . . ."

Cain listens incredulously to his friend. Get a grip! This was worse drivel than he used to hear back in the old Catholic church in El Paso, when he would sneak behind the confessional and listen to some pathetic old woman ask to be forgiven for any thought or feeling she ever had. And Ferron was always babbling about the dignity and solemnity of the church. This was *dignity*? Ferron Bell was on his knees like a beggar in the subway.

Suddenly, Bell stops in midbabble. Something is interrupting him, a sound that freezes the heart and minds of both men.

It is a long, low moan—far louder than anything they have yet heard. It seems to be coming from everywhere. It sounds almost human, as if an enormous person, at a great distance, were in unendurable agony. It isn't the wind, for the wind has long ago passed beyond sound into the white silence that has already terrorized them. Or has the wind moved up to some new, demonic level? Or is it another hallucination? Is it the sound of the whole world mourning for them? For itself?

The sound continues and mounts. The cottage continues to rock on its weary wet joists. Both men think the unthinkable thought at once. Has the sound something to do with the wall of water? Each man sees his private nightmares on the TV screen in his head: the Atlantic Ocean, green, swirling and angry, crashes through the southern wall; in slow motion it churns, grinds, and devours the room; death by drowning; the pink lung tissue, so delicate and airy, suddenly engorged by racing salt water, exploding bloated; the mouth widening and greedily sucking in not air but the dreaded green liquid; the eyes bursting out of the head; the silence; the dank eternal tomb; the intestines laid bare on a reef, petrified, algae-infested, a home for fish . . .

The moan grows louder still. It echoes in the room, which begins to vibrate. Books tumble off shelves and the candle in the alter starts to swing on its leather thong. Bell climbs back to his knees, and sinks low on his haunches. He intensifies his apology to the living eyes in his alter. "Forgive my whining excuses. You're right, I'm a wretched thing, a coward unworthy to call himself a servant of God. If, in his grace, he sees fit to spare me, I pledge—"

"Shut up."

Bell shudders. The voice of Merton again, refusing his miserable apology? No, the voice of Ralph Cain.

Cain's long bony arm is pointing out the window, and Bell's eyes follow it. The muscular pines are bending almost to the ground. Clinging to one of them, almost flattened against the bark, is a cat. It's an orphan calico, mangy and pathetic, that's been hanging around the neighborhood all week. Probably it was left behind by one of the summer people, who grew tired of it, or didn't have an apartment big enough to keep it. Now the poor thing was hanging on to life by a thread so thin as to be invisible. One erratic gust would blow it off the pine and into oblivion.

Watching it, Ferron Bell feels suddenly chastised, self-indulgent, and ridiculous. He turns his prayers intensely in another direction, away from his own enlightenment, and toward the life of the cat.

"Save her," he says, fervently.

Another image races into his mind. The redstarts, his dearest friends in the bird world. Where were they? Had they left? How far had they gotten? Had they found a spot to lay low, or (and this was the most depressing thought) had they been caught out over the water, with nowhere to go but down?

He remembers their council yesterday, on a dune. God, how the problem had weighed on them! To migrate, to risk the wind, . . . to stay? Without comprehending a note of bird song, Ferron could feel the question hanging, like frost on their tangerine wings. How rare a privilege it had been to sit there among them, these proud, private creatures who shunned even other birds, who trilled not from blooming branches but from dead, rotting trunks. The birds were almost human. In a sense they've always reminded Ferron of Ivan Bekoff, the recluse at the western end of the pines. But of course Ivan had stopped singing altogether, it seemed. No, old Ivan was more like a whippoorwill, that malevolent night flyer who will unnerve you with a hiss and a glare from its hot yellow eyes, should you dare to peek into the hollow log where it hides. No, really, the redstarts with their temperamental artistry, bore more of a resemblance to . . . Ferron Bell himself! Yes, maybe that was why he gravitated to them . . . and why they allowed him to. Ferron was a human redstart, or they were the Ferron Bells of the sky. So what advice would Ferron Bell have given them yesterday, in their deep dilemma, had he the gift or warbling?

"Save yourself," he would have said. "Do anything at all but face into this awful wind." And as if to confirm this, the wind keens again now, building, high above the tiny cottage. But if he would have given this advice to the redstarts, Ferron is thinking, why *did he not take it himself*!?

No sooner do the words form in his brain than the calico cat is ripped away, almost straight up into the wild air, its front paws simply torn out of the pine bark. Its receding screech is barely audible. Gone.

Just like that.

Reeling around the room, Cain gags in horror, fighting for breath. Ferron Bell remains erect.

The house is rocking jerkily but he struggles for balance and hangs on to the thought. Life! Life itself, whether it was feline, avian, monastic, heterosexual, homosexual, botanical, reptilian, *whatever*, was precious. That was what he felt, deep in his deepest heart. Wasn't that the lesson learned every day when some AIDS victim was lowered into the ground? Wasn't that the lesson of the poor cat? What wouldn't they have given, each and every one of them, for just a day, an hour, a *minute* more of what Ferron Bell was so carelessly pitching away? Plenty. So maybe sticking through this monstrous storm hadn't glorified God at all. Or even pleased him. As a casual waste of human life, perhaps it even pissed him off!

So if this was what he felt in his deepest heart, what was he doing here?

Chinaware, vibrating off the shelf, explodes behind him as the answer explodes inside his head.

He was paying for his sins. He was doing penance for having been the ringmaster of the most decadent circus on earth, for presiding over the Bo Peep parties of the seventies, for all the nude surfers painted silver and singing "The Man That Got Away."

But how twisted, he is suddenly thinking! It's one thing to do penance by getting down on your knees and apologizing to the ghost of Thomas Merton. It's another thing to toss your life away! That was *martyrdom*, for Christ's sake!

The eaves are fluttering, the wind is getting under the roof, he feels about five seconds from death, urine is soaking his pants, but he doesn't back down from this new line of thought.

Yes, there were the Mertons and many other sublime, enlightened creatures at Gethsemane and St. Basil, but there were also a few people there who were absolutely unhinged! What difference did it make who lived the grimmest life, or ate the blandest porridge on the most remote cliff? Why did that connect you to God, necessarily, any more than dressing like Myrna Loy? And what about fat little Harry who first brought the news of the hurricane yesterday, and even this frenetically pacing beanpole Ralph Cain, for God's sake? They were as decent a pair of souls as you'd ever find. But you wouldn't find them dug into cliffs; you'd find them sipping a cocktail at the Ice Palace. But so what? You go to your church, I'll go to mine, as somebody, *not* Thomas Merton, once said.

Now a high whine of wind interrupts his thoughts and rocks him, jolts him off balance. He feels a tearing motion, as the house fights to free itself and fly away. A gust of wind actually picks up a corner of the tiny bungalow, free at last, and pitches Ferron Bell violently into Ralph Cain, and the two men collapse into an antique china cabinet, shattering the glass.

Cain has come unraveled. The unearthly low moan pushed him to the edge, and now the horrible death of the cat has pushed him over it. After a moment of lying in the wreckage of the china cabinet, he extricates himself from Bell and the broken glass. Nicked and bleeding, he begins to pace again furiously, trying to burn off the anxiety of death. As he lurches through the room, the room itself moves and thrashes on its free side. The house is straining to be gone, to cut its earthly bonds, to join the cat in the wind! Through his terror he fixes on the central point around which he now spins with near centrifugal speed. It is a gleaming metal object he gave Ferron as a gift a couple of years ago, a tide clock. In the absence of a religious icon, it takes on that significance for Cain, and it shines for him and hypnotizes him as he moves around it.

Maddeningly, though the drunken wind is struggling to liberate the house and murder Ralph Cain, he does not review his life in a flash, but instead gets caught up in a piece of trivia, an anecdote he heard yesterday. It was about a man who received a piece of mail order bric-a-brac back in '38 similar to this thing Ralph gave Ferron Bell. It wasn't a tide clock, but it was the same general family of handsome nautical brass instrument, a barometer. The man unwrapped it only to find the dial reading twenty seven! The cheap piece of crap. You had pressure that low maybe on the moon. The man rewrapped the barometer and took it back to the post office. When he got back, his house was gone, washed away by the hurricane of 1938.

Very funny.

Now the demonic moan rises to a shrill wail and remains at this high frequency, almost inaccessible to human ears. The men stop and look at each other. Full of echoes, the near-silence is more threatening than anything that has gone before. It is the half-note hesitation before the big cymbal crash. The rocking of the house falls into a wide, easy rhythm. Something was about to happen. Was the killing wave, roaring beyond sound, curling at this moment into its arc?

Cain remains desperately fixed on the tide clock. What an ironic artifact to be found floating next to! He had thought it would make a nice gift, since Ferron walked the beach so often. He should have given him a fucking toaster!

How did the arcane instrument work? In his hour of obsessed pacing around it, he hadn't even figured it out. This gizmo here was obviously supposed to indicate something, probably low tide. *Was the big wave cresting now? Was that the first delicate spray pelting the*

———

roof? And this dial here was probably . . . well, the actual time. At least it was good for something; it told time! Well, maybe not. All the needles seemed to be stuck in the same place. But maybe all that meant was that it's low tide right now. That would explain . . . wait a minute. Low tide right now. Low tide right now? *Low tide right now!*

A pane of glass shatters behind him, soaking him with a blast of cold, salty air, but he clings to the thought. If the tide was low, lower than low with the full moon, the so-called "storm surge" might not be as bad as everyone thinks. If the sea only got lifted up fifteen or twenty feet, it may be no worse than high tide on any *Goddamn day of the year!* The implications begin to register themselves on a heart and mind that has been pushed to the limit. Was this right? Was he piecing it together right in his jangled brain? If the wind didn't get any worse, if it didn't manage to wrest the snug little cottage completely off its moorings and pitch it away, then in all probability . . . he wasn't going to die!

Now, as if in answer, the high pitch of the wind lessens imperceptibly, but enough to reinforce the precious infant of a thought in Ralph Cain's head.

He wasn't going to die! Neither one of them were going to die! He would swim again in the ocean; he'd have another brandy Alexander; he'd nibble again on those little goat cheese-and-basil hors d'oeuvres he had the other night at Jerry's; he'd walk down the boardwalk again, with that incredibly annoying splintered plank catching on his sandals; he would get stung by a bee again probably, by a mosquito certainly; he would have a political argument with Right Wing Roger Rifkin again; he would hear music; he would take a crap; he would read a bad novel, a good one, a dirty one, a clean one; he would take out the garbage; he would forget to take it out; he would see the moon; he would smell the earth . . . *He was going to live!*

He turns to his friend, who is on his feet staring soberly ahead at the wall. Cain starts to frame a sentence in his head. He wants to tell Ferron Bell that they're going to make it.

———

As the first word forms on his lips, a shaft of sunlight shoots through the pines in the backyard, illuminating like emeralds the bed of needles on the ground. The low moan is an echo and a memory. This sunlight isn't false, it's real. The storm is over. They have survived.

TWELVE

The thrush trembles in a shadbush. She pokes her head up and looks around. It will take more than a shaft of sunlight to move her. The winds have shaken her deeply and the ground is strewn with the corpses of her friends. They were lured out into the *last* burst of sunlight. It was a false, fatal sun. Why should this be any different?

She squirms to the top of the bush and feels the air. It is clear and heavy, the way sunlight should be. But the leaves, pasted with salt, are slippery to move on. She sinks back down. Let some other creature test the air. She licks and smooths her feathers, all of them profoundly ruffled by the storm. Now she sits still and lets the hunger, the awful searing hunger, eat away at her.

All told, it's been a very bad month. First, during the last full moon, her throat turned brown. True, it happens every year, but that doesn't mean she has to like it. For one thing it means that her little bird scam, her gimmick, her particular angle is played out and over with. All summer, while other songbirds competed brutally for food, swooping, diving, digging, clawing, even killing, she simply sat in this little shadbush with her mouth open. Bugs poured into it, thinking her bright orange throat was a flower. The thrush feasted. But now in September her throat has turned brown and unappealing and she has emerged from the bush starving, ready to hunt bugs like everyone else. Unfortunately, most of the bugs are gone. Without the foraging skills of her cousins like the scarlet tanager or the great kiskadee, the thrush has had to settle for what she can get. The easily accessible juniper trees are full of rough, powdery, blue-gray berries and she has been chomping them. The effect on her famous voice has been dreadful.

Some think the thrush's song the loveliest sound on earth. To Audubon, it came "in tumultuous eddies, enormously, as if to silence the very breathing of the unformed thought." In autumn, after a month's diet of juniper berries, it's a desperate rasp, the aging saloon singer's ten thousandth weary ballad after a lifetime of booze and cigarettes.

Nevertheless, God has today chosen her to announce the all-clear and peace on earth. Me? she asks. Are you sure? A washed-up chanteuse like me?

Yes you, comes the answer. She struggles to the highest branch on her shadbush. She reaches back for a note from her youth, when the woods were wet and green. The saloon is empty, it's 3 A.M. and there is her first love, looking divine after twenty years, sitting at a table in the back.

For you alone, baby.

The smoky sound of the thrush blankets the world. The storm is over. People, frogs, deer, fox, snakes, bugs, birds peer out of their shelters. Hearts beat again. *Macedonia*, sings the bird. *Sweet gone Macedonia Macedonia Macedonia.*

From a dark house on the bay, Ferron Bell and Ralph Cain blink into the sunlight of the new world. It is empty, clean and full of promise. There may never be another war, another wasted life, another regret, another tear. Blank. Scrubbed. New.

Whoooosh! A foot from their faces, the new world fills with the first event, a rhapsody of black and yellow. A nation of monarch butterflies flutters up in an instant, blocking out the sky. The delicate little pieces of God-silk have survived! Ferron Bell's heart floods with happiness. Always they have mystified and thrilled him, every autumn traveling three thousand miles to the same cliffside in Mexico, riding the wild winds and sucking their meals from the waxy seaside goldenrod.

Godspeed, clever beautiful little things! The birds will never touch you, disguised as you are like your cousins, the foul-tasting Viceroys. No wind, today has shown, can destroy you. Back into the sunny south wind, all ten thousand of you, more inexorable in your delicacy than all of Hitler's armies!

Ralph and Ferron step out into the new world. Bell is in the Wrigley estate of his youth, crawling after his father the gardener through great flowering bushes. Cain is in the Amazon in the dead of night, the apex of his greatest adventure. Any weariness in their hearts, spiritual or otherwise, is absorbed by the new world. Their hearts are thumping wet new muscles. It is Day One and they are naked babies. The storm is over.

Tomorrow, on Day Two, the cautious ones will return. The boats will dock and worried homeowners will pour off them. The new world will be a day old, and there will be a thin film of dirt and corruption over it. At first it will be imperceptible, barely changing the brand new colors, the bright blues, the deep wet greens. Then, as lies are told, as promises are broken, as complaints are made at the liquor store, as funerals are held for young men, the film will thicken, and darken the world.

But not today!

Around their heads the monarchs flutter and dance. The warmth of the sun comes to the men through the yellow wings, like a huge shifting parasol. They suck clean air in through their noses. The China blue veins that run through their lungs carry rich luminous blood. The pink soft cavities expand.

Had things turned out differently, of course, these very lungs might have filled with green water and burst, their edges finally turning rancid and black.

Why didn't they?

The United States National Weather Service, the most advanced meteorological organization ever to favor the world with its forecasts, gets its information from orbiting satellites, lunar bounces, infrared photographs, radar readings, and dozens of other intricate means. They have no more explanation for Hurricane Gloria than you do.

Oh it's clear, in retrospect, what happened. The storm grazed the coast of New Jersey and caromed off at a queer angle. Stretched out by the friction of dry land, the eye widened to a twenty-mile diameter, and shifted its axis. By the time it reached Fire Island it was lurching to the northeast and the feared eastern edge of the storm passed harmlessly out to sea.

The island was hit, but only by the storm's western edge, where the northerly movement of the storm and the southerly movement of the wind cancel each other out. Yes, houses were crushed, roofs flung off, walkways ripped up, trees blown away. But it could have been worse. Moving across the island at high speed, the weakened system had little time to rouse the sluggish low tide into the kind of destruction it might have. Gloria, billed as the greatest storm of the twentieth century, was something less than that. On Fire Island, it was no worse than a dozen other fierce hurricanes since the hurricane of '38—a nightmare, but not the Apocalypse. It disappeared whimpering several hours later off the coast of Newfoundland, a mild irritant to fishermen trying to get their nets up.

But why?

Why did the storm graze New Jersey? Why did New Jersey send it careening off at one angle and not another? Has the new construction boom in Atlantic City, all the landfills and the skyscrapers, altered the wind patterns? Does that mean that legalized gambling, which caused the building boom, saved Fire Island?

Martin Quartararo could have cared less. He was alive, the world was brand new and he meant to romp through it. He bounded out of his bayside cottage. The streets were empty. Was he the only one left on the island, the only one left alive, or what? He lit a joint and looked around. The marsh grass trembled in a mild west wind. The bay was turquoise and agitated. The wooden walkway was littered with shingles.

Something was different; not just the litter, or the vibrant colors, or the scrubbed molecules of the air. The landscape had changed somehow. He drew again on the reefer and again his eyes swept the horizon. Something was missing. That was the change. Something that had been there before was gone.

The Belvedere! He felt like he'd been kicked in the groin. The bell tower of the decadent old dinosaur of a hotel was gone. The wind had snapped it off like a twig.

Martin plunged into gloom. Gone was the elation and the sheer relief of surviving the storm. In its place was a kind of . . . mourning. The Belvedere was more than a baroque wreck of a hotel. It was a symbol of something beautiful and ridiculous and old and free. Just a few days ago, as Martin sipped cappuccino on the patio, people had gathered beneath the bell tower to observe some sort of strange bird, perched motionless for hours. It was the sort of thing that happened in the little hotel.

Wayne Duclos. The very subject of wreckage brings the name floating into Martin Quartararo's head. When the police had gone door-to-door the night before, they asked Martin if he had AIDS, too. Snide bastards! But that must have meant that an AIDS victim was sticking around, probably plucky little Wayne right down the street. Probably all alone too, since Jacques didn't come out till weekends. Martin drew on his reefer one last time, stubbed it out, and put the roach in the pocket of his blue-jean jacket. Kicking shingles out of the way, he moved up the walkway to Wayne's.

AIDS was not something Martin was comfortable thinking about. Too many of his friends had grown morbid over the subject. Granted, the daily funerals were a sobering thing. But that didn't mean that life itself had to turn into a funeral. On the contrary, it meant that you had to dance faster and turn up the volume higher just to stay even. If the black-hooded dude with the scythe was competing for your audience's attention, that just meant that the sequins on your gown better sparkle that much brighter, honey.

He turned onto the wooden ramp leading to Wayne's place. There was the new shed, with the washing machine that Jacques had installed in a desperate attempt to keep Wayne's laundry business alive until the little guy got better. That was devotion, to say nothing of self-deception! Wayne would never be able to do another stitch of work in his life. Nevertheless, Jacques had shelled out for the machine and spent half his vacation time washing other people's underwear. The rich hairdresser now almost looked like the victim himself, worn thin from pouring his energy and his money into his dying lover.

It was inspirational but it was also, thought Martin, another way for love to screw you. Jacques was a nurse chained to an invalid, and only death would turn him loose.

Martin wondered if there was anyone who'd do that for him. Well, certainly Cecil. Hell, *he* was willing to chuck his whole military career for love! And of course there was Bill, the older man from New Orleans in the gray dodge. Bill's devotion was as constant as the stars. Yes, in a catastrophe Martin would be well taken care of. But what about the other way around, he thought, knocking at Wayne's door. Is there anyone *I'd* sacrifice myself for? Anyone whose pills I'd buy, whose intravenous feedings I'd take care of, whose vomit I'd mop up, whose underwear I'd scrub?

Not particularly.

"I'll be devastated if anything happens to you," the army officer had said. But was there anyone Martin would be devastated to lose?

No, there wasn't. Not that Martin had anything against the

idea of commitment. For some people it was fine. But Martin would no sooner get into a relationship when his eye would be caught by someone younger and more interesting, someone that he truly *had* to have. Soon it became like an itch that simply had to be scratched . . . so Martin scratched it.

No one understood that. Or at least they claimed they didn't. Privately, they understood it perfectly, Martin suspected. The men who were settled into "mature," growing relationships had done just that, settled. They had made a bargain for their old age; they had traded excitement for security. If those people really faced the truth, Martin felt, they would agree with him that relationships, like evening gowns, wear out.

There was clear sunshine on his back now, but the wind was still shredding out of the west, making it colder. Wayne wasn't answering the knock. Martin pushed the door open. There was the little man lying on the couch with his eyes closed. Uh oh, thought Martin . . . trouble. He rushed to the sleeping form and started nudging, pushing, cajoling him. No response. The sleep was deep, if that's what it was.

Finally, mercifully, gloriously, Wayne opened an eye. "Frere Louis?" he asked softly. He was mistaking Martin for a priest from his childhood.

"It's Martin, Wayne. From down the walkway."

Wayne was coming out of a beautiful dream. While the hurricane rocked his cottage, he had been in a serene place, like the cable underneath the bay. The dream was of the time he and Jacques had traveled to Quebec, their ancestral home, in the dead of winter. It had been a succession of clear frozen days, bluer than blue skies meeting diamond white ice at the horizon. Forever after when Wayne heard the Canadian national anthem, the line about "the True North, strong and free," made sense to him. The truth is in the cold and the colors. It is so cold that nothing lives and the beauty is in purely lifeless things, like the sun and the etherized sky and the ice.

Maybe death would have this kind of beauty.

Though he didn't know it, Wayne had undergone a kind of

death since Hurricane Gloria started moving across the water from Africa. In that time a tumor the size of an egg had formed in his brain. It was the cause of the paralysis and sluggishness he had recently complained of. It was the latest assault on his immune system and this time it came from a bacterial spore found in cat urine. He must have been sitting too near somebody's litter box. You have to watch that kind of thing when you have AIDS. You can't live that fast and wide.

Martin cradled Wayne's head, unaware of its dark cargo.

"Is the storm over?" Wayne asked.

"Yes."

"Are we still alive, or are we in heaven?"

"If this was heaven, honey, what would *I* be doing here?" said Martin Quartararo.

This got a laugh out of the sick man.

"You want to go for a walk?" Martin asked.

Nodding feebly, Wayne propped himself up on the side of the bed. His clothes were still damp, and Martin changed them, trying not to register his horror at the gross scarlet lesions that studded the sick man's body. When Wayne was dressed and on his feet, they tottered out the door together, arms linked like ninety-year-old lovers.

The air was shimmering clean and the light was soft and diffuse. The wind was almost spent, a few wild straggling zephyrs kicking up and dying away. The men moved east, along the walkway beside the ocean.

The storm had reorganized everything. In the placid late afternoon were the frightening proofs of its power. Whole sections of walkway had been lifted and twisted and discarded, like orange peels. Here and there a house was without a roof, and a little farther on was the answer to the question "Where is it?" In someone else's yard, halved and upside down. It was as if a huge spoiled child had thrown a tantrum in a nursery. Walking through it, the two men felt the fragility of their own bones. The spooky thing was the tranquility of the weather. Nowhere in the air was there a hint of the struggle the houses made to keep their roofs, or of the violence with which the struggle had been lost. It had turned into a gorgeous day.

Martin and Wayne mounted the steps that led over the dunes to the ocean. The step unit wobbled, having been ripped out of its trench. The dune had been gouged and half-eaten by the sea. But the sea itself, having eaten, was never healthier. As far as the men could see, it rolled in in white, creamy folds. Its fury had not even begun to subside. It ranged and frothed wildly across the horizon, barely contained. The lions had been caged for now, but that didn't prevent them from pacing and snarling and showing you what you just missed.

The smell off the water was intoxicating. The whole Atlantic Ocean, from the Azores to Asbury Park, had been rearranged, the bottom churned and sucked up to the top and back again. Davy Jones's locker had been reamed out, and the smells they were getting were things never intended for nostrils, ossified pink-aqua things. Both men sucked in the queer scrubbed air, Wayne force-feeding it into his bum lungs, and they surveyed the whole 360 degrees of horizon.

Before them was the unruly sea, beside them the constant Sunken Forest, behind them the blurred green bay, and behind that, shorn now of its tallest trees, the purple landmass of Long Island. To their left was the Eastern Kingdom of Fire Island. First their own broken toy town, Cherry Grove, and way beyond it the opulent wilderness of Fire Island Pines. In between the two was the Meatrack. Rugged and pristine now, its tousled junipers and low bearberries looked every inch what they were—in nature's design, a transitional carpet from sea to land. But with the shadow of death still over one of them, the two men could not stand there without acknowledging what they knew.

The Meatrack was the Incubator of Death. This was where the Plague had spread. Here was where men in leather lurked for a week at a time, screwing anything that moved. Here was where diagnosed AIDS patients, bitter about their bad luck, had one last kiss-the-boys-goodbye fling and spread the bad luck around a little. The bastards! thought Martin. The sheer starburst of creativity that was the Eastern Kingdom lay in morbid ruin, and all because a handful of selfish men couldn't keep their cocks in their pants.

Martin pulled back a little on that thought. Who was he to talk? Besides, it was a little shortsighted to blame promiscuity for the death of the Eastern Kingdom. Promiscuity was the whole *point* of the Eastern Kingdom. The traditional lanes of family life weren't open to you, so instead of moping around and being ashamed about it, as you had done for centuries, you chose the other route: love for its own sake, not to muck up the world with more squealing babies. You loved madly, as if tomorrow would never come, and you bled every moment dry of its sensual possibilities. That's what those moments were for!

Yes, people would cry that the pleasure-seeking gays had been the moth too near the flame, and now they were paying the price. But that's what moths *did*, for Christ's sake. If you weren't going to play around with the flame, why even be a moth? Never was this clearer than now, with life everywhere hanging by a gossamer thread, with the muffled funeral drums deafening you. Life was to be lived!

This was the very notion that seemed to so unnerve the straights, thought Martin Quartararo. They could find a million reasons to stay home from the party that was life. They were planning something for the future, or they were getting over something from the past. They found things "inappropriate," they were "exhausted," they were a little "wary" of certain things. It was all a pile of crap, of feeble excuses for not opening up all your cylinders, incoming and outgoing, and saying YES!

Because the gays could say *yes*, the straights envied them and hated them and were willing to let them die.

Let them die. Yes, it was an extreme accusation, but it was time to make it. Martin looked over to Wayne as the gaunt, angelic man watched the sea.

But why? thought Martin. Why instead couldn't the straights just join the party, open those cylinders and say YES! themselves? It often reminded him of the old fable about the ant and the grasshopper. The grasshopper danced in the sunlight while the ants hauled huge crumbs into their holes for the winter. Naturally, the ants resented the grasshoppers, especially when they stuck their big green heads in with the first frost, begging for food and shelter. But the fable, Martin recalls, ended happily with a compromise. The way Disney handled the film version, the last frame had the grasshopper playing the fiddle by the ants' fireplace. In return for sustenance, the grasshopper gave the ants music to dance to. That much corresponded to human beings; didn't gay, rapacious Cole Porter, for instance, provide the music for millions of straight courtships?

Where the stories didn't match up, though, was right now, at this moment in history. Right now, the way to let the grasshopper into the hole was to find a cure for this horrific disease. At the moment, gaunt pockmarked grasshoppers were pleading at the door, and the ants were saying, "Keep walking."

But these were thoughts for another day. There was no space for bitterness on this perch above the wild ocean, and in this moment, delivered by the hand of God from death, and being shown His most sublime beauty.

God? Where was that quaint notion coming from? Maybe the old Biblical homestead in New Orleans was staying with Martin longer than he cared to acknowledge. But if there was a God, He surely had a hand in this; the sky over their head, brightening and reddening with the dusk, was like some raw, rich mineral. It bathed all of the Eastern Kingdom with its light in a benediction, even the Meatrack. It inflamed Martin's most romantic visions of his tribe and his adopted homeland. Even empty and storm-tossed, the place glowed with energy. If it was to inspire deep thoughts today, let them not be sour and regretful. Let them not have to do with the twisted, inglorious circumstances of the Kingdom's death, thought Martin, but of the vibrancy of its life.

Let the story be told one day like the story of the tribes of Israel in the black dusty books on his father's shelf; how once a tribe of men sang show tunes in the Valley of the Shadow of

Death. How they declared themselves, and stuck by it through humiliation, pain, and despair, on through to freedom. And finally, how they stood tall at the gates of heaven.

Martin had seen thirty-year-old men watch with courage and dignity as their mates were lowered into the ground. He had seen men agree to die publicly, to educate the public about the disease. These were men for all the human race to be proud of. It was almost enough, thought Martin Quartararo, to inspire you to commit yourself to a relationship.

Almost.

Wayne was turning up his collar now against the chill coming off the water.

"Want to head back, Wayne?"

"Think I'll stay awhile."

Martin had to go. He had just had a thought that led to a stab of guilt. Hercules the Doberman still hadn't been out. The poor thing hadn't taken a shit in a million years.

"Want my jacket?"

"No thanks, Martin."

The ravaged body was alert to infections lurking in the petals of a flower. In the scrubbed air of the new world it found none, and greedily sucked it in.

"Well, don't overdo it."

"I won't. Thanks, Martin."

Martin smiled and moved away down the path, leaving the sick man alone by the ocean.

T H I R T E E N

A short distance away, the twelve-point Buck's Doe lay hiding in a bower of leaves. Like the thrush, she refused to believe that the hell out of the sky was over with. The first sunlight had been false. Maybe this was, too.

Now, with even this new sun beginning to set and the sky growing darker, she was beginning to stir. She was hungry. She had galloped a full five miles out of the forest after the shock of watching the Holly tree die. That alone would have been enough to give her an appetite. Then the monstrous wind had picked up again and forced her into this little gully of bayberry. Now, two hours later, she was still here and she was starving.

There were sounds all around her. The rest of the animal kingdom was trusting the clear sky. If the birds could come out, she began to think, so can I. She got to her feet and walked on shaking legs to a beach plum bush. She stripped its fat berries, the few the storm had not shaken loose. They were good, as they always were just before mating time, but there was another taste that intrigued her even more. It was salt. The wind had whipped it off the ocean and pasted it everywhere.

She followed the path of the bushes along the sloping swale, stripping each branch as she went. Her eyes glistened. The taste made her heart pound. She licked a carpet of sourdough leaves, caked with the stuff. Her eyes widened and her rear end moistened and tightened. It made her want the Buck inside her.

She circled the edge of the Eastern Kingdom, sidestepping shorn branches, the carnage of the storm, still following the path of salt-drenched bushes. Each feast of leaves was richer than the one before it. And now, as she approached the ocean dunes, she felt the spray off the water. Even on an ordinary day it is powerful and constant. Today it was so thick the Doe could see it. She stood there and ate the air.

It made her want more.

She knew where to get it. Slurping salt as she went, she retraced her steps, moving back toward the bay. Now she found herself beside a small, still cove, just north of the thicket where she had passed the storm. Here, at water's edge, fruitless nude stalks floated stupidly, dominated by the tide. She took a mouthful and sucked. The salt sent the blood squirting into her head. But this stuff, which bathed in water only once a month, at the full moon tide, was only a tease, an hors d'oeuvre. Nearby was the feast.

She waded out into the dense, low marshgrass. Now she was where she wanted to be, in nature's opium den. Here the soak was daily, and the weeds were white with salt. *White* with it! Quivering, she chomped. The taste was pure and strong. The blood rushed into her sex organ. She sunk to her haunches in the muck and ripped off a mouthful of stalks, and sucked them dry. She was wild with it now. More of this, more! She jammed her pointed face into the cloudy water and pulled another mouthful of stalk into the air, its black bloated roots dripping down her chest. She ate it whole. More, more, more! Her heart raced. She was blind with the taste now. She rolled in the algae-infested muck, clouding the water. More, more, more! She was breathing fast and hard and staring up at the blue sky. Her rear end swam and twitched in the dense brown water, and the salt pushed, rushed, exploded the blood through her body so fast her eyelids began to flutter wildly, and great heaving sounds roared out of her. More more, more!

Then, at the brain-splitting height of it, she was through. Suddenly, she'd had enough. She was exhausted. She didn't want any more. She couldn't take any more. She couldn't *bear* any more. The twitching stopped. Her heartbeat began to slow down . . . to normal, then past it. Within minutes she was falling asleep heavily in the muck.

But one eye wouldn't close. She couldn't quite sleep, because a new craving was forming. Not for salt, for something else . . . something she wanted, now needed more than she ever needed salt.

Water.

Just . . . water. She needed a drink of fresh water, desperately. Her throat felt like the high dirt ridges of the forest after the summer had dried them out. Parched. Cracked. Bone dry. In another second she would flake into dust. She had to have water. NOW.

She rolled and rocked herself out of the mud, which had begun to cake around her. She got to her haunches and then to her feet, and bulled her way out of the muck back to land.

She looked around. Where would she go? Back home in the Sunken Forest, she knew where to find water. After a rain it floated for weeks like a lens over the salt-water bogs. Here, on the edge of the place where Men live, she didn't know where to begin looking.

But she needed water more than she feared danger, more even than she wanted the Buck. There was a fire in her mouth. Boldly, the Doe stepped into the Eastern Kingdom. She wasn't the first one, deer or human, to think that somewhere among these strange, sleek houses, somewhere, surely, she would find a drink.

The sun, beginning its languid plummet into the bay, blasted a tunnel of light through the dense, lush little walkways of the Western Kingdom. The most ordinary trees, the laziest drooping junipers, had been brought stiffly to attention by the events of the day. In the late light they were vital and muscular, dark liquid green edged with gold. The air was as sweet as lavender.

The Bahamas Swallow was having her first moment of grace in this strange place, so she chose it to make her first serious exploration.

Cautiously, she took to the air, her first flight since the wild thousand-mile journey in the eye of the storm. Like all other creatures, she mistrusted the sunlight, but she had no choice. Chances had to be taken if she was to survive. Already, she could sense that this place had no food for her—now, or anytime. And she knew that things would get worse before they got better. Her only hope was to get south, even as far back as this morning, when she had passed over places where bugs still filled the air. But even to get *that* far required sustenance, and the bird had no idea where to find it. Usually at this time of day she had luck with the cluster of bugs that hovered over rotting coconuts. Not here.

She crested the dune, and there was the sea she had fought for days to stay above. It looked no less threatening now. The surf was roiling and frothing.

And at the edge of that surf was another familiar sight—or at least what passed for familiar in this utterly strange place. Earlier in the day, just after her arrival, she had been frightened by a huge, brown, four-legged, horned creature poking through the bed of seaweed where she lay. Now, here in the foaming sea, were more of the four-legged creatures, without horns but just as big.

These were Dana Wallace's racehorses and they were prancing unbridled through the surf, romping like wild things. Free of fences and ropes, and of the land itself, they were mythical creatures, dancing in the ocean. They looked as if they might swim or even fly away.

It was getting onto high tide, and the sea itself was finally getting its chance to invade the land. A long carpet of white foam was spreading across Wallace's empire. Miraculously, the little beachcomber's shack was intact, surrounded, almost buoyed by the white water. The entire spectacle, merely strange to the Swallow, would to the human eye have been extraordinary—a vision out of a child's fairy tale.

One man observed it, but without innocence or joy . . . without even curiosity. Dana Wallace was so stone-still it took the bird a long time to make him out—the first human in this new place, the first human she had ever seen, in fact, whose skin was not black.

He stood on the long ramp leading up to his manorhouse, gazing on his sodden holdings. The look in his eyes would not have been a familiar one, even to those who knew him well. Truthfully, the look on Dana Wallace's face would not have been familiar to anyone at all, because it was not of this life.

Before him was his empire, submerged and battered, but more or less intact. When the water went down in the morning, there would be all the debris of hell to clean up. But the buildings still stood: the main house, the makeshift barn by the corral, and the beloved symbol of his soul, the beachcomber's shack. More important than nails and lumber, his animals had survived. His horses romped in the surf right before his eyes, and his faithful black Labs sat at his feet. Like the other survivors, maybe more than any of them, Dana Wallace had put big stakes on the table and won. Or at least not lost.

Why was there no elation, relief, serenity, or even weariness in his eyes?

The price that Dana Wallace paid for his seat in the sky casino was higher than he had expected. He had expected to pay physically and emotionally, and he had indeed done that. Bruised and cut and exhausted, he had been led through terror and back again. But he had been given an extra, special treatment, one reserved for those who didn't show the storm the courtesy and respect of cowering inland and fortifying themselves, reserved for those who showed no fear.

In the case of Dana Wallace, it was more of a Lifetime Achievement Award, in recognition of a long career of showing no fear, no respect for limits, no desire for comfort. It was an award presented without warm applause from a black-tie audience, and he was compelled to accept it utterly alone. The citation read like this:

Your friends are dead, or digging in against old age, ensconced in Major Medical Plans.

You won't even fill out the forms.

They're nestled into comfortable, secure relationships, but you won't settle for some half-baked passion; you want someone that will rattle your bones and be worthy of the kind of love songs your old golden throat longs to croon, having been so long silent. So you choose someone half your age, someone open to all of life's possibilities, including you, and when she moves on to explore still other possibilities, you weep tears from your surprised eyes and expect us to feel sorry for you.

When it comes to living arrangements, you camp out here by the edge of the sea, accepting no less of a smell in your leathery old nose than the pure brine, no less of a taste than a fresh thumping bluefish. You won't accept the very comfortable accommodations America offers its senior citizens, with its full schedule of social activities, its nutritional planning, its central heating. No, you insist on sticking around out here all by yourself and freezing your ancient butt off listening to the cry of a loon.

And when this nature that you love so much rears

up to smack you with all its fury, and give you the lesson you deserve, when men half your age and twice as smart quake with terror and flee inland, you decide to sit here and watch it through a picture window. So what did you expect?

Yes, the Award is yours, but it's not an award that gets put in your hand. Instead, this is how the presentation is made:

God picks you up in *His* hand and holds you out over the edge of life for a solid hour. It doesn't sound like a long time, but after the first ten minutes, after you've screamed and struggled and writhed yourself into exhaustion, then comes the prize, the thing that this Award is all about. Every second, as you hear it and feel it, a ferocious wind rattles your very soul. Every second, as you watch it, the ocean whose power you thought you knew shows you power you never dreamed of, boils up in your face, and threatens to swallow you and pulverize you and drop your sodden old body twenty fathoms to the bottom. So with death pounding and braying at the door *every second*, feeling that every second may be your last, you adjust to that kind of terror the only way you can. You pass beyond it to another place.

You release your fear of death and injury, you say good-bye to sunny days and music and frozen margaritas and laughter and kissing, you hurl your bitter accusations at the ones who hurt you in love and you apologize to the ones who were hurt by you, you whisper good-bye to your only son, you tell your dead wife and your father to make it a table for three in heaven, you wring every last tear and regret out of your heart and after all this you are left with . . . nothing.

Nothing.

And then you are given your life back again.

But you are so utterly blanched and drained that you come back to the living with . . . nothing. You've had a vision of the other side, and it has altered you, and you return a stranger. Men who have known you all their lives will barely recognize you. Nor do you have any interest in them, or in anything else remotely human.

Congratulations.

The Award Winner moved down the wooden ramp into the white water, which spumed around his ankles. He registered without emotion the fact of his dancing racehorses, lit up copper by the low sun. He waded out to the beachcomber's shack and looked blankly at the foam-swathed thing, as if studying it. He surveyed its bleached timbers, wondering without feelings how it had survived.

What happened next, which was Dana Wallace's concluding experience of Hurricane Gloria, was an answer to people who don't think there is a God, one with a sense of humor, and with an instinct for theatre that humbles Ibsen and Shakespeare.

The storm, which was gone, which now skittered harmlessly over the open Atlantic on its way to oblivion, pulled behind it shreds and tatters of its former self. The air of the evening was erratic, still punctuated by a curving little puff out of nowhere. Such a puff came . . . and destroyed Dana Wallace's beachcomber's shack. Just knocked it over, like the last playful swipe of the lion's tail that breaks your neck.

He watched the timbers collapse into the white water, recognizing each one of them as they fell. He saw his most precious personal mementos disappear into the brine and get sucked out to sea on the ebb tide.

Gone.

The old Dana Wallace would at this point have howled and roared above the sound of the sea itself. The post-storm Wallace continued to stare at the soaked wreckage, as if even this were of only mild academic interest to him.

The Swallow was close enough now to study his face. Its pinkness intrigued her, and so did a certain gleaming, like a bright bauble. In the corner of the Award Winner's eye, lit by the last of the sun, moisture had collected into a salty globule of a tear, only one, and slid down his cheek into the sea.

The Swallow flew past him, up the dune to his battered ranch house. The windows were in shards on the floor, so nothing prevented the bird from flying into the home of Dana Wallace and making the discovery that saved her life. There, on a kitchen counter littered with broken glass, was Wallace's cocktail mess. Half-squished limes lay in a sticky bed of sodden peanuts, salt, and cheap tequila. Clustered above the mess, reveling in it, was a delirious convention of flies and other assorted bugs. In another minute they would all be heading down the gullet of the big white bird.

F   O   U   R   T   E   E   N

Where was she?

The last hour of Gloria had totally disrupted the Buck's hunt for the Doe. First it forced him into a thicket of willows by the bay. Then it ripped away half the trees, their shallow pancake roots no match for the wind. The Buck found himself exposed, unable to shift his position lest he himself be blown away. So for an endless hour he had simply been battered. Now he was underway again in the placid dusk, but the wind had obliterated the scent of the Doe. Deer-nerves wrung dry, he headed wearily east.

Though the evening air was peaceful, he was still hearing that wind, as he would for days and nights to come. But as his hoofs found the wooden walkway of Fire Island Pines, a new sound broke through to him. It was a kind of low whine . . . a

———

228

deer sound, very much like the sound of his Doe. It could have been another doe—his chestnut ears had been so storm-battered he couldn't tell—but his every instinct told him to locate the sound and find out. This skill the wind had not diminished; deer have a radar for each other's sounds almost as infallible as the birds'. Without it (and its precision for establishing and communicating feeding ranges) the race would be long dead.

The Buck honed in on the sound, which took him circuitously through half the southwestern quadrant of the community, into several sassafras bogs, and finally out onto a wide space beside one of the structures of men. Obviously the open space was also the work of men, since it was flat and smooth and hard, nothing like the rough forest floor or the shifting, soft beach. And in the middle of that flat space was a hole with blue water.

This was a swimming pool deck and flailing away inside of it, splashing through the dusk-darkening water, was his Doe. Her eyes were wide with terror.

Many pools dot the Eastern Kingdom and it wasn't unusual for fawns to blunder into them. By the time anyone found them, it was usually too late. Swimming is bred into deer, but climbing pool ladders is not. The fawns simply swam back and forth until they were exhausted, and then sank.

But the Doe was not an innocent fawn, nor had she tumbled into the ornate pool by accident; she was driven in by the demon called salt. When she finally found her watering hole, this tile-by-tile replica of the private bath of a Roman emperor, she sank to her haunches and started slurping. In her enthusiasm she lost her balance. By the time the Buck found her, she had already been paddling for an hour.

Her eyes widened at the Buck as she swam and reswam her oval pattern, still looking for a way out. The Buck kept pace with her on the turquoise pool deck, stumbling over plants, urns, and stereo speakers. As it got darker they moved more slowly, she exhausted, he bruised and not keeping up. By the time the sky was the dark blue between day and night, she was treading water and he could do nothing but lie on his side on the deck . . .

breathing hard, wailing, and watching her. The light remained long enough so that he could see her eyes as they disappeared under the water.

The Ivan Bekoff that led three young marauders through the Eastern Kingdom was a changed man. Gone was the recluse who had holed up in a glen for twenty years. His step was light and his bearded face was fierce, proud, and radiant. He looked like nothing so much as the head of a great Scottish clan, leading his strapping sons down from the Highlands.

In fact these were Mitchell the houseboy, Timothy the chauffeur, and the terrified young man they had all pulled in from the storm-wracked walkway.

When they all closed their door against the last winds of Gloria, Ivan was losing a battle with his own bitterness. He had brought the young men through the long dark night and the nightmarish day . . . for what? Where was the gratitude for his sacrifices, past and present?

Nowhere. They simply cared about nothing but their own lovely asses, which they deeply feared were about to be blown into orbit by Hurricane Gloria. To the extent that Ivan could do something about that, they tolerated his dowdiness and his eccentricities. Apart from that, they had only this to say about his dour outlook: *"Get over it!"*

Get over it, indeed. By the time Gloria started to rock the bungalow, Ivan had secluded himself in its tiny kitchen. He was looking out for himself and didn't care if the rest of them got blown into the bay. But the storm's monstrous second half made a chemical change in Ivan Bekoff. It began by blasting out a window and slamming him against the very door he had just closed behind him, knocking him unconscious.

When he came to, he was floating in a pool of cold water, broken glass, and blood. The sounds of his young companions, still blubbering hysterically, reached him through the splintered door, and through his reeling, hazy brain. Instinctively, he rushed back in to minister to them again, this time even more intensely; even—and this is what shocked him—to the point of not caring about his own safety. As the storm mounted, keening dreadfully, pounding the tiny cottage relentlessly, he was literally standing over them, shielding them. That's when he knew what was going on.

This was his blood.

He was never going to reproduce and these were his sons. It was as simple as that. So he would protect them with his life. He would teach them, he would chastise them, he would boast of them to his friends. And if they were a little stupid and ungrateful . . . well, children sometimes are.

No, it wasn't like most families. In this family there were many fathers and many sons. Ivan was an elder of a tribe whose painful trials and deep gouging wars required the collective wisdom of all its members, from the young braves to the old queens. Ivan sat in the sacred circle of the council of the gay tribe with as much authority as anyone. Many were the honored feathers on his headdress.

True, he still thought there were better ways to spend an hour than cooing over cocktails about fabrics and musical comedy. True, he still mourned the passing of the haunted poets who had settled this kingdom, and he had trouble worshipping the disco queens who had taken their place. But like all wise parents, Ivan had lessons to learn from his sons. They had knowledge to trade. They could teach him to sip a daiquiri on a pool deck for the sheer light emptiness of the moment. He could learn to socialize again. For what other reason had he been spared by the worst storm of the twentieth century? Why had the wind and the sea been held back?

So that Ivan Bekoff could rejoin the human race.

The Grecian nights when a thousand men made love under the moon were gone forever, with the spread of the deadly disease. Ivan's youth was gone, too. Now was now, this was life, and a precious life it was, that an ocean or a virus could snuff in an instant.

*   *   *

Kreeeeeeeeeeeeeeee! An agonized wail came at the men through the bushes. What sound of distress pierced the new world? Surely nothing that the storm-hardened heros could not quiet. Intrepid Ivan cut through the brush, the leaves slapping his young lieutenants as they followed close behind.

Their first reaction, on seeing the pool, was bitterness. Whose was it? Why had they never been invited to a party here? Then, in the darkness, Calvin Klein's houseboy spotted the prone Buck. The men followed its doleful eyes to the pool, and made out the form of the Doe under the water. They got the sad picture right away. All five creatures, man, boys, and Buck, were hushed in mourning. All of nature in fact—the faint last rustle of the wind, the new sporadic bursts of birdsong—went silent in the presence of death.

Then the Klein houseboy gave a yelp. He saw something. A *bubble!*

"Get in there!!" screamed Ivan, shoving all three of them into the water. They dove under, scilliated down, and surrounded the motionless Doe. They couldn't budge her. They all had health-club muscles but rarely used them except to ripple them for a lover.

"Lift her up!" They could hear Ivan screaming through water level. With the last of their breath they heaved the brown sodden carcass off the pool floor. Once in motion, it floated to the surface with nudging and guidance from the young men. As they maneuvered it to poolside, Ivan wrestled onshore with the plastic rope that adorned the pool's phony life preservers: exact replicas of the *SS Normandie*'s, hollow and worthless.

A rope was a rope, though. Ivan tossed it in the water, and the young men made a crude harness for the Doe and climbed ashore. Then they all hauled away. Aaaaagh! No! Ivan's back was out! It always happened at the worst possible time! He lurched away in agony as the young men dragged the Doe onto the pool deck. By the time he straightened up, they had her laid out, soaking the concrete. The Buck sniffed around her rear end.

232

The others stood there. Nobody knew anything about artificial respiration, or how it applied to animals. Minutes passed and the sky grew very dark, with no more signs of life from the Doe. The Buck stared at her. The men looked nervously to each other. Obviously, the thing was dead. Was the Buck going to stand around stupidly over it forever, as it decayed?

His lower back in profound spasm, Ivan sank down on an urn. No one who's never had this kind of pain understood it, certainly not the three Adonises standing over him. He looked bitterly at the Klein houseboy, so beautiful, so sure of himself.

"She's breathing," said the boy.

Ivan's head snapped around. The others rushed to the Doe's side. It was true! The brown ribs were faintly rising and falling with breath! Ivan leapt to his feet, ignoring the pain he knew would crucify him in the morning. The four men began jumping up and down with their arms around each other, cheering and screaming. Beside them the Buck reared and snorted. Now, yesterday's party that had been so rudely interrupted by the dark clouds of death could reconvene. The liquor cabinet of their absent host was quickly located. So was the sound system. Hooked up to an emergency generator by Timothy the chauffeur, it was cranked up to an almost-unendurable level with the original cast album of *Kiss Me Kate*. The Doe's breathing became more regular still and she lifted her head to watch. Extraordinarily complex cocktails were mixed, and the dancing began—wild dancing, pagan, undisciplined things unimagined by Cole Porter when he wrote the music. The great party era of Fire Island Pines was for an instant rekindled and it would burn through the darkness for hours and hours. In the years of gestation, it had gone deeper. It was a tribal celebration. It was a blood ceremony.

After watching them awhile, the Buck guided his Doe shakily to her feet and the two of them disappeared into the deep woods.

From a distant hill, Ferron Bell heard the hubbub but was not attracted by it. The Gay Nation's Mamie Fisk and Krishna all-rolled-into-one was off on his first walk in the new world.

The air in his cottage after the storm had grown lousy. First Ralph Cain had run off worrying about his real estate. Then the phone had begun to ring—neighbors, wondering how their deck furniture had made out. One idiot wanted Bell to check on his collection of antique Christmas tree ornaments.

Christmas tree ornaments! In a hurricane! For Ferron, still in a monastic mode, the petty vibrations were undermining the whole event. He took off. Now he was alone in the dying light and the artist's eye was feasting even on the faint colors. The water-blues and the tree-greens and the sun-reds rushed into his soul with sexual urgency.

He needed all the rebirth he could get. He was no longer a sleek young gay star in a loincloth, but a portly middle-aged man. Like many artists who came to New York with great ambition, he had adjusted himself to reality; his current project was making T-shirts for the Hayden Planetarium's celebration of Halley's comet, which was expected in the spring.

The only thing that would neither compromise itself nor grow old was the ocean he stared at. He descended twisted steps to the pink beach. A small wind eddied out of the west and stung him with sand. Rather than face it he headed east, and soon was beyond the boundaries of the Pines, and into the even more sparsely populated place called Water Island.

Once a favorite retreat of Teddy Roosevelt's, Water Island had remained a curious mix of the primitive and the elegant, resisting until the last the electrification of its old open-flame candelabra and little jewel-box kerosene lamps. Now the place was enjoying a renaissance and a rediscovery by people rich enough to keep it empty. On this day it was as utterly deserted as everywhere else. From its high, wide grainy beach, the white tide was on its way back out again.

Ferron headed for it, a perfect perch for ocean watching. When he got close, he saw that a carpet of dark objects littered the sand. Jellyfish. Or maybe shellfish. Or maybe some strange flotsam the storm had dredged up. He couldn't begin to remember all the weird things he'd found along the water-line after bad seas;

belaying pins, turn-of-the-century condoms, you name it. Half of it had turned up in his art, jutting out of canvases, giving them texture.

He got closer still and saw that the gulls were feeding on the stuff; probably fish after all. But who knew for sure? Those gulls would eat anything. It wasn't until he was right up on it that he saw the graveyard of birds. More like a battlefield, scattered with corpses. Most of them showed tangerine bellies to the sky.

He stopped cold. They were his soul-mates the American redstarts. These were the solitary warblers who collected in deep forests by the ocean and preferred death to captivity. Each spring, they shocked him with the beauty of their sad song. Through the storm, the image of their frailty had come to him and straightened out his priorities in a hurry.

He stared at them, lifeless and still, the savage gulls drooling and pecking them apart. Some were still alive, their chests ripped open, their hearts still beating, stopping one by one in the raw wind.

Enraged, Ferron began to race up and down the beach like a madman, trying to chase the gulls away. No sooner would he crouch to minister to a broken songbird, than the cackling gulls would converge on another, a few feet away. So Ferron would run over there, like a living scarecrow, and the same thing would happen again. Life was draining away faster than he could stop it. Finally exhausted, he could do nothing but collapse in a heap and watch the carnage proceed to its end.

For a while he let the roaring ocean numb his thoughts and kill his pain. When it was over, and the last braying, sated gull had careened away, he pieced together the story in his mind. The day before, a few hundred of them had taken off for their winter homes. Sensing the urgency of time, they had headed out over the water; a shortcut, rather than hug the coastline that veered to the southwest. It was a disastrous gamble. The storm had picked up speed over the cold night water, and it met the birds out over the ocean. Had they been over land, the redstarts might have plopped down and holed up somewhere. Had it been a hundred years ago, with all manner of sailing ships still plowing the ocean, they might have settled on the wooden decks and ridden it out. Had they been big seacruisers of birds, circumnavigators like the white storm petrels, they might even have descended and ridden the waves.

As it was, a big wind meeting a little bird over the water, it was no contest. Forward progress was impossible. They did not even have the good fortune, like the Bahamas Swallow, to be caught in the placid eye. The redstarts were trapped in the most brutal part of the maelstrom, and it took their life's energy to keep from being slapped down and buried in the water, or just ripped apart by the gyre itself. Many of them died in just those ways.

The "lucky" survivors pushed and scraped and fought, giving in to the death wind enough so as not to be broken in half resisting it, but not enough to be sucked into a great arching zephyr that was going nowhere but down. So the ones with the biggest hearts in their tangerine breasts made it back here where they started, and the reward for their fortitude was the last, worst part of the nightmare . . . to be picked apart, as they lay exhausted, by the cowardly gulls.

By nightfall Ferron Bell was a forlorn army bugler, simply standing among the dead. Long after the last heart stopped beating and the last light left the sky, he could not bring himself to leave. For all his spiritual training, he was clinging to a whimsy from childhood. As the stars became visible he imagined that each was the soul of a bird, and he would go nowhere until all the stars were out, and all the souls were accounted for.

Martin Quartararo had no vote to cast on the issue . . . which way he would take Hercules the Doberman on the beast's first walk in the newly scrubbed world. After the first order of business—relieving himself joyously for about fifteen minutes—Hercules decided they would go west. So west they went, the dog pulling the man like a stallion pulling a chariot.

The area west of Cherry Grove was new territory to Martin Quartararo. The Sunken Forest was frequented by naturalists and tourists, but Martin was neither of those. For him the place was just a name on a map and a kind of blank spot in nature, a meatrack with no meat.

Had Martin been even a fledgling naturalist, he would have known better than to bring the panting, hulking Hercules anywhere near the place. The rangers would have had a fit. The dog would throw the ecosystem utterly out of whack for hours after his departure; deer would gallop off, toads would bound into thorns, snakes would slither in mad circles. But of course in the chaos after the storm, all of this was academic.

Martin entered the dense woods with the dog, and the effect on both was instant. Hercules went silent, his eyes wide and glistening. Martin Quartararo almost fainted. The last of the sun had invaded the Sunken Forest like a theatrical spotlight. The place looked like a lit-up sculpture, the way the sea spray had, over the years, molded the contour of the forest roof to the sweep of the south wind. Mauve shadows suggested endless depth. It was the most beautiful spectacle the small man had ever seen in a lifetime of seeking beauty out. It was like the set of a Wagnerian opera of his youth, and Martin began to dance about in the near-darkness, like a wood-sprite.

The two creatures proceeded farther, the one dancing, the other sniffing. In the deep woods, the thick, twisted old trees with all their limbs and branches started to block out the setting sun, and it became almost impossible to see. It was Hercules who showed the way now, with luminous yellow eyes, leading them still farther into the forest. Miraculously, they were in a place that seemed to widen out again, and admit again the faint light of dusk. They were where the Hollies grow.

Hercules's snout went down, burrowing into the soft floor of the forest, into the black viscous muck of centuries. Quartararo watched him forage awhile, and his eyes began to pick out knob-like shapes in the darkness. They were mushrooms. Martin picked one up and chomped it, then another. Tasty, he thought. He was unaware of what truly rare delicacies he had in his hands. Usually the deer were all over the mushrooms as soon as the rain stopped.

Today, most of the deer were still in hiding. Here and there were some deer droppings, some of it wet and steaming, but its manufacturer was long gone. Martin Quartararo squinted, trying to pick more knobby shapes out of the distant darkness. It was then that he saw the dead tree.

Since the Doe had watched it die, the giant Holly had marched an hour into history. Its rich marrow, the once-teeming xylem and phloem, was sticky and dry. Martin stood before it, feeling a rare feeling, feeling an awakening. It was the acute pain of loss. It was the first time he had had the feeling since being wounded in love by the traveling salesman in New Orleans. Knowing nothing about botany but everything about theatre, Martin understood in his bones that something very grand and very sad had taken place. He mourned the tree as he hadn't been able to mourn even the tragic young men being lowered into their graves, their bodies savaged by AIDS. His heart went out to the tree as it hadn't gone out even to himself, as he sat during the storm and pictured his dead body among the wreckage. Impenetrable Martin, invulnerable in love and able even to mask the horror of a hurricane with a modest amount of Jamaican marijuana, cried for the first time in twenty years . . . for a tree.

Wayne Duclos remained by the sea until he began to feel the first deep chill of evening. He would dearly have loved to stay longer, even long enough to watch the full moon bob up out of the water, but he didn't want to push his luck. AIDS could take an evening chill and parlay it into pneumonia.

He took in the panorama of dusk and tried to memorize it, as he did now with many island spectacles. He never knew which vision would be the last. He had a feeling he would soon be going back to the hospital. He was right. The tumor in his brain, throbbing and ripe, would in a few days be the object of a surgeon's search through his open skull.

But right now that brain was an organ of pleasure, registering the changing colors of the sky. Over the ocean it was dark, but over the bay, into which the sun was disappearing, it was salmon pink. The horizon was punctuated by the twinkling lights of the mainland. In all the little houses, Wayne imagined, fathers were reading bedtime stories to children. What would it be like to lead such a life? To reproduce? To grow old?

Take the Tysons, for example. Still together, man and wife, at eighty! Fancy that. He formed an image of the old couple. As he did, he winced. Why? A snatch of a conversation floated up from memory. Something overheard on the walkway. Something about the old people . . . refusing to leave! Good God! Had the frail Tysons stuck around? Could they have been so stupid? Their house was ten feet from the ocean! It was right across the walkway from Los Brisos, for Christ's sake, and that house was without a roof right now.

Wayne's eyes swept the horizon until they rested on that unfortunate structure. Los Brisos was eerie as hell, its jagged, roofless outline against the sky. What made it even eerier was that its owner had died the week before on his way out to the island. Never mind that. Where was the fucking roof?! Hopefully not lying across the ancient bodies of Allys and Robert Tyson. The sick little man got down off his perch and hastened off in that direction.

As he moved carefully among the debris (a nail puncture in the darkness would be a stampede on his immune system) he said prayers for the old people. He hoped it had been a rumor and they weren't even there. He truly loved them, not only for who they were, but what they were; just about the *only straight couple in Cherry Grove*, for God's sake!

Everyone more or less knew the story of how the Tysons had come to remain in Cherry Grove, but only Wayne, he thought with a little smile, knew the *whole* story. The old people had told it to him on a lonely April night in front of the fireplace, when everyone except the very old or the very sick was out at the Nights in Venice Ball. It was the story of another time, and it had filled Wayne's head with visions of another place in history.

Making his way to their little walkway, he remembers the story in the rasping voice of Allys Tyson, between puffs on her Virginia Slim cigarette.

It was the late thirties, the debris of the hurricane of '38 was everywhere, and the Tysons were arriving in Cherry Grove just as all the other straight families were leaving. But the Tysons, who saw no reason why different life-styles meant people couldn't be good neighbors, held their ground. For more than twenty years they had resisted the entreaties of their family and friends to pull up stakes.

But with the arrival of the sixties, everything changed. The wild gay orgiastic explosions all around them were no environment in which to grow old. Allys dared not even venture outside for fear a naked man, in her parlance a "three-legged man," would saunter past. The aging couple became prisoners in their own home. They made complaints and got complained about, as the dowdy couple on the ocean. They were mocked, and they were provoked. It was a strange, unhappy time. The summers became long and grim. Again the entreaties came, this time from their own grown son, to pull out. Finally even Allys could no longer maintain her passion for the island in the face of Bob's irrefutable logic: The string was played out. Things were only going to get worse. It was time to go.

The morning the realtor was coming to appraise the property, Allys was awakened at dawn by a whoosh and a flap and a splat. She peered out the bedroom window to discover, to her great unhappiness, that a northeaster had come up during the night and blown her favorite quilt off the clothesline. Now the frail, antique thing was sitting in a gully of mud! It would be hell on earth to get clean. Ah well, it wasn't going anywhere, sodden as it was. She'd deal with it when she got up.

As it turned out, that wasn't until noon. She had a bit of a flu coming on (or maybe she just dreaded facing that smarmy realtor) and she had lingered in bed awhile. She made herself a cup of coffee, threw on a housecoat, and ventured outside, reluctantly, to deal with the quilt. The sun was out and the thing would be dry-caked with slop.

The first thing she saw was the little rain-washed gully, empty. No! Had the heirloom been blown away? Then she lifted her eyes. The quilt was hanging from the line, spotlessly clean. There was movement in the window of the house across the way. Behind pulled blinds, two pairs of eyes flickered above two mustaches. These were her neighbors. They had cleaned the quilt. They were making an offering of peace.

First, there was a small, conciliatory tea between the two couples. Then a cautious dinner. The two species sniffed each other out. Casseroles were exchanged. An invitation was extended to the older couple. Would they attend the Norma Shearer Memorial Ball? They graciously declined, but extended their own offer, for bridge the following night.

The four players sat stiffly around the table, the two young men trying not to gossip too rapaciously, the older pair trying not to be too boring. Then the Tysons made a grand slam and the gay couple got pissed off. They began to play in earnest and forgot, forevermore, about the differences between them.

The story of the Tysons from then 'til now, this storm-tossed day in 1985, is legend in the Eastern Kingdom. The natural instincts to be neighbors came gushing out of everyone. There was never a party, no matter how wild a gay bacchanal, to which the Tysons were not invited. The young men began to respect Allys's sensibilities, and cover themselves when they passed. When one of them forgot himself and sauntered past in the nude, profuse apologies followed. Allys would get angry, then blush, then accept the apology, then worry about him catching a cold.

The old couple were revered and treasured like a pair of ancient doves. No one made a trip to the Orient or Europe or South America without returning with a bauble they knew would please Allys. No strange or delicious cake was anywhere baked, but that two slices were quickly brought to the old couple in the house by the ocean.

The young men were thanking them for sticking it out.

The Tysons responded with what they had. Bob gave them legal advice as they and the Law grappled with new questions, like the marital rights of gay lovers, and wills in the era of AIDS. Allys worried constantly about the young men's health and repaid their slices of cake with meat and fresh vegetables. Growing old in America, so grim for so many, became for the Tysons richly infused with love and beauty. They had a thousand sons. In return, they held themselves out as an anchor for the doomed, sensual young men.

As Wayne moved quickly and evenly through the dark streets, trying not to raise the fatal sweat, he had to wonder about the old people's sanity. If they had indeed stuck around for the storm, why? Why pitch away such a rich, comfortable old age?

The answer, no doubt, had something to do with Bob Tyson's monstrous ego. With the skills of reason honed through fifty years in the courtroom, old Bob had probably cut through the sensational bullshit surrounding Hurricane Gloria and gleaned onto the hard facts; the storm was moving at a certain speed, and the speed would increase at a certain rate as it passed over colder and colder water. Given that, and the direction it was taking, and the inflection of its curve, and so on, it could be expected to arrive precisely at noon on the twenty-seventh at low tide.

Hence there was nothing to worry about.

That had turned out to be a pretty solid theory. Only one question remained. *Why was he willing to put his and Allys's lives on the line to back it up?* Yes, hers too, for the passionate woman was not leaving the man she loved at this stage of the game, not after sixty years of marriage. So what was the old coot thinking of?

Maybe he needed to prove that an old barrister can still think straight. Maybe the "live for now" mentality of his neighbors had made its mark on him. Maybe he was punishing her for some strange grudge inside the relationship. Who knew? Romance could get pretty weird sometimes, and no one knew that better than Wayne.

He was outside the house now and took a moment to breathe

deeply a couple of times. His lungs were full of crap again, a weird hangover from the AIDS-related tuberculosis he had recently shaken (he thought). The place was quiet and dark. He stepped carefully through the rubble around the back door. Squoshh! Suddenly, he was ankle deep in a mixture of oatmeal and coffee grounds. The overturned garbage. He felt a sudden gloom. His socks would stink all night, but the implications were far worse than that. Garbage was collected on Thursday mornings. Fresh trash meant that the Tysons had not left. They were in there somewhere.

Wayne scoured the house again for a light or a sound, or any other sign of life. Nothing. Should he probe further? No. As much as he loved Bob and Allys, this was futile and dangerous. The house was as still as a mausoleum. Either it actually contained the corpses of the only straight couple in Cherry Grove, or the two of them had holed up somewhere else. Either way, if Wayne spent any more time climbing through this debris in the night air, he was a candidate for tetanus and pneumonia.

As he started to pick his way gingerly out of the garbage and the ruins, a burning smell came to his nostrils. Coffee grounds? Was it even real, or just another symptom? By now he was used to the fiendish tricks of AIDS. A strange scent meant another complication.

No, this was real, unless the smoke coming out the vent was an apparition. He climbed on top of a wooden planter and peered in the window. Deep in the darkness, a faint glow. Fire! His heart raced and sank. A fire would spread across this dry rubble like contagion. The whole island would go up in a flash.

A sound! What was it? He leaned in closer. A human voice! Had one of the Tysons survived? Were they trapped? How could Wayne, frail as he was, pull anyone out of anywhere? He climbed down and raced around to the patio. He threw his small body at the back door. It was unlatched and he went tumbling in. Startled, Bob and Allys Tyson turned from their living room sofa to face him. Before them, on the coffee table, a candle burned. There was lipstick on Bob's face. They had been necking.

"What are you trying to do, cramp my style?" barked the old man. The lovebirds laughed uproariously. Wayne was stunned. He sat on the floor like a bewildered pet.

"Get up, you'll catch a chill," rasped Allys, lighting a Virginia Slim.

"Are you all right?" Wayne finally managed to stammer.

"Great," she said, "except for arthritis and senility. Come give me a hand with dinner, unless you expect to be waited on like the King of France." Still dazed, the little man struggled to his feet and followed the old woman into the kitchen.

The Tysons had, indeed, stayed for Hurricane Gloria. Wayne had been right about that, and he was right about why. Old Bob had figured the whole thing out. He had weighed all the factors and concluded that everything was going to be all right. And he had insisted on backing it up with his own life and his wife's, despite the pleading of his son and his grandchildren to cross the bay to safety. Worry warts, he called them all.

With a perverse pleasure he had watched the ocean boil up beyond the point where an emergency vehicle could reach them. And he had kept the smile on his face even through the severe tongue-lashing administered to him by his wife, who was obliged to pay the price for his monstrous stroke of ego.

But the first part of the storm had borne Bob Tyson out. Beaming like a mad scientist, he had watched from an upstairs window as the angry sea and the parallel winds stalemated each other for an hour . . . just as he had anticipated. He even allowed himself a celebratory glass of whiskey during the eye, out of the same bottle of Cutty Sark he had earlier purchased under the horrified eye of Martin Quartararo.

Prematurely, it turned out. The second half of Gloria was a lesson in humility for old Robert Tyson. He learned that a hundred-mile-an-hour wind blowing off the water is also off the slide rule. It bows to no laws and reasonable judgments. It comes under the category of Act of God.

Shortly after the eye, the wind moved through its silent high harmonics into the low, almost human moan that had shaken the souls of Ralph Cain and Ferron Bell. For the elderly Tysons, it was not only frightening, it was painful to their brittle eardrums. And, felt the suddenly sobered and humbled Bob Tyson, it was ominous. He was right again. He watched the wind slowly tear the roof off Los Brisos, and then, suddenly, fling it at him.

"Rob Roy," announced Wayne Duclos, laying Bob's favorite cocktail in front of him. The old man's eyes widened with delight. His daily ablution! Dinner would not be far behind! Fortified, he watched the little man amble away and rejoin Allys in the kitchen.

Truly, Wayne was about his favorite neighbor. The other men yakked endlessly over bridge about chintz, or kitsch, or whatever it was, but Wayne was a regular guy. That such a good, radiant soul was headed for an early grave brought tears to the old man's eyes. He had no desire to outlive his little friend.

The self-righteous bastards who thought AIDS was "God's way" of chastening the gays! If God was making some kind of point with AIDS, thought Bob, it was more likely directed not at gays but at their tormentors. Turn around and pick up your stricken brother, God might be saying. Find a cure, or the whole human race will go down the toilet, and I won't lift a finger to stop it. The sickness of Wayne Duclos was a call to arms for the decent. He was a modern-day Tiny Tim. With his stool empty by the fireplace, thought Tyson, who among us can sleep peacefully?

Oh, the intolerance of gays was something he understood very well. He'd practiced it himself in the early days of the Grove. Back at Princeton, in the twenties, such people were only whispered of in the eating clubs. Queers were ostracized, black-balled. Hell, in the rest of the country, they were *hung!*

Tyson sipped his Rob Roy. Too sweet, as usual. Didn't any-one know how to mix a drink anymore?

But no, the persecution of these for-the-most-part gentle souls was downright irrational! Long before AIDS, strong, good people were totally unnerved by gays. Why? Maybe the old theory was true, that the ones who were the *most* unnerved, who hooted and lisped the loudest when gays walked down the street, were fearful of the woman within themselves. Even Bob had to admit to being shaken by a long, lascivious look from a man. Was he terrified of the awakening of some total, all-encompassing, nondiscriminating, dark, lubricated sensuality inside himself? Possibly, but why? The old barrister's mind kept probing. Was it a racial thing, a reaction of the species? Were we afraid of screwing other men because at some level it would be a threat to the human race not to reproduce?

Even that didn't make sense.

Hell, with the race threatened by overpopulation, maybe the gays were even doing us a *favor* by not reproducing. Helping the species to survive. Oh, not that the leather-clad, muscle-bound jerks parading down Christopher Street knew anything about Darwin, or even cared about saving the human race . . . *but why were people so damn scared of them?*

It defied logic.

But so did a lot of things. In fact the day had been a lesson in the impotence of logic. Only one thing was certain, thought Bob Tyson. You could get a nice buzz off a Rob Roy (as his granddaughter would put it) no matter how badly it was mixed. The booze and a smattering of evening senility were sanding the rough edges off the old lawyer's mind, and he was feeling pretty good. As his companions joined him on the couch with dinner, he resolved to think no more today.

The menu was a little disappointing. The chefs had proved helpless without an electric stove, and all three diners held in their hands open cans of Chicken of the Sea Tuna. As they dug in, they turned their attention to the living room window. The absence of a roof on Los Brisos was affording them a magnificent view of the sea, the only impediment to which was a huge black telephone cable. But Bob Tyson figured he really shouldn't complain about that; if not for the cable, the only dinner going on around here would have been the gulls pecking out his eyeballs.

Two hours earlier, no sooner did the winds of Gloria fling the roof off Los Brisos, than that big black telephone cable intercepted it, snapped it in half, and dropped it into a ditch without so much as scratching the Tysons's paint job. So how could you figure it?

You couldn't.

All three of them were settled now, and silent. Before them was occurring one of nature's great spectacles, the rising of a full moon. First a sliver of crimson peeked over the still-churning sea. They could see it move, inch by inch, revealing more of itself, until it was a wedge of bright copper. Then laboriously higher, until it was the red of good farm soil.

Old Bob watched Wayne's face change colors. It was the face of a child, absorbing the event as if it did not know the outcome, did not know if the moon would manage, this time, to climb dripping out of the sea. The lurid history of his tribe and the imminence of his own death notwithstanding, Wayne was an utter innocent. He was without bitterness or cynicism. That was what was so rare about the man, thought Tyson, and perhaps that was what people really feared and envied and hated him for.

Suddenly, the moon sprang full into the sky as if it had been catapulted by an unseen primitive mechanism. It was three dimensional, an orb bursting with golden blood. The water lit up with the color, and Wayne had a sudden vision of himself, it was spring, the first boat was plowing the bay back to Fire Island, and he was on it. Not in a sackful of ashes, but on the top deck, with the spray hitting his face.

The three fragile people watched the moon ride through the sky.

Not far away, a natural event far rarer than a moonrise was taking place. The purple martins were assembling for their fall migratory journey. That in itself was not rare. The martins have darted sleekly around here forever, their beaks wide open to suck the insects out of the sky. The Secatogue Indians loved the feisty birds, who scared the vultures away from their venison. In gratitude, they hung great hollow gourds for the martins to live and breed in.

Then, as now, the martins stayed until the last leaf fell in autumn, and were back with the first breath of spring. Often that was a fatal mistake. Seduced north by a warm wind, they were sometimes clobbered by a late frost, or a long spring storm that kept them and their insects out of the sky. The hurricane of '38 had been the end of one of their most tragic chapters; in the preceding week of rain, thousands of them had starved.

Now, far earlier than usual, they were leaving. What made it doubly strange was the hour. Always the martins traveled by daylight, feeding on the wing; at night the bugs were sparse and impossible to see. The chimney swifts, themselves always gone before the first hearth fires chased them from their homes, were shocked to see their cousins clearing out before them, in the middle of the night, no less!

Great councils of purple martins were arriving at the appointed spot, hovering in by fifties and sixties. Soon there was a waving iridescent line of them, a quarter of a mile long, on top of a dune.

There was chattering and flapping.

One end of the line lifted off, and the rest of it followed, a long undulation. As it rose into the light, a fluttering of the man in the moon's eyelash, a dot straggled below it. It was the Bahamas Swallow, so far from home, fighting to join her cousins.

Finally together, the line moved out over the water and swung south.

E P I L O G U E :
M U R M U R S

Hurricane Gloria took no human lives, but it complicated many of them. In the remaining weeks of temperate weather, Fire Islanders dug themselves out. The storm's damage had been arbitrary but harsh. A dozen small tornados had twisted off the mother maelstrom, and struck fiercely and specifically. Calvin Klein's roof was gone, but his neighbor's chinaware hadn't budged an inch on the shelf.

The electricity and even the water were a long time being turned back on—days, and in some remote places, weeks. The islanders lived during this time like their grandparents: working and cleaning with handtools, hauling water from community wells, and passing their evenings by flamelight. Finally, when the walkways and living rooms were clear of sludge and debris, celebrations were held.

In the Eastern Kingdom, everyone converged on the small clapboard house in Fire Island Pines that serves as the library and post office. Each household brought food in a casserole. Whether chastened by AIDS, or Gloria, or their own middle age, the citizens, with their history of excess written in purple, were holding an extraordinary event. It was a Covered-Dish Supper, like the ones that were taking place in churches all over Iowa that very night.

But what covered dishes! Here were recipes from the nerve centers of Manhattan's swankest restaurants, whipped up by their very creators. The fellowship was warm and genuine. Ralph Cain moved about enjoying mild celebrity status as a hurricane survivor. Mario Herrera, the owner of Spirits of the Pines liquor store, surprised everyone by revealing that he, too, had remained through the storm in his house by the bay. And as usual, the highlight of the evening was Ferron Bell's slide show. Here were pictures from each epoch of Ferron's island life: self-portraits of the sleek young man in one of his own handcrafted sharkskin jockstraps, and dazzling color slides of the wildest moments of the Nights in Venice Ball. Then there were the austere winter pictures: familiar walkways frozen over, snow on the beach, frigid dawns.

Ivan Bekoff didn't attend. He wasn't ready for a mob scene. Instead, he had a few people over for tea on his small verandah. None of them could remember as large a gathering there in the past.

Across the Meatrack, Cherry Grove was dark. The old Tysons were gone, like the birds, to Florida, where they would remain until spring. Martin Quartararo made a game attempt to spark the last wild party of the season, showing up dressed as Rita Hayworth, but the event was poorly attended and fizzled. The action seemed to be over. All sorts of agencies were recommending "safe sex" as a way for gay men to have their fun and avoid

AIDS, but the pall over the Grove had gone far beyond that. Now, the men associated sex and death together in their minds—not a festive or erotic combination. This great creative burst of American Gay History was over. In its next phase their courage and boldness would take more subdued forms; legal, political, and medical ones. The rest of mankind would have to wait for some as-yet-unknown group, perhaps some happy immigrants, to shout its next unalloyed shout of joy.

Wayne Duclos had recovered from brain surgery, but had suffered a relapse of AIDS-related tuberculosis and was back in St. Luke's Hospital. Now, in late October, he was improving. The doctors could make no sense of the little man's resilience. They had written him off long ago. They were bemused and saddened to hear him insist that enduring Gloria had given him the strength and confidence to beat AIDS, and that he expected to do so.

Out on the water, the big breakers teemed with silver fish. The homeowner's loss had been the fishermen's gain. The migrating bluefish, driven to deep water by the storm, had feasted on exotic fare and grown huge. Now they were intimidating sizable weakfish, and stampeding them to shore, into the fishermen's pails.

Most of the birds in the sky were now waterfowl, ducks and geese who were not leaving for the winter, but arriving from frozen Canadian ponds. The tragedy of the redstarts had been avoided by most of the songbirds, who had made the ageless voyage south and chattered now among blooming branches in Mexican squares. The birds by and large had been lucky; an average storm in the Irish Sea breaks the necks of enough seabirds to more than fill the graveyard of the redstarts on Fire Island. And on Halloween night, after what must have seemed a dream, a Bahamas Swallow dropped out of a tropical sky and landed on the beach where she had hatched.

Of all the Fire Island animals, the hardest hit were the deer. Not only did many of them die in the swimming pools of Fire Island Pines, but many more were still to die of winter starvation. The same salt spray that had driven them wild with thirst had browned and desiccated the evergreen leaves that were their winter food.

But naturalists would not be sad to find the spring ground littered with their corpses. There was an enormous pressure on the Parks Department to solve the deer overpopulation problem. Not only were the voracious, fearless bucks and does chomping every flower and vegetable garden in sight, but they were now vilified for a different reason. They were the primary carriers of Lyme disease ticks, which they left on leaves and branches throughout the woods. Many islanders who worked or spent time in nature had been at one time or another the victims of a tick bite and the degenerative, arthritic symptoms of the disease.

Even though, like AIDS victims, a case could be made for their innocence (field mice actually spawned the insidious ticks), the deer had become pariahs. The rangers had tried everything to curb their growth, even once condoning a bow-and-arrow hunt . . . but they called it off when hunters were found shooting deer with rifles and jamming arrows into the wounds. Recently someone had proposed a solution bizarre to the point of lunacy: Why not turn a bunch of wild pumas loose in the off-season? That the suggestion even found its way into print was a measure of the problem's urgency. It was a great relief to the rangers when nature herself took care of the problem, as she was now doing.

For the Buck and Doe of our story, the ending was happy . . . from their point of view. In late October the twelve-point Buck, now full of rack, led his Doe back to the Western Kingdom, where the vines of several abandoned gardens still hung heavy with tomatoes. The Doe ate her fill, and shortly afterward, at mating time, conceived a fawn, who five months later, brown, wet, and newborn, would add to the overpopulation problem.

And over in the Sunken Forest, the Holly tree was a far more affable host in death than in life. Its machinery shut down, the great ochre channels had dried and shriveled, opening cavities that now teemed with insect life. When the bark decayed, it would be a food festival even for soft-billed birds. A whole new species might be tempted to settle here.

---

* * *

As it turned out, Dana Wallace had not been alone in the Western Kingdom during Hurricane Gloria. Bill Roesch, the sewage plant supervisor, and Ted Minski, the town manager, had been in the firehouse undergoing a rite of manhood. All their lives, from their fathers and mothers and uncles and aunts, they had heard tales of '38. Now, huddling in the Ocean Beach Firehouse, they had matched themselves against ghosts long dead. A little farther down the street, Jimmy Viles, the remarkable and erudite gardener who grew all the plants of the world behind his bamboo fence . . . even old Jimmy had stuck around. If the plants were going under, then so was he, was the way he figured it. Over in Point O'Woods, Chuck Doersam, a young WASP prince who has eschewed his throne for the open air of construction work, had stayed around to keep an eye on things. And Bobby Ferguson, the construction worker with the incendiary temper, had stayed put in Ocean Beach looking for a thrill. He got more than he bargained for. Throughout the two hours of the storm he had been obliged to hold down the skylight of a newly built home with his two aching arms lest it—and he—be blown away. And a mile to the east, James Lindsey, having packed away his parents and his children to the mainland, enjoyed a second honeymoon with his wife, Virginia, in a world without people in uniforms.

Now, after forty-eight hours of emergency work on power lines, all these men were welcomed like heros to the celebration of the Western Kingdom. The rotting food of a thousand powerless refrigerators had been gathered and an immense banquet was prepared by John Palermo, who runs the Italian restaurant in Ocean Beach.

But up by the ocean, Dana Wallace was not celebrating. Whatever light the storm had extinguished in his soul seemed permanently out. Something had simply been beaten out of him. For days afterward he seemed to disappear from the life of the community. Occasionally someone spotted him shuffling around town with a glazed look in his eye, but for the most part he remained at home, sitting listlessly amidst the wreckage of his empire. He had barely the passion or energy to keep living, let alone rebuild. For what? To have it all demolished again by the next big wave?

Then one morning he heard a sound in the basement. He went downstairs to a shocking spectacle. His son's wife was holding a huge pushbroom and she was sweeping out the sand. It was impossible for Dana Wallace to believe. There had always been bad blood between the conservative young woman and the flamboyant old man. She thought he was the most dissolute soul on earth, and the worst possible father. He in turn blamed her for the rift between him and Dana Junior and thought she was as cold as steel. But there she was, inexplicably, with a broom, ankle deep in the dreadful muck.

"Well," she said, "are you going to help me?"

He gave her a long hard look to see whether this might be some kind of a cruel joke. He had endured many of them at the hands of young women. She returned his look with unflinching dark eyes. Finally he picked up a dustpan and held it, and into it she pushed the first broomful.

She was calling him back to life.

Old muscles stirred and something kicked into gear. He opened his eyes and looked around. There were running acres of silt to be siphoned out of basements, cords of firewood to be hacked out of flooded forest, a corral fence to be rebuilt, a seawall to be refortified, and all the crap of the universe to be hauled out of his front yard. He made a phone call down to his breeding farm in North Carolina. Could his foreman Charley Davis get his family together and come up north to do a little work?

They would be there in a couple of days, they said.

When they arrived they found Dana Wallace sitting on his porch, turning his old Speed Graphic camera over in his hands. It had been years since he'd picked it up, and dozens of years since he'd done so without bitterness. He felt the textured black casement of the thing with his fingertips. He lifted it and squinted through the sight at Charley, a full-blooded Cherokee Indian. Behind him stood his brood—a strong wife and three teenage boys, two of them with wives. It would be a tough picture; there wasn't much light, and there had to be a little depth of field to get them all in.

Click.

His heart began to pound like the surf.

Click. Click click, click.

In October of 1985, Dana Wallace came back to life. Within a couple of days he was standing on the porch, screaming orders at Charley and the crew. The phone was ringing off the hook. There was action in the house. Maelstrom ran third in a sprint at Belmont. His dogs were yapping and he was pouring margaritas for anyone who walked in the door.

One day shortly afterward Charley hung the Half-Moon door back on the beachcomber's shack. Now fully rebuilt, it stood again on the edge of the sea and challenged the waves to take it away. About an hour later, a National Parks Ranger arrived with a permit to tear it down. A new environmental law, bitterly detested by Wallace, empowered the government to finish demolishing any structure the storm had begun to demolish. What storm damage? said Dana Wallace. He led the vexed ranger out to the shack, and defied him to find so much as a scratch on a windowpane. Outfoxed, the ranger got back in his Jeep and angrily drove away.

That night Charley's wife, Marie, made a little dinner to mark the occasion. It was southern cooking to die for: fried chicken, yams, black-eyed peas, and homemade biscuits. Afterward Marie served up coffee and some unbelievable rhubarb pie. Charley's oldest boy Kimmy began to pick out a tune on the guitar. It was an old Duane Eddy tune—"Pipeline" or "Apache," one of those—and Kimmy picked pretty well. Dana Wallace's eyes filled up with tears at the amount of love in the room, and at the sweetness of life.

He drifted out to look at the ocean. A half-moon hung on a nail, over a dead calm sea. From his corral, Maelstrom noted his master's presence with a whinny. Wallace moved down the ramp to the fence, and called the colt over. A bridle hung on a fencepost

---

and Wallace grabbed it and in one fluid motion insinuated the bit between the horse's gums. He buckled the throat latch under the massive jaw, clipped on a couple of rope reins, and swung himself up.

It felt good to feel Maelstrom's warm back between his legs, without the interference of a saddle. Kind of like screwing without a rubber. Wallace urged the colt mildly, and in a moment they were lightly cantering out to the water. Now Wallace craned over to the big bay ears and said "Go," and they were gone. First they galloped at water's edge, kicking up spray into the gray light of the half-moon. Then he dug his heels into the horse's ribs and they accelerated into the highest gear, the racehorse gear. They simply flew. Wallace stuck his ass in the air and lay his body along Maelstrom's neck, the way the jockeys do.

To his right the sea glistened faintly. The old man turned his face to it, said a couple of words heard only by the moon, and rode on.

—

A   F   T   E   R   W   O   R   D :

F   C   H   O   E   S

Time is more implacable even than a dark wind. By the seventh anniversary of Gloria, in the fall of 1992, half its survivors were dead.

The night of the hurricane, as the moon rose out of the ocean, Wayne Duclos shared a vision with the old Tysons: of himself returning to Fire Island in the spring. Astonishing his doctors, he did just that. He left St. Luke's Hospital in December of 1985 and was on the first boat back the following April, the salt spray hitting his gaunt, smiling face.

But AIDS leaves no survivors. Despite his immense personal will and the ceaseless devotion of his lover Jacques, Wayne Duclos died in Manhattan on May 6, 1987, a full twenty months after Gloria. At his request he was cremated, and his ashes were deposited in the compost pile that would soon feed the soil of his Fire Island vegetable garden.

In the spring of 1992 AIDS also claimed Martin Quartararo, who had once so dreaded the disease. The resolutely carefree man had spent his last years in great physical pain. And before his own illness began, he had endured the prolonged sorrow of nursing and finally burying his lover Hal. The romance had begun not long after Gloria, and it was the first mutual, stable one of Martin's life. Many thought the storm had made a dent in the little man's armor, and made a relationship possible.

But for Ivan Bekoff, the lessons of Gloria seem only to have been temporary. In the fall of 1990, after years of growing reclusiveness, Ivan was discovered dead in his hand-hewn shack, having refused for weeks the ministrations of passersby to his mysterious illness. Many suspected it was AIDS, but since Ivan had refused to see a doctor, it may also have been the lingering effects of an earlier bout with hepatitis. No one knew. Upon his death it was learned that the rarely glimpsed man was a virtual millionaire, leaving behind him extensive land holdings not only on Fire Island but also in the Florida Keys.

Allys Tyson died in the fall of 1991 under the relentless assault of old age. Toward the end her arthritic symptoms were so agonizing that even Bob, her husband and lover of sixty-six years, wished only for her release. Bob, now eighty-eight, lives alone in Florida.

Not long after Gloria, Ralph Cain relocated to Hollywood, a move that surprised many of the conservative man's friends, including Ferron Bell. Bell himself divides his time between Key West and Fire Island Pines, but continues to paint Fire Island scenes almost exclusively. As his style has grown simpler and his craft surer, recognition has come. Nineteen ninety-two saw two major Bell exhibitions, canvas after canvas of plain objects against deep blue skies.

Dana Wallace still lives in Ocean Beach, although these days he is rarely seen stalking the bars of that tiny village. He is far more likely to be found at his compound by the sea. By all reports he has relaxed into old age and made certain concessions to it . . . but physical comfort has not been among them. In recent years he has spent more and more time in the beachcomber's shack. Last summer he lived in it almost fulltime, while his nearby modern ranch home stood empty.

The disease that claimed the lives of Duclos, Quartararo, and possibly Bekoff has become a national issue, the first one mentioned by the youthful American President upon the night of his election in 1992. In the Gay Nation itself, the black bunting has been removed. AIDS is a fact of life and the very youngest of the men can't remember when it wasn't. The most spectacular party of the year drew five thousand people. Although it was a medical fundraiser, it did not want for gaiety, exuberance, even madness. In this respect it was an echo of the great parties of the seventies, with one startling exception; it took place at ten o'clock in the morning. Darkness was the only unwelcome guest.

The bird migrations continue unchanged, the disturbance of Gloria an insignificant glitch in a timeless design. A new colony of American redstarts has discovered the Sunken Forest, as if the memory of the dark place was somewhere in their genes. But the entire race of songbirds is now threatened by a more insidious force than any hurricane. As man continues to pave over the birds' northern breeding grounds, their tropical wintering range, much of it in rain forests, vanishes with the spread of slash-and-burn farming. Squeezed from both directions, their number is dwindling and their song is fading.

On the slim positive side, the Brown pelican, hitherto unknown this far north, has been seen offshore . . . though no one can say why. And the same peregrine falcon that left Fire Island shortly before Gloria is still flying. Her old age may even be warmed by the sight of more falcons in the air, if current experiments to save the species succeed.

The deer overpopulation problem has grown steadily worse

and the new solution is immunosterilization; the does are injected by air gun at a distance with a tiny dart that will render them barren for a couple of breeding seasons. Everyone agrees it has to be done. Apart from carrying Lyme disease and chomping flower gardens, the deer are now felt to threaten the island in a more profound way. By eating all the low plants, they compromise the whole network of roots and vegetation that hold the island together and protect it from the assault of wind and sea.

The hurricanes themselves have been relatively mild since Gloria, although the Halloween storm of 1991 was bad, and the winter storms of the '92–'93 were worse. They dragged a few dozen houses into the sea, gouged great expanses of dunes, and even breached the island from bay to ocean in several places. But eventually the water went down, and no new inlets were created . . . although an old one, buried since 1700, was briefly re-glimpsed.

But by and large, barring something worse than the Hurricane of '38 (still mythic in the imaginations of naturalists and weathermen) the island will endure . . . and shrink. The rangers have conducted their five-year fly-over survey and concluded that the inexorable westward tide has indeed chipped another couple of feet off the southern beach . . . the house percentage.

What this suggests is that Dana Wallace's beachcomber's shack will not be swallowed by a dramatic tempest after all. Instead, long after the old man is gone, it may simply tumble into a calm sea.